Gothic Bodies

Gothic Bodies

The Politics of Pain in Romantic Fiction

Steven Bruhm

University of Pennsylvania Press

Philadelphia

Excerpt from "Hanky Panky" (Madonna Ciccone, Pat Leonard), copyright © 1990 by WB
Music Corp., Bleu Disque Music Co., Inc., Webo Girl Publishing, Inc., No Tomato Music.
All rights on behalf of Bleu Disque Music Co., Inc. and Webo Girl Publishing, Inc. and
Madonna Ciccone administered by WB Music Corp. for the world. All rights reserved.
Used by permission.

Portions of Chapter 4 previously published in *Eighteenth-Century Life*. Reprinted by
permission.
Portions of Chapter 5 previously published in *Studies in Romanticism*. Reprinted by
permission.

Copyright © 1994 by the University of Pennsylvania Press
All rights reserved
Printed in the United States of America

Library of Congress Cataloging-in-Publication Data
Bruhm, Steven.
   Gothic bodies : the politics of pain in romantic fiction / Steven
Bruhm.
      p.   cm.
   Includes bibliographical references and index.
   ISBN 0-8122-3291-7
   1. English literature — 18th century — History and criticism.
2. Gothic revival (Literature) — Great Britain.   3. English
literature–19th century — History and criticism.   4. Horror tales,
English — History and criticism.   5. Politics and literature — Great
Britain.   6. Mind and body in literature.   7. Body, Human, in
literature.   8. Romanticism — Great Britain.   9. Pain in literature.
I. Title.
PR448.G6B78   1994
823'.087290936 — dc20   94-33221
                                                              CIP

Frontispiece: Eugene Delacroix, *The Death of Sardanapalus* (courtesy of Musée du Louvre) for my parents, Lawrence and Helen

It is by [sympathy] that we enter into the concerns of others; that we are moved as they are moved, and are never suffered to be indifferent spectators of almost any thing which men can do or suffer. For sympathy must be considered as a sort of substitution, by which we are put into the place of another man, and affected in many respects as he is affected.
    —Edmund Burke,
       Enquiry . . . into the Sublime and Beautiful

Hmmmmm . . . my body hurts just thinking about it.
    —Madonna, "Hanky Panky"

Contents

Acknowledgments

Preparation of this manuscript was assisted by a Doctoral Fellowship from the Social Sciences and Humanities Research Council of Canada, and by a Research Assistantship from McGill University. Thanks to the English Departments at Bishop's University, Lennoxville and to the Université de Montréal for their generous support.

I would like to thank the editors of *Eighteenth-Century Life* for their permission to reprint an article entitled "William Godwin's *Fleetwood*: The Epistemology of the Tortured Body," which comprises a substantial part of Chapter four of this work. I am grateful also to the editors of *Studies in Romanticism* and the trustees of Boston University for permission to reprint "Aesthetics and Anesthetics at the Revolution," Chapter five here.

I would also like to thank the people at McGill University who read this manuscript and made invaluable comments: Christopher Heppner, David Hensley, John Ripley, Faith Wallace, and especially Maggie Kilgour, who painstakingly anatomized this work from start to finish. Alan Bewell generously provided a number of insights at an earlier stage of the manuscript, and Nancy Johnson and Catherine Burroughs gave me important references to check and kept me honest. Thanks as well to Frances Restuccia and John Allen Stevenson, the readers at the University of Pennsylvania Press, for their precise attention and helpful suggestions. I express my appreciation to the participants in my aerobics classes at Maison Alcan, and at the Montréal and Halifax YMCAs for allowing me to practice torture techniques on them during the writing of Chapter four. And finally, thanks to Peter Schwenger, who heard about the headaches and the backaches and sympathized all the while.

Introduction

Eugene Delacroix's 1827 canvas, *The Death of Sardanapalus* (see front-ispiece), is not about the death of Sardanapalus. The moment captured by the painting immediately precedes the one in which the Assyrian king of Byron's drama will drink poison and immolate himself on his own bed. What Delacroix has chosen to present is a king who watches others die, a king who, in the painting, remains untouched. Poised with seeming insouciance on his bed, surrounded by riches and lushly attired, Sardanapalus watches the assassination of his concubines by the soldiers of his treasonous satraps. The painting is not about the death of Sardanapalus so much as it is about Sardanapalus's contemplation of death. It indulges what Norman Bryson calls the "beauty of barbarism" (*Tradition* 186) to contrast the thinking about pain with the experience itself. It sets the life of Sardanapalus's mind squarely against the lives of the harem's bodies.

This division of body and mind is replayed through another division, a veritable separation in the canvas. As Jack J. Spector notes, the painting is troublesome for the split between the background and the foreground, between the "opposed moods of pensive melancholy and animal energy, and of the detachment of the mental from the physical" (*Death* 23). The concubines' life-sized bodies eclipse the king who looks on from a

> dark background [that] seems rather more like a somber stage setting than a
> believable receding space, especially in view of its apparent division from the
> brightly illuminated foreground, across which figures move like actors down-
> stage under the spotlight. (17–18)

This intensified, focused light emphasizes the immediacy and vulnerable corporeality of these bodies. Like the bodies of their murderers, the women are mostly naked and exposed. Their glowing skin is set off by deep velvets of red and green, and by the lush pearls on earlobe, arm, and ankle. This sensuous nakedness, against which the sadistic violence is committed, depicts Delacroix's fascination with the violent in the erotic—that familiar Freudian paradigm of sex and death—a fascination that has resulted in critical dis-ease with the painting since its appearance in 1828 (see Spector,

Death 18). Sensuous exposure here becomes synonymous with vulnerability, and the body, once the site of Sardanapalus's pleasure, is, in the painting, a proclamation of human fragility. The women's susceptibility to pleasure bespeaks their bodies' susceptibility to pain. Moreover, this fragility is absent in the depiction of the king. His body is fully covered, except for the forearm, face, and toes; his gown is not disheveled, let alone bloodstained. The servant bearing the cup of poison that will kill him is recessed, almost invisible, the deadly urn just one more glittering bauble in the palace's splendor. At the moment in the canvas, Sardanapalus is both surrounded by carnage and immune to it; he is an interested, and yet a disinterested, spectator.

Norman Bryson finds in the painting those two moments that, for Delacroix, must be "taken together [to] define the work of culture: a primitive state from which culture emerges, and a later or higher state where it risks the return of that which has been repressed" (205). *The Death of Sardanapalus* isolates that moment of Romantic apocalypse when a holocaust is rendered necessary to destroy an existing culture in order to save it. Bryson argues that for Delacroix, as for Freud, culture is a move away from primal urges, but only to have those urges return as various forms of discontent. In the story that Delacroix gets from Byron, Sardanapalus has refused slavish submission to what could be called primal urges by declaring himself unwilling to wage war, to assert power unduly, and to inflict pain. His peaceable kingdom is ordered by adherence only to pleasure. This order is destroyed by a return to war, violence, and carnage — in short, by a return of the repressed. But with the return of that repressed comes another kind of order, and another kind of repression. While Sardanapalus has outlawed certain primal urges, he has indulged others: he has been eating, drinking, and loving in typical Byronic fashion, and his passions are threatening the country with destruction. By eschewing repression of the body, by indulging food, sex, and freedom from pain, Sardanapalus has evoked the greatest repression of the body that is possible: the murder of his subjects, and his own eventual suicide. In this painting, as in Byron's play, the repression of physicality is essential to the social order.

Repression is, of course, essential to a theory of the Gothic, that poor cousin and contemporary to Romanticism. In one of the most important early essays to influence criticism of the Gothic — Freud's "The Uncanny," written in 1919 — Freud discusses the Gothic as a study in the uncanny, a study in the return of various repressed experiences. The uncanny, says Freud,

is in reality nothing new or alien, but something which is familiar and old-
established in the mind and which has become alienated from it only through a
process of repression . . . , something which ought to have remained hidden
but has come to light. (*Complete* Vol. 17, 241)

One of these repressions, a very important one for Freud, has to do with the
body. Freud recalls the story of Hoffman's Sand-Man, a mythical agent of
terror "who tears out children's eyes" (227). Then he reminds us: "Many
adults retain their apprehensiveness in this respect, and no physical injury is
so much dreaded by them as an injury to the eye" (231). This fear of bodily
violation, Freud argues, displaces another, more primal, yet equally physical dread: the fear of castration. The castration complex, he suggests, is
symptomatic — indeed a *foundation* — of our fear of injury, death, and the
dead body that constitutes our experience of the uncanny. In one sense,
then, it is a repressed body — the eye, the penis, physical power in general —
that returns in our daily experience to be defined as the uncanny.

From this opening premise, Freud goes on to enumerate a number of
instances in which the uncanny is a return of repressed anxieties about the
body:

> Dismembered limbs, a severed head, a hand cut off at the wrist, feet which
> dance by themselves . . .   all these have something peculiarly uncanny about
> them. . . . To some people the idea of being buried alive by mistake is the most
> uncanny thing of all. (244)

As an experience rooted in the body, and marked by a return of the body's
repressed fragility and vulnerability, Freud's uncanny can in some ways be
said to define Sardanapalus's experience. He has repressed the ever-present
political reality of violence; he has sublimated his kingly responsibility to act
aggressively into a love of eroticism; he has privileged a life of pleasure over
a life of pain. In the moment captured by Delacroix's painting, that repressed violence returns, and the body — afflicted, severed, cut — proclaims
its primacy, its irrepressibility, its material existence.

The depiction of the Assyrian king as distanced contemplator of carnage and violence aligns him to some degree with the Romantic tradition of
which Delacroix was both apostle and critic. Sardanapalus is not only the
haughty, Byronic hero standing outside the sphere of human action, but
also the subject-spectator who tries to make sense of what is happening
before him. He is the exotic avatar of Wordsworth or Coleridge, Blake or
Shelley, all of whom, in their different ways, drew on German transcenden-

talism to construct an intellectual, imaginative theory that would transcend the carnage around them, especially carnage associated with the American Revolution (as in Blake and Wordsworth), the French Revolution, and the violent responses to France that England manifested in the 1790s and periodically throughout the Napoleonic campaign. Like Sardanapalus, authors at the turn of the nineteenth century sought to process violence through the point of view of a distanced, transcendent spectator. The split between Sardanapalus and his harem, then, is in a general way the split between Romanticism—or a certain version of it—and the Gothic, between the life of the mind and the immediacy of the body. Robert Hume argued in 1969 that the key difference between Romanticism and Gothicism is that while the former offers escape through transcendence (theoretically, at least), the latter is bound by fixity and limitation ("Gothic" 289). Such a division, I believe, is misleading, for while it may emphasize what Romantic authors *tried* to do, it does not account for what often they *succeeded* in doing. It is one of my premises in this book that the major Romantic authors share with their Gothic cousins a fascination with physical pain, and much Romantic production concerns itself with the implications of physical pain on the transcendent consciousness. To speak broadly, Blake and Wordsworth were greatly troubled by local explosions of violence in England, explosions often having to do with oppressive government policies regarding the revolutions in France and America; Shelley and Keats were intensely aware of the ways physicality circumscribed Romantic idealism; and Coleridge and Byron were constantly plagued by their own physical pain, which became both a catalyst and a deterrent to literary production. (And these categories are by no means fixed: Keats too was troubled by physical pain; Byron and Coleridge were overtly conscious of revolution; the later Blake became suspicious of his own early idealism.) In Delacroix's painting—and, I believe, in Romantic fiction as well—that essential limitation is the body, a body whose pain and vulnerability repeatedly signal its return from the repressions of the transcendent Romantic consciousness. Thus to read the Gothic and Romantic together is to set in high relief the Gothic delimitation of the Romantic body.

Sardanapalus's temporary disengagement—his thinking *about* pain rather than thinking *in* it—is part of the problem raised by this book. *The Death of Sardanapalus*, like much Romantic fiction, is replete with painful bodies, but they are most often viewed by a poised, distanced spectator. This distance has usually earned the king the condemnation of critics who see his spectatorship as morbid and irresponsible. But such condemnation does not allow the validity of the activity Sardanapalus is performing on the canvas, the activity of *thinking* about pain. It does not allow that thinking about pain may itself be a legitimate and necessary enterprise. Indeed, we are reluctant to think about pain. When describing this project, for example, I have often been met with responses like "Don't you think that's rather sick?" (the "sick," it would seem, being morally suspect); or "Wouldn't you rather think about Romantic *pleasure*?" (as if that had never been done). These regulatory responses reflect the dearth of Romantic criticism dealing with physical pain. It should become evident throughout this book that, while there are numerous studies dealing with Romantic agony in the sense of emotional suffering, disenfranchisement, alienation, and grief, these studies assume — or subsume — the category of the physical, which raises its own, particular problems. There is no extended analysis that attempts to locate *physicality* and physical pain as a concern for the Romantics. Pain is the great repressed in criticism of the Romantics, just as, for Freud, the body was the great repressed in the constitution of the social order. The Gothic, and the Gothic elements of Romanticism, invite the repressed to return; they bring us on stage with pain, and force us to see what fascinates us at the same time that it disgusts us.

Thus what I am calling the "Gothic body" is that which is put on excessive display, and whose violent, vulnerable immediacy gives both the Delacroix painting and Gothic fiction their beautiful barbarity, their troublesome power. Sardanapalus contemplates pain, and has the luxury of doing so because he is not feeling it (the same could be said, I suppose, for the author of this study). Pain for Sardanapalus is filtered through spectacle: it has that curiously fascinating quality that inflicters of pain have exploited in different ways from the Roman coliseum to the contemporary slasher film. And for writers in the late eighteenth and early nineteenth centuries that spectacality takes on particular importance, for it underlies the ways writers saw and thought about their world. In Chapter two, I discuss Ann Radcliffe and the young Wordsworth, both of whom are indebted to the sensationalist literature of sensibility, and both of whom are suspicious of its effects. For both Radcliffe and Wordsworth, the imagination itself is a site of spectacle, where the pained body is evoked to register the hero/poet's engagement in the sad music of humanity, the social violences of which the sensitive writer had become so aware. But like Sardanapalus, their acts of imaginative contemplation put them outside the suffering rather than in it; they are spectators in the theatre of carnage, as they expose the limitations of the imagination to figure shared physical suffering. This imaginary spectatorship is literalized in Chapter three, which deals with the Romantic theatre and the spectacle of suffering. In this chapter, I emphasize the contradictory move toward representing "things as they are" in the realist/historical dramas of Byron, Coleridge, and Shelley, a representation that is constantly plagued by the distaste for sensationalist representation itself. In Radcliffe and Wordsworth, imagined pain isolates the imaginer; in the Romantic drama, however, that isolated spectator risks being infected by the violence he or she contemplates. If, as Blake said in *Jerusalem*, we become what we behold, then the effects of imagined violence — like those of stage violence — become much more difficult to control. The imagination itself risks becoming the stage for the playing out of Gothic violences.

The contagious effects of this spectacle were not confined in the Romantics to self-conscious literary production; they extended across the boundaries of the social, materialist concerns that many of these writers addressed directly. Legal reform, military revolution, medical developments: all were events whose emphatic physicality inspired the Romantics to think about physical pain at the same time that it troubled that thinking. Thus it must be emphasized that my focus on scenes of revolutionary and riotous violence in this book points to the degree to which France (my central example) was not only the source of anxiety about pain, but also a convenient nexus for figuring a wider range of problematic discourses about pain. France, in other words, acted as a site around which coalesced a myriad discursive considerations of pain as it displaced the immediacy of that pain. To understand these phenomena more fully, I have structured this book to discuss both the documents of social reform in the late eighteenth and early nineteenth centuries and the ways in which literary writers used those documents in their fiction. If the chapters herein feel somewhat discrete and disconnected, that is because I am interested in tracing the phenomenon of what I am calling the Gothic body across a number of discursive projects; if this book proves anything, it is how the pained body troubled the intellectual enterprises of *all* revolutionary Romantic endeavors.

One such discursive consideration is judicial policy-making. Chapter four situates the spectacle of pain in legal reform, as European authors sought to purge the last vestiges of judicial torture from the courts. As one of the fundamental influences on legal questions in England, William Godwin becomes an important player in this move, for it is to Godwin that many of the early Romantics looked for the foundations of a humane jurisprudence. However, in this chapter as well the contradictory status of Sardanapalus gets inscribed. Legal discipline and punishment following from the age of sensibility evidences a crisis in the subjective response: if imagining the ontological space of another always ensures that we are outside that space (as it does in Chapter two), then how are we to determine the complex world of *motivation* so necessary to an accurate and humane jurisprudence? On the other hand, if imagining the ontological space of another threatens us with an emotional infection by that other (as it does in Chapter three), then what hope can we have for a rational, utilitarian legal system that is not swayed by the rhetoric of sensibility? Into this quandary Godwin invites the spectacle of torture, at once the most moving example of spectacular pain and, often, the most efficacious of judicial procedures. His 1805 novel *Fleetwood, or the New Man of Feeling*, does so not with an eye for carving out policy — Godwin had taken care of that twelve years earlier, in *An Enquiry Concerning Political Justice* — but rather with a view ultimately to domestic affairs: in *Fleetwood* the scene of torture becomes an exercise in epistemology, through which the Godwinian hero can know with more certainty the delimitations of domestic affection as opposed to rationality. Torture becomes, among other things, a trope for emotional affliction and, as in *The Death of Sardanapalus*, the spectacle of another's suffering is channeled through the spectator's more self-centered concerns.

That the personal is political is no longer an insight — not since the projects of psychoanalysis, Foucault, and feminism have deconstructed the illusory centrality of personal agency outside of cultural inscription. However, it may be that the way the political becomes personal is what is really at stake in Romantic representations of pain. Marshall Brown's rather broadly stated thesis that *"books do not exist in history, but that history exists in books"* (363, emphasis original) foregrounds the Romantic authors' intention to achieve some personal goal in literary representation. In Romantic representations of pain, that goal is often to reconcile the political and social spectacle of pain with one's own experience or personal crisis. Thus Chapter five, perhaps the most ambitious in the book, tries to incorporate the personal experience of pain with a change of medical representations of that pain, and to do so in the context of military revolution. The theatre of revolution, that most widespread and grandiose of conflicted sites, is also paradoxically the most intimate space, in that its very scope allows Matthew Lewis and Byron to isolate the pained individual within it, and to analyze the dynamics of that pain. Like torture for Godwin — indeed, like all the pain in Romantic fiction — war is not only an abstract discursive event, nor is it merely a nexus for all the contradictions I noted above; war is also a personal, private experience. If there is a spectatorship in war, it is often a spectatorship of one's own private body. And here we come full circle to that problem Delacroix raises so forcefully in his painting: the problem of the Gothic body, and the self that is both always involved and always removed.

This history of pain, then, is in many ways a history of looking; it is a narrative of watching a pained object while occupying a contradictory space both *within* and *outside* that object. And within that narrative is a multitude of discourses that mediate the way a culture — or indeed an individual — experiences pain at any given time or place. Of interest here, obviously, is the later eighteenth century, and the way the pained body of the cult of sensibility gave way to the pained body in the Romantic consciousness. What, in particular, was involved in that liminal and amorphous transition? How did the representations of the body, and the very experience of pain in a given individual, change with the consolidation of what has come to be called the "Romantic consciousness"? Chapter one presents a history of pain that documents the way aesthetic, judicial, and medical revolutions were altering the whole arena of physical sentience, creating a new signifi-cance in the feelings of pain. In this sense, I treat pain here as a cultur-ally mediated experience through which authors and characters come to "know," in some sense, their own bodies. However, there is something innately curious about the assertion that pain is culturally mediated, given that pain is also that which has the ability to destroy our consciousness of it. The experience of pain is mediated and culturally specific; yet pain can destroy that mediation by rendering paralysis, numbness, and loss of con-sciousness. One of the contradictions I want to sustain through this book, then, is that pain is created and yet it also creates (even if only in the way it destroys). I want to resist the current critical trend to talk about "the body" — as if this were no one's body in particular, not a body at all, a no/body — and the "political space inhabited by the body" — for bodies themselves are three-dimensional; they have their own internal spaces. Bodies have physiological mechanisms that are always regulated, but that also always regulate. At the same time that I ask the constructivist question of how Romanticism articulated the experience of pain — and much of Chapter one is devoted to this — I also want to reverse the question and ask one similar to that of Diana Fuss in *Essentially Speaking: Feminism, Nature, and Difference*: she suggests that, in thinking about gender, we move the

1. Pain, Politics, and Romantic Sensibility

I

Pain and danger, sickness and death—these ideas, according to Edmund Burke's 1757 *A Philosophical Enquiry into the Origin of our Ideas on the Sublime and Beautiful*, give rise to the strongest passions of which we are capable, and can be a source of pleasure leading to the sublime (39). Even stronger than pleasure itself, pain, when rightly experienced and contemplated, can produce an "elevation of the mind [that] ought to be the principal end of all our studies" (53). Burke's proclamation on the aesthetic pleasures of pain was part of a larger fascination with physical pain at the end of the eighteenth century, a fascination that, according to Mario Praz, underlies much of its literary production (*Agony* 27). Burke is echoed, unwittingly, by that other great master of pain, the Marquis de Sade, whose thesis in his 1795 *Philosophy in the Bedroom* is similar in some ways to Burke's:

> there is no doubt that we are much more keenly affected by pain than by pleasure: the reverberations that result in us when the sensation of pain is produced in others will essentially be of a more vigorous character, more incisive, will more energetically resound in us, will put the animal spirits into circulation and these, directing themselves toward the nether regions by the retrograde motion essential to them, instantly will ignite the organs of voluptuousness and dispose them to pleasure. (*Justine* 252)

The location of pain in Sade differs from that in Burke: whereas pain stimulates Sade's "nether regions," it appeals in Burke to the *mind*, a mind capable of intense excitation. But the effects of pain are similar: both theorists attribute to pain the most intense experience they can imagine, an experience that both excites and exhausts.

The fascination that Burke and Sade articulate—although on very different moral planes—is part of a widespread concern of writers at the end of the eighteenth century, and goes to the very heart of England's understanding of the cult of sensibility. The concern as Burke and Sade define it is, among other things, an aesthetic one: sensibility deals with the way we respond to physical distress, both in ourselves and in others; sensibility gives us the categories by which we interpret those responses. Sade and Burke attempt to create pleasure out of physical pain, and to collapse the distance we usually place between the two experiences. This collapse has a long history in the development of sensibility, one that begins with Newton and John Locke.

In *An Essay Concerning Human Understanding*, Locke reifies and moralizes the distinction between pleasure and pain:

> Things then are Good or Evil, only in reference to Pleasure or Pain. That we call *Good*, which *is apt to cause or increase Pleasure, or diminish Pain in us; or else to procure, or preserve us the possession of any other Good, or absence of any Evil*. And on the contrary we name that *Evil*, which *is apt to produce or increase any Pain, or diminish any Pleasure in us; or else to procure us any Evil, or deprive us of any Good.* (II,xx,2, emphasis original)

Here Locke establishes the tradition that Burke will modify, which argues that "the removal or *lessening of a Pain is* considered, and operates as a *Pleasure*: And the loss or diminishing of a Pleasure, as a Pain" (II,xx,16). Physiological and moral life operate in proportion: an increase of pleasure designates an increase of the good, and an increase of pain designates an increase of evil. But this somewhat mechanical equation of pleasure/pain with good/evil assumes that one gets no pleasure in someone else's pain, an assumption that later eighteenth-century thinkers did not wholeheartedly accept. Man as he was described by Hobbes exists in a state of selfishness. Such a selfish creature may glean something more precious from the observation of pain than the mere ability to designate it as evil. For Joseph Addison, imagined suffering can "teach us to set a just Value upon our own condition, and make us prize our good Fortune which exempts us from the like Calamities" (*Spectator* 418, 298). The pleasure we feel in literature—a pleasure we *cannot* feel, says Addison, in "actual" observations of suffering—arises as we compare ourselves to the literary victim: "we consider the Misfortunes we read in History or Poetry, either as past, or as fictitious, so that the Reflection upon our selves rises in us insensibly, and over-bears the Sorrow we conceive for the Sufferings of the Afflicted."[1] Like Walter Benjamin's "Storyteller," the Addisonian reader is drawn to novelistic suffering in "the hope of warming his shivering life with a death he reads about" (*Illuminations* 101). From Addison's pioneering distinction, we find the eighteenth century moving away from a distinction between pleasure and come out of a lack of interest, but rather out of a concern to keep some semblance of focus and structure. I hope that what follows here might be a starting point for further critical thinking about pain. Elaine Scarry has suggested that intense pain destroys all words (*Body in Pain* 19–20); conversely, I think it might inspire many.

debate away from "How is the body articulated by the social?" toward asking "How is the social articulated by the body?" (52). My question here is not "How did the late eighteenth and early nineteenth centuries articulate the experience of pain?" (which, while important to this project, is closer to Foucault's formulation of the question), but rather "How did pain articulate the late eighteenth-century experience?" *Gothic Bodies*, then, is meant to explore the transition from the age of sensibility to Romanticism by analyzing the move Marshall Brown has noted from sensibility as a sense of "selflessness" to Romanticism which puts the self in the foreground as the mediating consciousness of all things. Pain in this study becomes the ontologically significant focused experience which, even if it comes sympathetically from the outside, is incontestably present in the self that feels it.

Finally, a few words on what this study doesn't do. I have tried to incorporate biographical and literary considerations into my analyses of the novels, plays, and poems, but I have not tried to provide an arch-theory or master discourse that would offer the last word on the author in question. While in many cases the author's medical history offers striking parallels to the problem of pain in the work, my concern is the text, and the problems it raises on its own terms, and in the terms of the circulating discourses in which it was written. Of course, I have not discussed all the Gothic novelists, nor all the Romantic poets. In fact, the words here and in Chapter one that concern Blake and Keats are the last on them. Texts were chosen on the ground of their applicability to the questions raised, and on my own personal interest in them, and not on their canonical status. Neither have I tried to follow a linear history in which I chart the changing conceptions of pain through the first days of the Gothic to the first and second "generations" of Romanticism. At times, later writers have a less sophisticated and interesting treatment than earlier writers on a given question (Godwin's discussion of torture, for example, is much more complete than Shelley's, even though Shelley's came later). Rather, I have organized the chapters around certain *theoretical* problems, which are not necessarily elaborated by a strict adherence to chronology. And finally, this work does not treat all the questions it could about pain in the late eighteenth century; it is not the key to all pathologies. For example, there is no discussion of pain as it comes out of a Protestant and Calvinist tradition, although such a discussion would no doubt illuminate the texts of Byron, Maturin, or James Hogg. Nor is there a chapter on gender politics, to which Wollstonecraft and Mary Shelley would contribute (and, I admit, which seems to be begged for by the chapter on Radcliffe and Wordsworth).[1] These deficiencies do not pain, toward the beginnings of a pleasure *in* pain, and more problematically, toward an aesthetic pleasure in someone else's pain.

The pleasure we derive from someone else's pain becomes the foundation of much of the literature of Sensibility in the mid- to late eighteenth century. As numerous studies are beginning to show (Barker-Benfield, Brissenden, Brown, Todd), both physical and emotional distress became pedagogical moments of sympathy in the moral sensibilities of authors like Richardson, Sterne, Mackenzie, Goldsmith, and Radcliffe (by no means an exhaustive list). From the transformative, salvific effect of suffering on Richardson's Robert Belford, through the sites of suffering Yorick encounters on his sentimental journey, to the moving tableaux of the pained hero in Radcliffe's novels, to the complacent heart of Wordsworth upon leaving the Discharged Soldier, sensibility exploited the experience of suffering to induce in its reader a proper sentiment: pity for the victim whose body is in distress. Yorick perhaps makes the case most strongly, as he contemplates the caged starling who cries that it cannot get out of its cage. Yorick writes with selfless ardor, "I vow, I never had my affections more tenderly awakened; or do I remember an incident in my life, where the dissipated spirits, to which my reason had been a bubble, were so suddenly called home" (*Sentimental* 96). With this incident he immediately pities all those prisoners who are born to slavery, whereas earlier he had assumed that suffering was good for them. With sentimental cliché, Sterne makes of suffering an ennobling, purifying experience.

As the century moved on, the preoccupation with suffering in another, and the pedagogical effect that suffering could have, became transformed into a preoccupation with the experience of pain in the self. Whereas Burke was interested in another's pain as "the principal end of all our studies," Sade focuses on his own "animal spirits"; for Sade, pain is indistinguishable from pleasure, an obfuscation he seems to share with the Romantics, who were intensely conscious of their own pain. Moreover, whereas Burke's "pain" exists in the imagination, Sade's stimulation goes directly to the "nether regions"; it inscribes itself fully on the body. This shift in focus from mind to body characterizes a shift in Gothic and Romantic fiction from contemplation of suffering to the experience of suffering. For Lord Byron, the "great object of life is Sensation — to feel that we exist — even though in pain" (*Letters* III 109). The idealistic optimism of Shelley is often defined to a great extent by falling upon the thorns of life and bleeding. Keats sees "mortal pains," the "worldly elements" that prey upon sensation, as necessary to the soul's formulation. In his famous letter of

21 April 1819 to George and Georgiana Keats, the "World of pains" is an
essential teacher of consciousness; pain is necessary to the Romantic construction of the identity (*Letters* 336). And for Coleridge, poetic production often arises as a direct result of pain. He writes in the *Biographia
Literaria*,

> I am well aware that in advanced stages of literature when there exist many
> and excellent models, a high degree of talent, combined with taste and judge-
> ment and employed in works of imagination, will acquire for a man the name
> of a great genius; though even that analogon of genius which in certain states
> of society may even render his writings more popular than the absolute reality
> could have done would be sought for in vain in the mind and temper of the
> author himself. Yet even in instances of this kind, a close examination will often
> detect that the irritability which has been attributed to the author's genius as its
> cause did really originate in an ill conformation of body, obtuse pain or
> constitutional defect of pleasureable sensation. What is charged to the author
> belongs to the man, who would probably have been still more impatient but
> for the humanizing influences of the very pursuit which yet bears the blame of
> his irritability. (20)[2]

Literary distinctiveness—what we see as irritability in a writer like Pope,
Byron, or even Coleridge himself—often proceeds from physical pain. Pain
in the self actually helps to formulate a sensibility. In Coleridge's view, pain
often helps to construct the same self that it abuses.

The exquisite distresses which are a benchmark of late eighteenth-
century prose come out of a movement to define the concept of "aesthetics"
in the 1750s—a concept that gave the cult of sensibility its clearest definition, and which continues into the production of Romantic literature. As
Terry Eagleton explains, the term "aesthetic" was first used by the German
theorist Alexander Baumgarten in his *Aesthetica* of 1750. Baumgarten's
formulation of the aesthetic, says Eagleton, designated "the whole region of
human perception and sensation, in contrast to the more rarefied domain of
conceptual thought" (*Ideology* 13). "Aesthetic" suggested the materiality
of sense perception as it grew out of Lockean empiricism and sense awareness, and it emphasized the importance of the perceiving body in the
material world as the privileged source of knowledge. In original aesthetics,
"things" were privileged over "thoughts"; physical sensations were more
closely attended to than were abstract ideas. This privileging of bodily
reactions manifests itself in Burke's *Enquiry*, as in so many other works. In
the *Enquiry* we are given a long dissertation on the physiology of pain, fear,
sublimity, and beauty. The anatomical descriptions that Burke provides

relate to what John Beer describes as a change wrought by eighteenth-century medical discoveries and their relation to ontological aesthetics. Beer says that in the eighteenth century experiments on the human heart changed the way the educated person saw its functions: no longer a simple metaphor for social sympathy and community, the heart came to be seen as a thermometer of one's emotional state, in that the heart beats faster and more perceptibly when one is excited (*Wordsworth* 11). Thus, for Beer, "the actual movements of physical heart and physical bloodstream can be intimately involved" in our relationship with other animate beings (16), a relationship he locates in Wordsworth's appeals to the human heart as the source of love and sympathy. This physiology, part of a growing interest in Natural Philosophy, marks the culmination of a process begun in the 1750s, one that Eagleton describes as "the first stirrings of a primitive materialism — of the body's long inarticulate rebellion against the tyranny of the theoretical." Hence the assertion that begins *The Ideology of the Aesthetic*: "Aesthetics is born as a discourse of the body" (13).

As the concept of "aesthetics" sought to validate one's existence in the material world, it began to obscure the distinction between pleasure and pain that Locke had assumed. Addison's revision of Locke suggests that pleasure is not the binary opposite of pain, but rather exists on a continuum with pain. By the late century and early into the following one — in the writings of Sade and Maturin, for example, and indeed, in the entire mode of Romantic agony — the continuum had been redefined as a pleasure in pain and, more interestingly, as a pain in pleasure. In the 1791 *Justine*, Sade writes,

> What is the aim of the man who seeks his joy? is it not to give his senses all the irritation of which they are susceptible in order, by this means, better and more warmly to reach the ultimate crisis . . . the precious crisis which characterizes the enjoyment as good or bad, depending upon the greater or lesser activity which occurs during the crisis? (*Justine* 603)

And to increase this irritation and enjoyment, Sade asserts, "there is no more lively sensation than that of pain" (606). For Sade, pain is syllogistic: aesthetics validates feeling; the greater the feeling, the more aesthetic the experience; pain is the most intense of all feeling; therefore, pain is the most aesthetic experience we can have. As I have already noted with Byron, the "great object" in the late eighteenth-century post-Lockean tradition — that which philosophy was seeking to affirm — was sensation. Thus, the fascination with pain seems to come from a need for the ontological confirmation that comes with the validation of physical sentience, a validation whose strongest expression is pain.

However, to see pleasure in aesthetic excitation of all forms is to do so at one's peril, for the boundary between pleasure and pain is a precarious one. I have already noted how, in Burke's *Enquiry*, pain was stronger than any other experience, including pleasure. For Burke, pleasurable pain, the pain that can lead to the sublime, "has no resemblance to absolute pain, which is always odious, and which we endeavour to shake off as soon as possible" (37). Absolute pain, as experience tells us, is always unpleasant. One thinks of Blake's Thel, who willingly explores the underworld of her sexuality until she is confronted by the pain of virginal intercourse, when the "little curtain of flesh on the bed of our desire" is violently torn. It is at this moment, the moment of sensory awareness to physical attack, that she shrieks and flees to safety (*Blake's Poetry* 68). Moreover, absolute pain is an aesthetic experience that threatens to render us unconscious, oblivious to any sensation or aesthetic experience. As the stereotypical fainting of the wounded hero or distressed heroine makes all too clear, pain is both an aesthetic intensity and an aesthetic vortex. It takes on that curious status of being too much feeling and not enough. It threatens the very aesthetic continuum of which it is a part. Sade himself complained in *Justine* that the "desire to increase [sufferings] . . . 'tis, I know, the reef upon which the fantasy is doomed to wreck" (*Justine* 598), and the "aesthetic" pleasures of pain can all too easily drown themselves in their own excesses. Somehow, the boundary between pain-as-pleasure and pain-as-numbness must be maintained at the same time that it is being obscured. In maintaining that boundary, the literary representations of pain at the end of the eighteenth and the beginning of the nineteenth centuries turn on a binarism of sensibility/insensibility or feeling/numbness that is constantly being established and at the same time threatened by the dynamics of pain.

The threat that excessive feeling (i.e., pain) provided to its own continuum becomes the foundation for a widespread, multivalent approach to the problem of pain management in the 1750s and beyond. One response to aesthetic theory's validation of corporeal sentience was to subject pain to a head-on attack. The later eighteenth century was the age of an emphatic reform in the management of physical sentience, a reform whose primary agenda was to rid the world of unnecessary pain. In utilitarian judicial theory, for example, sweeping changes in the procedures of punishment sought to reduce pain and corporeal affliction, thereby replacing torture and flogging with more humane, gentler methods of correction (Taylor, *Sources* 331; Foucault, *Discipline*; Spierenburg, *Spectacle*). Perhaps the most paradoxical development in this reform was the emerging popularity of the guillotine — the very symbol of French Revolutionary barbarity — named after the French physician J. I. Guillotin who recommended it to the Revolution as a *humane*, efficient, painless method of execution.[3] This emphasis on "humane" procedure made the execution akin to a surgical procedure,[4] and connects judicial pain-avoidance to changes in medicine as well. The late eighteenth century, targeted as the birth date of modern medicine (Foucault, *Clinic*; Morris, in Rousseau, *Languages* 298), saw as its major contribution to the history of health the development of effective, clean anesthetics that would render surgery painless. Indeed, as Foucault and Morris point out, medicine took the form of a "master discourse" in defining the healthy body against the painful body. And finally, the move to eradicate pain was making itself felt in thinking about theatre, spectacle, and artistic production, so that by the time we get to Shelley and Byron, the violence of late eighteenth-century melodrama, although popular with mass audiences, was distasteful to a new aesthetic demand for subtlety and psychological realism. This distaste for violence was mirrored in Wordsworth's disdain for the German influence on the Gothic novel. Such a disdain depicts a move in the Romantics away from the body's immediacy and toward a redefinition of "aesthetics," one focused on the abstract, the Kantian ideal, the disembodied — the "Sublime" in Burke's and Wordsworth's sense of *intense* feeling. What the debate on stage violence ultimately represents is the existence of the paradoxical forces suggested by the aesthetic: it signals a boundary between the aesthetic as that which is rooted in the body and the aesthetic as that which is opposed to the body.

I am suggesting, then, that Romantic fiction can be read as occurring in an intersection of pain and numbness that raises some important questions: as the late eighteenth century devoted remarkable energy to thinking about the Enlightenment continuum of pleasure and pain, and to the way that continuum could collapse into a pleasure *in* pain or a pain in pleasure, this thinking co-existed with a move toward the eradication of the *existence* of pain. This complex of contradictions bequeathed to us by the late eighteenth century raises a number of theoretical questions, the first of which is the very definition of pain itself. Burke says that actual physical pain is "always odious," and in no way a pleasure, but such a preclusion was not so easy for eighteenth-century aesthetic theory. As the *OED* tells us, pain is a "primary condition of sensation or consciousness, the opposite of *pleasure* [sic]; the sensation which one feels when hurt (in body or mind)"; but it also has a "specifically physical sense: Bodily suffering; a distressing sensation as of soreness (usually in a particular part of the body)." That pain should be on the one hand "specifically physical" (what medical discourse calls "nociception," that is, the activity of nerve endings to signal tissue damage) and on the other hand a property of "body *or* mind" (and therefore very much a matter of "perception") makes pain into something other than purely physical. Wilbert E. Fordyce, quoting J. Liebeskind, says that the usual way of describing pain as "physiological" versus "psychological" denotes "'a Cartesian dualism [that] should have been discarded long ago'" (in Sternbach, *Psychology of Pain* 49); David B. Morris identifies in the tendency to separate physical from psychological pain an "artificial division" which he calls the "Myth of Two Pains," a myth which fallaciously assumes that the experience of pain is separate from the sufferer's understanding of it (*Culture* 9). The discarding of this myth, as we shall see, occurred in the eighteenth century and has manifested itself in a number of ways: medical treatises on pain since the 1750s no longer entertain the notion of a physical pain that is not to a significant degree mediated by the patient's culturally determined understanding of that pain (see Browne in Mann, *History and Management* 40; Merskey in Smith, *Pain* 71; Sternbach, *Psychology* 226; and Morris, *Culture*); the constructivist standpoints in literary and critical theory since Foucault discuss bodily sensations as products of social discourses that define, regulate, and to a degree *create* those sensations in the conscious or politically unconscious subject; and literary criticism (especially that of Romantic fiction) conflates the physical aspect of pain with the emotional, so that "human suffering" comes to denote the mixture of nociception and perception. Since the 1750s, then, pain has been re-mapped as a dialogue between body and soul.

But while we may no longer see pain as a purely physical phenomenon, we do, I would suggest, continue to accord it a dualistic status in the way we describe it. "There is only one antidote to mental suffering," wrote Karl Marx in *Herr Vogt*, "and that is physical pain" (quoted in Scarry, *Body in Pain* 33). What Marx indicates here is that we treat nociception very differently from perception; we usually fear a broken leg with more intensity than we do a broken heart. In his essay, "On Narcissism: An Introduction," Freud states the case forcefully:

> It is universally known, and we take it as a matter of course, that a person who is tormented by organic pain and discomfort gives up his interest in the things of the external world, in so far as they do not concern his suffering. Closer observation teaches us that he also withdraws *libidinal* interest from his love-objects: so long as he suffers, he ceases to love. (*Standard* Vol. 14, 82, emphasis original)

To return to the Coleridge quotation for a moment, we see a kind of Romantic crankiness that is not the product of Coleridgean performance anxiety, Byronic alienation, or any of the other stock emotional agonies; rather, it is physically based, resulting from a body in pain that forces libidinal investment into itself. The pained body often operates not only in tandem with the mind, but also in spite of it.

The pained body's privileging of itself over the mind helps to explain our culture's antagonism to our own inescapable corporeality. In her 1985 book *The Body in Pain: The Making and Unmaking of the World*, Elaine Scarry suggests that, regardless of the physiology of pain, the *experience of pain* reinstates a Cartesian antagonism between body and mind by attacking the "self" with pain: "The ceaseless, self-announcing signal of the body in pain, at once so empty and undifferentiated and so full of blaring adversity, contains not only the feeling 'my body hurts' but the feeling 'my body hurts me'" (47). While critics like Peter Singer are right to be troubled by such a definition—how can pain be "at once so empty . . . and so full"? ("Unspeakable" 27)—Scarry's conclusion is helpful. In our thinking, pain is not "natural"; it is adversarial. Our English word "pain" comes from the Latin *poena*, meaning penalty or punishment. The body in pain attacks the self that recognizes that pain. This sense of being attacked by one's own body, says Scarry, explains why metaphors for pain are so often those of weaponry, assault, and violation (pounding, burning, tearing). Pain evokes an antagonistic relationship between the body and the self at the same time that it allows no distinction between body and self: I hurt and I am being hurt; I hurt myself. Thus what pain effects is a return of the body to a pre-Cartesian body—where mind and body are inseparable—at the same time as it pits the mind firmly *against* the body. Pain confounds one aspect of dualism (the primacy of mind over body) by evoking another aspect of dualism (the body's perceived estrangement from the self). What is perhaps most singularly remarkable about this confusion, then, is the way pain destabilizes Cartesian thinking, in which the mind is separated from and privileged over the body. And this destabilization seems to make its birth cries in the literatures of sensibility, and emphasized in its descendent, the Romantic novel.

I do not wish to suggest here that physical pain is ever free from cultural mediation, or that we can have direct access to nociception that is not in some way framed by the symbolic. That kind of dualism, physicians tell us (and rightly, I think), is no longer tenable, and is not my interest in this study. But I do believe that pain, as it attacks our bodies, reinstates *in our perception of it* a dualism: by trying to use the mind to control the pained body, we reinforce the mind's estrangement from the body. And in so doing, we invoke a complex series of confusions about the way we think about the body. These confusions become particularly acute for the late eighteenth century, in which the pleasurable perception of others' pain was colliding with the distressing perception of one's own odious pain. The dualism that Scarry suggests exists in pain can be read as part of a Romantic dualism of self-perception, one that depends upon nociception at the same time that it tries to eradicate it. I want now to turn to a more linear analysis of the history of nociception and discuss its implications for Romantic modes of thinking about the body. As pain manifests itself at the turn of the nineteenth century, we can ask Eagleton's question, "What kind of aesthetic was born as a discourse of the body?"

II

The complex slipperiness of pain began to manifest itself profusely in the mid-eighteenth century as physicians attempted to reorganize the landscape of the human body and its responses to stimulation. Until the early 1750s, pain was understood through the model provided by Descartes. For him, one's reaction to pain was a purely mechanical process, a reflex action. In his scheme, the soul was immaterial and made contact with the body through the pineal gland at the base of the brain. From there, it directed animal spirits toward the part of the body receiving the painful stimulation. L. J. Rather offers a lucid summary of Descartes's account of the body's encounters with potentially dangerous or threatening stimuli:

> According to Descartes the observation of something strange or threatening sets up a movement of animal spirits (material substances in the Cartesian scheme) in the nerves that (a) turns the neck and head, and moves the arms and legs appropriately, (b) moves the pineal gland in such a way as to incite fear or anger in the mind (not in the *brain*), and (c) in the same mechanical, reflex, fashion alters the size of the orifices of the heart and thus alters the "rarefaction of the blood." . . . The movements of the body are not primarily caused by the mind, but are rather of the nature of the reflex. (*Mind and Body* 57)

The experience of pain, of direct nociception, followed the same path. Because the soul is immaterial, it could in no way dictate involuntary motions of the material body, such as that of drawing one's hand out of a flame, or even of contracting the lungs in breathing. Instead, the soul activated the pineal gland, whose secretion of animal spirits would direct the body toward the proper protective behavior. For Descartes, then, one's response to the stimulus of pain was a purely mechanical physiological response, mediated through the pineal gland, and in which the mind and soul played no direct part; they merely engineered the mechanisms by which a reflex response could take place. This mechanism, expounded by Enlightenment physiologists like the Dutch Herman Boerhaave, constituted the most widespread source of understanding of pain until the mid-eighteenth century.

But for many physicians the reflex model of pain and its attendant behaviors was unsatisfactory, and its hydraulic, mechanistic implications did not explain the complexities of the patient's behavior in pain. The most famous of these physicians was Robert Whytt. Born in 1714 in Edinburgh, Whytt became the first physician to challenge seriously Descartes's theory of the reflex. For Whytt, Cartesian mechanism was too systematic and general. Descartes's reflex model may have explained how individual body parts respond to pain, but it did not account for the role that emotional disposition seemed to play in the behavior of symptoms. Nor did it explain why disparate body parts seemed to respond to pain that did not threaten them directly—why, for example, nausea often accompanies headaches. In other words, Cartesian mechanism failed to explain why the parts of the body seemed to act interdependently. In 1751, Whytt's *Essay on the Vital and Other Involuntary Motions of Animals* began to explore the principle of human sentience as it relates to neurophysiology. What Whytt would eventually propose was a re-evaluation of Descartes's centralized, alienated soul. For Whytt, the soul was not sequestered in the fortress of the pineal gland, there to issue orders but never to take part in battle; rather, Whytt hypothesized that the soul extends from the brain down the spinal column, through the nerve endings, and to all parts of the body. This principle he called "coextension," to contrast with Descartes's dualistic "thought" and "extension" (French, *Robert Whytt* 152), and he suggested through it that the body is interconnected at the level of physiology.

From this decentralizing model, Whytt advanced his famous "sentient principle." For Whytt, "nerves are endued with feeling, and . . . there is a general sympathy which prevails through the whole system; so there is a particular and very remarkable *consent* between various parts of the body" (*Works* Preface to "Observations"). This "general sympathy" gathers information from all parts of the body and discharges stimulation to all parts of the body, so that "every sensible part of the body has a sympathy with the whole" (493). The movement of spirits is no longer unidirectional, but rather dialectic. All stimulation is perceived by the mind, as Descartes maintained, but since "the mind is only affected thro' the intervention of the optic and auditory nerves" (493n), it too is affected by physical stimulation, and can no longer be considered to dominate the body's experiences. Nothing exists in the *mind*, to modify Berkeley's claim, but as it is perceived by the physical body—a principle that came to Whytt via Locke's reading of Newton's *Optiks* (Barker-Benfield, *Culture of Sensibility* 5). The sentient principle, then, overturned the hierarchically structured image of the body as a Cartesian system of mechanistic reflexes, and replaced it with the image of the body as an interconnected, feeling entity. Whytt's medical discoveries proved that "the old distinctions between *animus* and *anima*—mind and soul—or between thinking and feeling, were misleading and unnecessary" (Brissenden, *Virtue* 42). As Christopher Lawrence writes,

> The upshot of these conceptual shifts was a move from Cartesian dualism to monism, with the nervous system itself as the bridge which possessed attributes of both mind and body. In consequence certain key terms such as "sensibility", and "susceptibility of impressions" were used interchangeably as definitions of the properties of the nervous system or of the soul. ("Nervous" 24–25)

By the late eighteenth century, the physical had become one with the metaphysical in the medical body.

What comes to be valorized by late eighteenth-century moralists as "sympathy," then, is physiologically based. Galenic medicine had discussed sympathy, but only as the product of moving humours throughout the body. As John Mullan notes, Whytt firmly connects the term "sympathy" not just to the bodily organs, but to a kind of mutual awareness that these organs share with each other (*Sentiment* 230). With Whytt—and a group of physicians doing similar work at Montpellier, France (see Outram, *Body* 54–55)—sentience in general and pain in particular are no longer monologic reflexes. Rather, corporeal feeling becomes part of an internal integrity, wholeness, and unity of the body, one that can be rendered visible by the physician's penetrating gaze (Foucault, *Clinic*; de Almeida, *Romantic Medicine* 46). No longer a victim of an alienated and immaterial consciousness—a superstitious *ancien régime* of metaphysiology—the body contributed to its own aesthetic awareness and make-up by contributing to the signals which constituted its psychology, and thereby contributing to the psychology that constituted the sentient signals it received. Physical sentience became the raw material of sympathy — that joining together of all aspects of the body in fellow-feeling. Thus both sympathetic pleasure and sympathetic pain became inscribed in nerve endings and physiological processes.

However, the same corporeal sentience that could give full body pleasure could also take it away, and Whytt's text is troubled by the very problem of insentience that he wants to overcome. Whytt's critique of prior modes of understanding physical sentience — most notably Albreckt von Haller's — begins with a reference to Hippocrates that substantiates the omnipresence of sentient nerve impulses in the body. In response to Haller's assertion that dissected organs have no feeling because they display no symptoms of pain, Whytt quotes

> an observation made by Hippocrates, *viz.* That a greater pain destroys, in a considerable degree, the feeling of a lesser one; an observation which is confirmed by daily experience. Thus, pricking any part of the body so as to give considerable pain, will so obliterate the irritation in the left orifice of the stomach, which is the cause of the hiccup, as instantly to stop that convulsive motion. (*Works* 260)

From this he concludes "not that the parts above mentioned [in Haller's study] are wholly without feeling," as Haller had argued, "but that they are much less sensible than many others" (261). Here we begin to see how the sentient principle relies on *in*sentience, in that feeling in one body part depends upon lack of feeling in another. This orientation toward insentience, Whytt suggests, is endemic to physiological structures:

> The membranes of *tela cellularis* [cell tissue] are, in a natural state, soft, flexible, and ductile, and have little feeling; but, in every wound or ulcer, when they acquire some more firmness, they are sensible of every touch and every acrid application. After a cicatrice has for some time covered the parts where the sore was, and they have returned to their natural softness, these cellular membranes lose again their sensibility, as appears on making a new wound through the cicatrice; and recover it again, whenever they become firm and tense, by the new inflammation and suppuration. (*Works* 267)

From this wounding and healing Whytt concludes that "the parts of muscles, which in foetuses and children are lax contracting fibres and very sensible, become in a great measure insensible" (267). Here the Marquis de Sade would surely agree: nerves, once sensitive, lose their sensitivity unless wounded or violently stimulated. Both through the natural toughening of the nerve endings and through the Hippocratic principle that a greater sentience usurps a smaller one, Whytt seems to suggest that the body, theoretically united by the sentient principle, gets broken down by the experience of pain into smaller, insentient parts, rendered insentient by abuse in pain. The sentient principle in Whytt betrays its dependence upon — and its *causation of* — insentience; it fragments the body even as it unifies it.

The well-ordered, harmonious, and sympathetic eighteenth-century body that Whytt's research claimed to be expounding provided a model for the social body as well. As L. J. Jordanova remarks, the image of the body as naturally sympathetic became an important model both for the family and for the body politic (in Barker, *1789* 16). The physiological beginnings of social sympathy are, once again, founded in Whytt. From the "remarkable sympathy" which Whytt observed between various parts of the body, "there is a still more wonderful sympathy between the nervous systems of different persons, whence various motions and morbid symptoms are often transferred from one to another, without any corporeal contact" (583). Physical symptoms become "infectious" as they imprint themselves on the sensorium commune. For Descartes, the immaterial soul's alienation from the body effectively isolated and encapsulated subjectivity. This isolation, when transposed to public life, formed the social basis of selfishness and individualism (which would get picked up and developed by thinkers like Hobbes and Mandeville). For Whytt, on the other hand, the interconnectedness of body and brain — of object and subject — ensured the interconnectedness of all animate, sensitive beings (Brissenden, *Virtue* 42–43). In fact, this sympathy could even be induced by literature: "By doleful stories or shocking sites," writes Whytt, "delicate people have been often affected with fainting and general convulsions" (*Works* 493).[5] Whytt's theories provided "empirical physiological evidence . . . that it is through sympathy that human beings are basically able to communicate with each other" (Brissenden, *Virtue* 31). Toward the end of the century, John Hunter (one of Byron's doctors) would make a similar point. Hermione de Almeida states the case:

> John Hunter's teachings on the "sympathy" between organs and parts commonly observed by clinicians in the hospitals of England led him in 1794 to address a parallel "sympathy of the mind" vital to the study of life by the creative artist or physician: "One of its chief uses is to excite an active interest in favour of the distressed, the mind of the spectator taking on nearly the same action with that of the sufferers, and disposing them to give relief or consolation: it is therefore one of the first of the social feelings." (*Romantic Medicine* 35)

Thus democratized physical sentience underwrote democratized communal sentience. At the level of the medical body, sympathy, especially for the distressed sufferer, makes society possible.

As numerous scholars have shown, the sympathetic body propounded by the Scottish medical academy established in its moral implications the foundations for Moral Sense Philosophy that, in the eighteenth century, became Cartesian rationalism's most vigorous opponent (Lawrence, Mullan, Barker-Benfield).[6] However, the same vicissitudes that troubled the sympathetic medical body would trouble the body in Moral Philosophy as well. Perhaps the most famous of the Moral Sense Philosophers after Shaftesbury is Adam Smith. In his 1759 *Theory of Moral Sentiments*, Smith argues that, while we can have no direct knowledge of someone else's afflictions and pains,

> By the imagination we place ourselves in his situation, we conceive ourselves enduring all the same torments, we enter as it were into his body, and become in some measure the same person with him, and thence form some idea of his sensations, and even feel something which, although weaker in degree, is not altogether unlike them. (*Theory* 9)

For Smith, as for Burke and Whytt, it is the experience of pain that constitutes community; at the heart of society is that familiar contemporary cliché, "I know how you feel." However, in *The Surprising Effects of Sympathy: Marivaux, Rousseau, Diderot, and Mary Shelley*, David Marshall notes a contradiction in Smith: for Smith, says Marshall, "sympathy is based on an act of the imagination in which we represent to ourselves an image of what we think the other person is feeling" (169). Sympathy is fraught, then, with the possibility that another's feeling might be nothing but our own self-interested construction. Thus any theory of the sympathetic body must precede the actual sympathetic behaviors of the body. "Sympathy" is discursive, not physiological at all. In his discussion of Diderot, Marshall summarizes the main thrust of his book:

> since we are unaware of what other people feel, we can appreciate what takes place inside them only if they represent the exterior signs and symptoms of their sentiments. The danger in this situation is finally not that we might not believe other people, but that we might not believe in them. (*Surprising Effects* 134)

Smith himself says that "we have no immediate experience of what other men feel[;] we can form no idea of the manner in which they are affected, but by conceiving what we ourselves should feel in the like situation" (*Theory* 9). Rather, Smith writes,

> the emotions of the spectator will still be very apt to fall short of the violence of what is felt by the sufferer. Mankind, though naturally sympathetic, never conceive, for what has befallen another, that degree of passion which naturally animates the person principally concerned. That imaginary change of situation, upon which their sympathy is founded, is but momentary. The thought of their own safety, the thought that they themselves are not really the sufferers, continually intrudes itself upon them. (*Theory* 21)

For the Moral Philosophers, of whom Smith is the pinnacle, failure in sympathy is ultimately a failure in imagination. One cannot imagine another's pain; ergo, one cannot feel it. What you don't know won't hurt you, and the community established by pain is really a solitude based on the inability to feel that pain. Like Whytt's medical body, Smith's political body depends on insentience for cohesion.

While Marshall is right to argue that the attempt by Moral Philosophy to undo Cartesian alienation was doomed to failure, that does not mean that thinkers gave up trying to find ways to construct community. At the same time that Smith is betraying doubt as to the possibility of sensibility's imaginative sympathy, the developing concept of aesthetics is trying to find ways out of that doubt, and to shore up the aesthetic of shared suffering. I have already referred to Robert Whytt's discussion of physical sympathy, which argued a thoroughly involuntary construction of community: one was simply "infected" by another's symptoms; one's ability to *imagine* another's pain did not enter into the equation in any way. This more complete inter-changeability of bodies is bolstered by Edmund Burke's *Enquiry*, written, like Smith's *Theory of Moral Sentiments*, at the end of the 1750s. While Burke is not a Moral Philosopher,[7] he is interested in the construction of sympathetic community. And whereas Smith locates individualism at the limits of the imagination, Burke envisions an almost limitless imagination that can create community. To authorize the possibilities of this imagination, Burke draws on the evidence of the body:

> It is by [sympathy] that we enter into the concerns of others; that we are moved as they are moved, and are never suffered to be indifferent spectators of almost any thing which men can do or suffer. For sympathy must be considered a sort of substitution, by which we are put into the place of another man, and affected in many respects as he is affected. (44)

By placing ourselves in someone's situation, by substituting our bodies for the bodies of others, we share their physical feelings. Despite his optimism, Smith has brought Enlightenment scepticism to its peak, resulting in individualism; Burke, conversely, overwrites the limited imagination with intersubjective capability. Thus the crisis in Moral Philosophy is somehow alleviated by a new "aesthetic" definition of sympathy, one that writers like Hazlitt (in "Self-Love and Benevolence: A Dialogue") and Shelley ("A Defence of Poetry") would later argue as passionately in favor of as Sade and Maturin would argue against. In Burke, as in many later students of his *Enquiry*, the sympathetic body in medical and aesthetic philosophy was the site that proclaimed the potential imaginative transference of self into other, a transference so powerful that it would *kill* Henry MacKenzie's Man of Feeling who felt another's suffering too fully. With this new aesthetic, the unified, sympathetic body was invested with the power to close the subject-object gap, and it heralded the migration from what we call the Enlightenment to what we call the Romantic.[8]

However, just as the pain of a migraine could, in Whytt's observations, be replaced by the displeasure of nausea, so could the sympathetic pain of Moral Sense Philosophy isolate the sensible onlooker. Aesthetic philosophy may have undertaken to rewrite the subject-object gap that Descartes had opened, but it was still plagued by the precarious aesthetic boundary I noted earlier: how do we keep feeling from becoming numbness? Like Smith, Burke maintains the distinction between subject and object, but he does so in a manner strikingly different from Smith. We have seen through Marshall the anxiety expressed by writers in the mid-century that sympathy was an act of imagination, and often doomed to failure. While Burke entertains no such limits in the imagination, he does leave an escape clause that keeps him from getting too close to the pain with which he claims to sympathize. For Burke, the idea of pain is a "delight" only by virtue of the perceiving subject's distance from it, his contemplation of it. For when

> danger or pain press too nearly, they are incapable of giving any delight, and are simply terrible; but at certain distances, and with certain modifications, they may be, and they are, delightful. (*Enquiry* 40)

A comparison to Smith here is illuminating. For Smith, "we have no immediate experience of what other men feel"; there is never enough feeling. For Burke, on the other hand, sympathetic pain can "press too close"; we can feel it too much. And when pain presses too near, it evokes that desire for self-preservation which, for Burke, destroys community (*Enquiry* 46). But when pain is experienced at a distance — through literature, or imaginative projection, or any experience that does not threaten us directly — we feel a sense of delight:

> If this passion [i.e., the sympathetic sharing of pain] was simply painful, we
> would shun with the greatest care all persons and places that could excite such
> a passion. . . . But the case is widely different with the greater part of mankind;
> there is no spectacle we so eagerly pursue, as that of some uncommon and
> grievous calamity; so that whether the misfortune is before our eyes, or
> whether they are turned back to it in history, it always touches with delight.
> (*Enquiry* 46)

For Burke, aesthetic distance is necessary because the ability to feel another's pain is *all too strong*: for that reason, the experience of another's pain
must be regulated and diminished. Like Smith, Burke constructs a boundary between pain and pleasure, and between sympathetic identification and
distance, but he does so for very different reasons.

Thus the problem Romantic fiction will inherit from the literature of
sensibility seems to be a problem of the imagining self's role in the intersubjective, communal sharing of the other's pained body. While this body
makes possible an interconnection of subject and object, it does so by
inducing pain in the observer who wishes to unite with the pained subject.
From this threat, I would suggest, comes the generating principle of the
Gothic's fascination with and treatment of pain. Gerald Bruns describes the
"limits of Romantic hermeneutics" as the recognition that it is impossible
to "[exceed] the finitude of reason that withholds the other from me . . .
[which] is born of the impossible desire to possess the self-possession of
the other, knowing the other from the inside out, with the self-certainty of
Descartes's self-experience, not doubting the other as one not-doubts oneself." This limit, Bruns hints, is drawn at the body, and by the body: "The
grave, like the body, seals us off from the other"; "We cannot know another's pain" ("Wordsworth" 402–403). For Elaine Scarry, these hermeneutic limits are the necessary product of pain, which invokes the "absolute
split between one's sense of one's own reality and the reality of other
persons" (*Body in Pain* 4). In this sense, the limits of Romantic hermeneutics are similar to those which Marshall locates in Marivaux. But I would
suggest an even more complicated state of affairs for literary renderings of
pain after the 1750s. The literature of sensibility, and by extension Romantic fiction, fostered the myth that pain *could* be shared through the medium
of the sympathetic body. Thus pain became a proclamation of ontological
presence both for the victim and the spectator of pain; the distinction
between them could no longer be said to exist. As Elaine Scarry argues, pain
is "so incontestably and unnegotiably present . . . that 'having pain' may

come to be thought of as the most vibrant example of what it is to 'have certainty'" (*Body in Pain* 4). However, as I shall discuss more fully in Chapter two, this shared pain deconstructs its own community, since by centering itself in the observer who shares it, it becomes "the most vibrant example" of an *individual* experience, one that is not communal at all. Hermione de Almeida argues that the social awareness of pain's tyranny at the end of the century made the sympathetic voice of the poet—in her study, Keats—all the more necessary as intermediary spokesperson or ventriloquist for the private experience of someone else's pain (*Romantic Medicine* 56–57). But in my analysis the attempt to construct this coherent community through the fluidity of the sympathetic body is always troubled by the vicissitudes of sympathetic pain as they are inscribed on the body. Pain is always and never a communal moment.[9]

By this logic, pain constructs a binarism of privacy and publicity that its theorists sought to overcome: whereas observed pain is at the heart of Moral Philosophy's theories of substitution and community, it is really that which guarantees the solitude, individuation, and privacy that have come to be associated with Romanticism. This dual role helps explain why pain became such a fascination at the end of the eighteenth century. Plagued by the attempt to reconcile individual privacy with social community, philosophers from Locke and Hume on tried to find a system that could connect one's feelings to the outside world of others' feelings, but without compromising the private interiority of those feelings. As Frances Ferguson explains, debates about population, the growth of cities due to the development of industrial capitalism, and the emphasis on personal and private aspects of individual consciousness generated a feeling that one's self could get lost in the crowd, that one's individual consciousness was competing against *many* individual consciousnesses (in Scarry, *Literature* 106). Sympathy, then, became the perfect mediation. It acted as a way of feeling oneself in the world—an "aesthetic," in Terry Eagleton's sense—that facilitated social behavior at the same time that it allows a person to act autonomously.[10] For Stephen D. Cox, "sympathy" both destabilizes the solitary Cartesian prison by melting the boundary between the inside and the outside, and guarantees the preservation of that inside/outside division: sympathy's emotive experience (Burke's "delight," Smith's "effect") assures a distance and protection to the perceiving self that is enjoying this experience. The social fabric or body politic here is built on sensibility and the aesthetic, but it is constantly being threatened by the individualist protection of insensibility and anesthesia. In the chapters that follow, then, I want to discuss the way the hermeneutic limits as they are dictated by the body both invoke a community and at the same time destroy it.

III

If sympathetic substitution is the agency by which we reconcile our public life with our need for privacy, then sentimentalism has an overtly political aspect. In the late eighteenth century, this political aspect of the pained body was extremely important (but not limited) to representations of the French Revolution. Long before the Revolution exploded on 14 July 1789, Cesare Beccaria, the most famous of Enlightenment European judicial reformers, declared in his essay *On Crimes and Punishments* that "no lasting advantage is to be hoped for from political morality if it is not founded on the ineradicable feelings of mankind" (10). These "ineradicable feelings," as we have seen, not only legitimate the subject in a previously Cartesian rationalist universe, but they connect that subject to all other subjects as well by the substitution of painful bodies. For Carl Woodring, this ability to imagine oneself into another's experience constitutes "the politics of English Romantic poetry." For the Romantics, in Woodring's analysis, the new community that would replace the *ancien régime*, its tyrannical superstitions, and its mind-forged manacles, in Blake's phrase, was possible only through the ability to place oneself imaginatively in another's experience (*Politics* 330). But as we have seen, the possibilities for imaginative substitution — and hence, political affiliation — are not only most strongly invited by the body in pain but are also precluded by the body in pain. Thus, sentimental appeals to pain could both further the radical republican cause of much Romantic fiction, and also undercut that same cause.

To the degree that Romanticism's radical political discourses were fueled by Rousseau's *On the Social Contract*, they sought a political community based, like Beccaria's legal reforms, on the "ineradicable feelings of mankind." Rousseau sought to unlock the chains into which every citizen is thrown after birth by reducing unnecessary force and legal conscription. Law, for Rousseau, was preceded by sentiment, "what everybody has already felt" without "art and mystery" (*Writings* 203–204). This doctrine of sentiments, which is natural, although corrupted, in social man, unites the multitude into one body, and assures the individual freedom of each body within the social contract (150); thus the affirmation of aesthetic sensibility is essential to the momentum of the French Revolution, that most important repository of radical English Romantic thought. As R. F. Brissenden argues, the "French Revolution, at least in one of its aspects, was an attempt to create the conditions under which men would be free to express their good impulses" (*Virtue* 33). Brissenden believes that the moral truths and social programs expounded in the French constitution were grounded, like eighteenth-century aesthetics, in *feeling*:

> that is, they were grounded in the belief that man's capacity to act morally is related to the degree of psychological and physical sensitivity with which he can spontaneously respond to the world about him, related, in a word, to his *sensibility*. With this belief went the hope that if people were allowed to exercise their sensibilities freely they would act in a "humane" way. (57, emphasis original)

This physical response, this "aesthetic," then, is overtly political, and overtly revolutionary. The voice of the heart (which, by the late part of the century is called the "sentimental," and becomes indistinguishable from "feeling") cries out for the fellow body in distress and thereby confirms for us our "solidarity with our fellow creatures" (Taylor 370). This naturally sympathetic voice, that which arose from Shaftesbury and his school as a "natural morality," guaranteed the primacy of "natural rights," not only for writers like Thomas Paine and Mary Wollstonecraft (Poovey, "Ideology"), but even for the Marquis de Sade. In his attempts to persuade Frenchmen to become Republicans, he argues (atypically) that "happiness consists in rendering others as fortunate as we desire to be ourselves," that the Republican fabric is woven with threads of natural feeling and material improvement (*Justine* 303). This interweaving, which comprises the rhetoric of Revolutionary propaganda, is perhaps most famously displayed in Wordsworth's reminiscences on France: as he walked through Paris with his friend Beaupuis,

> we chanced
> One day to meet a hunger-bitten Girl,
> Who crept along . . .
> . . . in a heartless mood
> Of solitude, and at the sight my Friend
> In agitation said, " 'Tis against *that*,
> That we are fighting." (*Prelude* IX, ll.511–520)

"*That*" is the highly charged body in pain, the victim of the *ancien régime*. Pain is the product of political tyranny.

But "*that*" can be more than one victim; it can be any victim, including the French king himself. Beaupuis's appeal to sentiment as political rhetoric demonstrates an emotional effect that anti-Jacobin critics of the Revolution were also able to exploit. As Ronald Paulson notes (*Representations* 42), reactionary English Tories used images of French barbarism to argue the anti-Jacobin cause: the French, after all, paraded decapitated heads on poles, the French cheered during public executions, and worst of all (according to Burke), the French invaded the sacred bed-chamber of Marie Antoinette and attempted to stick her full of sabers. Pain could be used not only to support one's revolutionary sympathies, but also to argue *against* Revolutionary sympathies. In the *Reflections on the Revolution in France*, Burke concludes his long tirade on the attack on the Queen by discussing *why* he feels the way he does. In so doing, he outlines a politics of sentiment:

> Why do I feel so differently from the Reverend Dr Price, and those of his lay flock, who will choose to adopt the sentiments of his discourse? — For this plain reason — because it is *natural* I should; because we are so made as to be affected at such spectacles with melancholy sentiments upon the unstable condition of moral prosperity, and the tremendous uncertainty of human greatness; because in those natural feelings we learn great lessons; because in events like these our passions instruct our reason; because when kings are hurl'd from their thrones by the Supreme Director of this great drama, and become the objects of insult to the base, and of pity to the good, we behold such disasters in the moral, as we should behold a miracle in the physical order of things. (175)

Whereas pain and violence catapult the young Wordsworth, Coleridge, or Thomas Paine into revolutionary political fervor, they make Burke (and the older Wordsworth and Coleridge) all the more suspicious of revolution. Pain and violence conjure up different notions of the "natural man": in Paine, it is the man moved by sentiment to change the political structure of oppression, to effect a "revolution" that will be a complete break from the past; in Burke, pain and violence move one to return to the order of tradition and natural self-control, to effect a "revolution" that is a return. Clearly, the sentimental response to pain is problematic, in that it can work for or against a political movement, depending on whom you cast in the role of victim. It could be used by both Jacobins and anti-Jacobins alike to further the emotional appeal of their cause, and at the same time, as Janet Todd tells us, its unpopularity could be exploited as a way of accusing the other side of acting unreasonably (*Sensibility* 130). Thus, by the end of the eighteenth century, "sentimentalism" — the moral directives of sensibility — came to demonstrate not only false, hypocritical, affected, or superficial feeling, as Brissenden notes (*Virtue* 7); it also suggested a highly politicized, highly effective, and highly dangerous mode of argument, one that could win one's case rhetorically by transferring the moral weight of the pained body to the side one wants it to be on.

Of course, the sentimental manipulations of Gothic bodies were not limited to France, or to representations of revolution coming out of France. Shelley saw Italy as the site of barbarism, a barbarism that could most fully be associated with Catholicism. The violence inflicted by England on America returns, like an infectious disease, in Blake's *America: A Prophecy* and Wordsworth's *Salisbury Plain* series to obfuscate a clear-cut notion of who was tyrannical and who was victimized. And in England itself the spectacle of pain could work at cross purposes. To take one example, the persecution of suspected sodomites in England presented the activist Jeremy Bentham with a tactical problem. As Louis Crompton argues in *Byron and Greek Love: Homophobia in 19th-Century England*, self-satisfied English liberalism was troubled by the fact that, at the turn of the nineteenth century, the British criminal code contained more than two hundred offenses punishable by death (18). In the case of sodomites alone, England "invoked its parliamentary statute to hang sixty men in the first three decades of the nineteenth century and . . . hanged another score under its naval regulations" (17–18).[11] Nor was this homophobic barbarism limited to the clean and efficient execution at the Tyburn gallows: Bentham noted the propensity with which sodomites were sent to the pillory, where they might have "'a jaw broken or an eye beat out',"and which, because of the public love of committing violence, "'is almost as good as death'" (22). However, as Crompton argues, if Bentham were to argue against this practice as cruel and inhuman, he had to do so carefully: to invoke too much sympathy for the tortured sodomitic body is to align oneself rather too closely with the sodomitic practice, to express a sympathy where only moral outrage would do. Thus Bentham cast his arguments in the somewhat abstract and disembodied rhetoric of utilitarianism, one that left the sentimental body out of the picture. Like the Frenchman (with whom the sodomite was aligned, sodomy being a "French vice"), the sodomite could represent a profound threat to (homophobic, xenophobic) English bodily integrity by feeling too much for the pains inflicted on him.

I have made this side-excursion into a discussion of sodomitic persecution in order to underscore that the predominance of pain in the late

eighteenth and early nineteenth century cuts across both national boundaries and discursive fields — it is both a French and an English problem —
but that it often circulates around fears of French influence and French
invasion. Within this context, pain presents a confusion because, among
other things, it invites us to sympathize physically and emotionally with
someone whom we might abhor morally and politically — someone like the
sodomite, or like Louis XVI or Marie Antoinette, the objects of Jacobin
scorn. Similarly, pain presents problems because it is sometimes seen as a
necessary result of fighting injustice; the infliction of pain is essential to
fighting the tyranny that inflicts pain on others. The necessity of inflicting
pain, and the moral questions it raises, underlie much Romantic fiction, like
Shelley's *The Cenci* or Godwin's *Caleb Williams*, and also Jacobin tracts such
as Paine's 1791–92 *The Rights of Man*, Wordsworth's 1793 *Letter to the Bishop
of Llandaff*, and Godwin's 1793 *Enquiry Concerning Political Justice*. These
writings demonstrate the problem of determining whose pain we should
feel and whose pain we should remain insensible to. Wordsworth, for
example, chides Richard Watson, Bishop of Llandaff, thus:

> At a period big with the fate of the human race, I am sorry that you attach so
> much importance to the personal sufferings of the late royal martyr and that an
> anxiety for the issue of the present convulsions should not have prevented you
> from joining in the idle cry of modish lamentation which has resounded from
> the court to the cottage. . . . [Bishop M. Gregoire] declared at the opening of
> the national convention, and twenty-five millions of men were convinced of
> the truth of the assertion, that there was not a citizen on the tenth of august
> who, if he could have dragged before the eyes of Louis the corse of one of
> his murdered brothers, might not have exclaimed to him, Tyran, voilà ton
> ouvrage. (*Prose* I, 32)

The sentiment here, if it can be so called, is Godwinian and utilitarian: "It is
right that I should inflict suffering, in every case where it can be clearly
shown that such infliction will produce an overabundance of good" (*Enquiry* 635). Unlike Wordsworth, Paine is at least willing to invoke the
humanity of Louis XVI, but only to write it off by claiming that the
Revolution "was not against Louis XVIth, but against the despotic principles of the government" (*Rights* 47), as if that should make Louis's ghost
rest any easier. Paine's careful separation of the abused human body and the
abused body politic forces him to make another careful distinction in his
definition of proper sympathy. He accuses Burke of not expressing "the
language of a heart feeling as it ought to feel for the rights and happiness of
the human race," but rather of constructing "tragic paintings" that are "very

well calculated for theatrical representation, where facts are manufactured for the sake of show, and accommodated to produce, through the weakness of sympathy, a weeping effect" (*Rights* 49–50). The "weeping effect" of sympathy is an unnatural response, a pale imitation of the language of the heart. Natural sympathy, then, presumably includes the utilitarian recognition that regicide is acceptable and preferable to the status quo. Sympathy here has to do not only with political *sensibility*, as Brissenden would have it, but with political *insensibility* as well.

If sympathy as fellow-feeling can perform the dual function of telling us what to feel and what not to feel politically, then it furthers the mediation between the public and the private I noted earlier. Paine's ambivalent sympathy, marked as it is by the binarism of sensibility/insensibility, is representative of a larger structure of sentiment and Stoicism that runs throughout the imagery of the Revolution. Ronald Paulson notes a central paradox in aesthetic representations of the Revolution: while the sans-culottes sought as their ultimate goal to replace previous definitions of order and monarchichal structure with a democratic system founded on natural morality, they employed a Neo-classical mode of representation to figure that replacement. Suspicious of the rococo decadence and frivolity of Louis's court, the revolutionaries, argues Paulson, brought order and harmony to their newly envisioned political system through a classical reference that both structured and legitimized the republic (*Representations* 36). For Dorinda Outram, this Stoical nostalgia — such as one sees in the paintings of Jacques Louis David — was not only essential to the superstructure of the Revolution, but also to the individual within the new body politic. For Outram, the repeated references to Stoicism in Revolutionary productions were intended to provide a model of *self*-government that the individual could emulate (*Body* 36). And essential to this self-government was the citizen's withdrawal from the object world. Each member of the new republic had to be freed from a sensibility that, as the previous discussion makes clear, obfuscates one's political alignments and one's physical sympathies.[12] "The 'Stoicism' of the Revolution," Outram argues, "is about the definition of an autonomous self through an autonomous, impermeable, controlled body" (*Body* 81). This impermeable body, what Norbert Elias called the "*homo clausus*," constructed a dialectical citizen, one who, like Wordsworth, was moved by the sympathetic impact of the hunger-bitten girl, but one who, again like Wordsworth, found the deepest and most profound sentiments in privacy, "[in] the last place of refuge, my own soul" (*Prelude* X, l.415).[13]

IV

To the degree that much Romantic fiction constructs the hero as *"homo clausus"* in order to isolate him or her from the body in pain in general, and from the Revolution in particular, it presupposes that the reader of the Gothic novel will strike a similar relation to the body. We are already familiar with the argument that Romantic fiction is a literary expression of the desire to connect subject and object: in *Natural Supernaturalism*, M. H. Abrams discusses the importance Schiller placed on art's unification of the unself-conscious subject with the self-conscious subject-as-object (215); René Wellek argues that Romanticism is the attempt to reconcile the perceiving subject with the perceived object world[14]; as John Jones notes, Coleridge's work is permeated by Schelling's thesis that art makes the external internal and the internal external (*Egotistical* 6–7). To the degree that Romanticism arises from an aesthetic, sentimental tradition in which political community is founded on individual sensation, it becomes what Janet Todd describes as "a kind of pedagogy of [the senses] and of the physical reaction that [those senses] should produce" (*Sensibility* 4). However, it is also not new to suggest that this attempt at connection is problematic for the Romantics, or that the Cartesian gap can never be bridged by any self-conscious strategy. James Averill traces the effect on Wordsworth of a literary tradition that emphasizes one's own intense feeling in the face of human suffering, arguing from this that once we recognize our own feeling we can never hope to get back to an unself-conscious identification with the object in distress (*Wordsworth* 30; see also Nuttal, *Common Sky* 136); in their discussions of painting and theatrical spectacle, Michael Freid (*Absorption*) and John Bender (*Imagining*) talk about qualities of self-conscious voyeurism that are intended to highlight the spectator's status as observer, as standing *outside* the actions of the artistic subject; William Patrick Day relates this self-conscious voyeurism to the dynamics of parody, which for him is the underlying mode of the Gothic and its distancing of the reader (*Circles*). While this debate is firmly established in criticism of the late eighteenth century, I would suggest that it does not take into account the dynamics of imagining pain as I have outlined them above. Romantic fiction, in its fascination with pain and physical limitation, registers a crisis of sensibility that both engages and distances. Someone else's corporeal sentience always demands a sentient response from the spectator — what Marshall Brown sees as the "selflessness" of sensibility — yet it also always invokes the awareness of the limitations of that sentient response. In this sense, corporeal sentience is "aesthetic" in both aspects of the word: it points to a feeling of physical being-in-the-world at the same time that it disembodies and abstracts that physical being.

Up to this point, I have tried to explore the eighteenth century's fascination with pain in terms of the contradictions it presented. These contradictions — pleasure/pain, publicity/privacy, sensibility/insensibility, sentimentality/Stoicism — cut across a number of fields of enquiry, including the aesthetic, the ontological, and the political. Given this rich and complicated intersection of problems, I want to define as clearly as I can what I mean by "the politics of pain," the subtitle of this study.[15] The vicissitudes of the sensitive body, going back at least as far as the 1750s, combined with the possibilities for self-delusion and misconstruction of the "real" by the Romantic consciousness, constitute in Romantic fiction what Jürgen Habermas calls a "legitimation crisis" (*Communication*) for the notion of a community based on sympathy. Politics, both as it relates to the bonding with others and to the management of the self, circles around the image of the pained body and affirms both the bond and the alienation of the perceiving individual. Thus the politics of pain becomes at least three-fold. The first is a cultural politics. In Romantic fiction, pain demonstrates a general bourgeois interest in constructing the individual self that is *part of* but *separated from* the larger society. This construction is achieved by exploiting the ambivalences that sympathetic pain embodies: pain signifies both a threat to health — whose logical extension is death — and an assurance of health — in that it guarantees that he or she who is feeling it is not dead. By blurring the gap between the perceiving subject and the pained object, sentimental Romantic responses to pain create a community of shared pain. But, as I have already noted, pain is ultimately a completely individual experience that isolates the sufferer from all others. Pain destroys Cartesian individualism only to end up re-inscribing it.

The second sense of the politics of pain comes from the first, and emphasizes the political implications of the breakdown in dualism. Given the slipperiness of a definition of pain, a definition of its politics becomes difficult to pin down. As I have already shown, medical theorists and physicians since the eighteenth century have discarded what David B. Morris calls the "Myth of Two Pains," the separation of nociception, or tissue damage, from the patient's culturally determined perception of it. While this mind/body relation must be assumed, it also presents political problems. To argue that pain does not exist but as it is perceived, and that cultural, class, and gender differences always shape the way pain is experi-

enced, is to open up the possibility for differences in the political signifi-
cance of pain. As G. J. Barker-Benfield notes, the eighteenth-century physician George Cheyne claimed that "'There are as many and as different
Degrees of *Sensibility* or of *Feeling* as there are Degrees of *Intelligence* and
Perception in *human* Creatures. . . . One shall suffer more from the Prick of
a *Pin*, or *Needle*, from their extreme Sensibility, than others from being run
thro' the Body'" (*Culture of Sensibility* 9; emphasis original). And Barker-
Benfield makes clear the political implications of this distinction by recog-
nizing it in the mouth of Richardson's villanous Lovelace: "'Some people
are as sensible of a scratch from a pin's point as others from the push of a
sword; and who can say anything for the sensibility of such fellows?'" (9).
Lovelace is hardly the authority one would want to speak for the signifi-
cance of one's suffering. In a very different context, David Morris argues
that racist whites in nineteenth-century America assumed that black slaves
were less capable than they of feeling and responding to pain; thus slaves
could be whipped without the moral implications that accompany violence
being inflicted on another human being (*Culture* 39). By privileging the
mind — and its alleged capabilities and incapabilities regarding the perception of pain — whites could then justify the oppression of the body. As I will
demonstrate in Chapter four, this problem is replicated in Gothic discussions of torture, where the body of the "criminal" becomes useful to the
degree that it can help to expose and to regulate the mind. Because the mind
can be used to justify abuse on the body, the attempt to negate the body as
something distinct from the mind does not destroy mind/body dualism,
but actually risks reinforcing this dualism all the more. Politically induced
pain — as in torture, war, or revolutionary violence — is intended to exploit
the body's connection to the mind, and to get at the mind by way of the
body. In so doing, it ultimately attempts to reinstate the primacy of the
mind as the site of truth, pain, subjectivity — in short, of "real life." Thus I
am proposing here a study of the body and physical pain as something not
separate from the mind but also not able to be *subsumed by* the mind, because
the body is too often the site of pain in its political manifestations.

The third and final sense of the politics of pain is more partisan:
depictions of pain in turn-of-the-century fiction often set the problems of
pain within the context of the French Revolution (or historically distant
revolutions that connote the French). These depictions use pain to exploit
English responses and ambivalences toward events in France, and to the
often violent means England employed to squelch Jacobin and other kinds
of undesirable behavior. Pain both enlists and destroys Revolutionary sym-

pathies; it both engages the British subject (in the two senses of the word) in the cause of liberation and isolates that subject from a Revolution that might spread to its own front yard. It enlists the discourses of sensibility from the earlier part of the century, the discourses of imaginative sympathy and substitution, and weaves them throughout with an individualized pain that exploits the imagination that perceives this pain. Thus I want to turn now to two writers in the 1790s, Ann Radcliffe and William Wordsworth, both of whom were fascinated by the implications of pain on the imagination, and by the ambiguous politics that pain could inspire.

2. Imagining Pain

I

> We had not travelled long ere some mischance
> Disjoined me from my Comrade, and, through fear
> Dismounting, down the rough and stony Moor
> I led my horse, and, stumbling on, at length
> Came to a bottom, where in former times
> A Murderer had been hung in iron chains.
> The Gibbet mast had mouldered down, the bones
> And iron case were gone, but on the turf
> Hard by, soon after that fell deed was wrought,
> Some unknown hand had carved the Murderer's name.
>
> (*Prelude* XII, ll.231–240)

> This spot seemed the very haunt of banditti; and Emily, as she looked down upon it, almost expected to see them stealing out from some hollow cave to look for their prey. Soon after an object not less terrific struck her, — a gibbet standing on a point of rock near the entrance of the pass, and immediately over one of the crosses she had before observed. These were hieroglyphics that told a plain and dreadful story.
>
> (*Udolpho* 54)

In 1793 Wordsworth traveled across Salisbury Plain, where he had the experience that would provide the "spot of time" for the section of *The Prelude* quoted above. The same year, Ann Radcliffe published not her first, but certainly her most popular and critically successful novel, *The Mysteries of Udolpho*. And in that novel Emily St. Aubert, like Wordsworth, comes upon a gibbet which has been the site of someone's intense physical pain, and Radcliffe records her terrified reaction to that place. Both authors are writing in the same mode: Radcliffe is, of course, the "mother" of the English Gothic novel (so named by Keats), and arguably its most famous practitioner; Wordsworth began his career in the Gothic mode with poems like *The Vale of Esthwaite* and the unfinished "Gothic Tale," which are conventionally sensational in tone and subject matter. Indeed, *The Vale of Esthwaite* sounds like a Radcliffe novel in verse.[1] Yet, in both scenes, the act of imagining pain is somehow foreclosed as it becomes a depiction not of the suffering victim but of the dynamics of the subject doing the imagining. Like Sardanapalus in Eugene Delacroix's painting, Emily St. Aubert and the young Wordsworth behold the site of pain only to eclipse it by the act of looking.

This act of eclipsing is organic and temporal, as Wordsworth's original depiction of the gibbet experience in his 1793–94 *A Night on Salisbury Plain* undergoes radical revision before becoming a boyhood memory in *The Prelude*. In an early manuscript addition to *A Night*, the traveler finds an existing gibbet where "In clanking chains a human body hang [and] / A hovering raven oft did round it fly" (39r, *Salisbury Plain* 116). The effect is only intensified in the second version of the poem, *Adventures on Salisbury Plain*, where the traveler is a murderer, and so the gibbet symbolizes a direct physical threat to him. The boy of *The Prelude*, on the other hand, sees only "monumental Letters . . . inscribed / In times long past" (XII, ll.241–242); the landscape poses no real danger for him.[2] And it poses even less danger for the adult poet looking back on this childhood incident. Similarly, Emily reads the "plain and dreadful story" of the gibbet as posing the threat of murderous banditti who imprison their victims; yet this story's status as "hieroglyphics" helps to distance it in the past, to make it less personally threatening, despite the terror it inspires. In fact, even though Emily associates the gibbet with great personal danger — she expects to see banditti steal out and attack her — the danger is, like most others in *Udolpho*, greatly exaggerated by the excesses of the imagination and, in the end, poses no real personal threat.[3] Emily and her caravan reach their destination of Rousillon with hardships no greater than tired mules and windblown clothing.

Both Radcliffe's and Wordsworth's depictions of terror reduce a "dreadful story" of past physical suffering to a benign scene of reading. In so doing, the descriptions use the gibbet to instruct us on the proper use of the imagination. Betraying their mutual suspicion of the mode in which they are writing, both authors advocate restraint in the way such a scene as the gibbet should be looked at. Wordsworth's early descriptions in the *Salisbury Plain* poems border on the "application of gross and violent stimulants" which are the property of those "frantic novels, sickly and stupid German Tragedies, and deluges of idle and extravagant stories" (*Prose* I,128) that the older Wordsworth so intensely disliked, and which the later *Prelude* tries to tame. Similarly, Ann Radcliffe was suspicious of the potentially excessive passions of contemporary literature. The best-known spokesperson for this suspicion is Emily St. Aubert's father who, as he lies on his death bed, warns:

> Above all, . . . do not indulge in the pride of fine feeling, the romantic error of amiable minds. Those, who really possess sensibility, ought early to be taught, that it is a dangerous quality, which is continually extracting the excess of misery, or delight, from every surrounding circumstance. And, since, in our passage through this world, painful circumstances occur more frequently than pleasing ones, and since our sense of evil is, I fear, more acute than our sense of good, we become the victims of our feelings, unless we can in some degree command them. (79–80)

While there may be important differences here between the German *Sturm und Drang*, which Wordsworth condemns, and the novel of sensibility, which is Radcliffe's subject, the warnings are the same: literature seeks to move us through intense stimulation, but that stimulation can be dangerously excessive. It can make us slaves of our own imaginings.

A common interest of Wordsworth and Radcliffe, then, is in how the ingenuous spectator imagines a scene of physical suffering. Wordsworth's encounter with the gibbet gives rise to a whole series of meditations on physical suffering, both in the *Salisbury Plain* poems and in the *Lyrical Ballads*; Emily views her experience as a dreadful story of human vulnerability, and of the susceptibility to violence she shares with all other travelers. Yet the very act of imagining pain seems, in both authors, to be treated with suspicion: imagining pain opens up the possibility for self-delusion, for a slavish submission to the spontaneous overflow of powerful feeling that is not regulated by thinking long and deeply. The paradoxes that the gibbet scenes engender for both writers mark one of the primary contradictions of pain that I outlined in the previous chapter: pain is both an immediate physical experience and one that is mediated through a transforming consciousness. It is both antagonistic to and defined by the imagination. And this contradiction underlies the literary depictions of Wordsworth and Radcliffe as they think about the effects of pain on the sensitive subject. The Gothic convention of imagining pain demonstrates the power of the imagination, but only by demonstrating its impotence and limitation.

II

The most famous theoretician to discuss the power and impotence of imagined pain in the eighteenth century, and the one to whom Wordsworth and Radcliffe are most indebted, is Edmund Burke.[4] In Chapter one, I discussed how, according to David Marshall, imaginative sympathy in Marivaux and Adam Smith was a construction that always suggested its own artificiality and limitation. One could never know how another person felt. In Burke's *Enquiry into . . . the Sublime and Beautiful*, however, pain could be an actual moment of sentient transference, in that the observer could put himself in the place of the actual sufferer of pain. This substitution is itself an act of imagination, but seemingly without the boundaries imposed by consciousness. In Burke, the subject's body is imaginatively interchangeable with the victim's body. In fact, imagined pain — what Burke calls "fear" or "terror" — behaves in exactly the same way as "real" or experienced pain, if only to a lesser degree. To illustrate this point, Burke borrows a passage from Lucretius in which he asks us to imagine "a man in great pain[: he] has his teeth set, his eye-brows are violently contracted, his forehead is wrinkled" and so on. For the observer looking on,

> Fear or terror, which is an apprehension of pain or death, exhibits exactly the same effects, approaching in violence to those just mentioned in proportion to the nearness of the cause, and the weakness of the subject. . . . The only difference between pain and terror, is, that things which cause pain operate on the mind, by the intervention of the body; whereas things that cause terror generally affect the bodily organs by the operation of the mind suggesting the danger; . . . they agree likewise in every thing else. (131–132)

In the experience of terror, the mind imagines a certain physical experience which it reproduces on the body as the experience of pain. It then transmits that pain to the part of the anatomy where it was located in the observed object experiencing pain. In other words, we feel the "wound" in our limbs or organs through a kind of sympathetic identification, one produced by the imagination. In Burke, the direction of the sentient process (mind to body, body to mind) is what distinguishes physical from imagined pain, but the ultimate effect in the mind is the same. What separated Burke from Adam Smith, we remember, is that for Smith, the imagination could never replicate the experience of the sufferer, whereas for Burke, the imagination can replicate it all too well.

However, Burke is emphatic that pain can never be a *pleasure*, only a *delight*, by which he means that observed pain can only be pleasurable because it is characterized by *distance*, by the fact that the pain is not the observer's. Pain and danger are delightful — and possibly sublime — only to the degree that they are removed from one's immediate experience: Wordsworth and Radcliffe can anatomize their characters' reactions to pain only because that pain *suggests* an intersubjective threat without really providing it. Absolute physical pain, says Burke, is "always odious" (37), and the affliction we suffer as observers "has no resemblance to positive pain" (35). Thus Burke constructs a contradiction between the pained object and the imagining subject who "agree likewise in everything" on the one hand and "[have] no resemblance" on the other. While pain is identical to that which can be replicated by the imagination, that imagination depends upon the spectator not really coming into contact with physical pain. "Imagined pain" is both marvelously embodied and oxymoronic: its potential is always and never realizable.

The contradiction of imagined pain that Burke sets up in the *Enquiry* is part of his attempt to negotiate a complex terrain of the private and the public. For Burke, the imagination makes us public beings, and the potential for public interconnection is all the more present when we imagine ourselves into another's pained body: "The delight we have in such things, hinders us from shunning scenes of misery; and the pain we feel, prompts us to relieve ourselves in relieving those who suffer" (46). However, this body, which opens up the possibility of community, also threatens to foreclose community. If pain "press[es] too nearly" (40) or "too close" (46), it freezes the sensibilities and closes us off from feeling anything whatsoever for anyone else. Pain, danger, sickness, and death, says Burke, are those emotions that inspire "self-preservation," emotions that he contrasts to the "social" (38). If the imagination allows us to substitute ourselves for another, then it risks that odious experience of pain, the experience which forces us to close in upon ourselves and destroys the very community it claimed to construct. Thus Burke's imagined pain must be carefully regulated to keep it from destroying itself: it must exhibit "exactly the same effects" as real pain, yet bear no resemblance to it. In order to constitute the social fabric, the imagination of pain must have limits imposed.

To understand more fully the psychological roots of those limits, we can turn to Elaine Scarry's *The Body in Pain: The Making and Unmaking of the World*. In one way, Scarry re-inscribes the distinctive incompatibility of imagination and pain — of mind and body — that philosophers of sensibility like Burke were attempting to destroy. In her analysis, pain is differentiated from any other state of consciousness because it is totally interior in its referentiality. To explain:

> Contemporary philosophers have habituated us to the recognition that our interior states of consciousness are regularly accompanied by objects in the

external world, that we do not simply "have feelings" but have feelings *for* somebody or something, that love is love of *x*, fear is fear of *y*, ambivalence is ambivalence about *z*. (5)

But the experience which is least likely to have an external referent is pain, because pain needs no object to give it meaning:

> physical pain — unlike any other state of consciousness — has no referential content. It is not *of* or *for* anything. It is precisely because it takes no object that it, more than any other phenomenon, resists objectification in language. (5)[5]

Explaining the contradiction as it appears in Burke's *Enquiry*, Scarry delineates how, in pain, we are usually incapable of imagining anything other than our own bodies. Pain eradicates the external world and proclaims the primacy and irreducibility of hurting.

By Scarry's logic, while pain foregrounds the body's immediacy, the imagination depends upon the body's distance. The body must make no demands upon the imagination that might distract it from its functioning *as* imagination.

> The only state that is as anomalous as pain is the imagination. While pain is a state remarkable for being wholly without objects, the imagination is remarkable for being the only state that is wholly its objects. There is in imagining no activity, no "state," no experienceable condition or felt-occurrence separate from its objects: the only evidence that one is "imagining" is that imaginary objects appear in the mind. (162)

From this lack of external referent, Scarry reasons that all imagined materialities are by definition *im*materialities. The imagination "may well provide an object for other forms of sentience, an imaginary object of hearing . . . or an imaginary object of touch . . . but the object it provides is never provided for any experienceable form of sentience unique to itself" (162). As Burke has said, pain and imagination have "no resemblance."

In Scarry's discussion, pain and the imagination are the "extreme conditions" of our consciousness; when we are in pain, we are aware of nothing but the existence of our bodies; and when we imagine, we are aware of anything *but* the body, whatever external object occupies the imagination at a given moment (even if that object is an imaginative reconstruction of the body itself). Pain and imagination become for Scarry the " 'framing events' within whose boundaries all other perceptual, somatic, and emotional events occur; thus, between the two extremes can be mapped the whole terrain of the human psyche" (165). At one level, these extremes appear to recapitulate a rather discomforting Cartesian dualism in which all experience rests on a battlefield between *res cogitans* (here, the imagination) and *res extensa* (the body in pain). Moreover, we must pause at such essential and totalized categories as "the human psyche," "the imagination," and "the body"; as I discussed in Chapter one, such categories are always specific to history, culture, religion, and gender. But despite her claims to universality, Scarry does not envisage a body free from cultural, material effect; rather, she stresses that imagination and pain always shuttle within the frame of human experience. The imagination always responds to some perceived lack in bodily necessity: we imagine things in order to imagine away some physical limitation or disturbance, some part of our embodied, acculturated existence. (We invent a saw, for example, because our hands are not strong enough to pull apart wood.) And significantly, we imagine specifically to heighten our sense of being in the world. Imagination has the effect of increasing our physical sentience (so that the experience of sawing wood becomes itself an embodied, sentient act). We imagine ourselves into different places, experiences and embodiments — including the bodies of gibbeted prisoners. Thus imagination is always an at least partial attempt to increase our physical sentience, and physical sentience is always a source for imaginative activity.

The mutual constitution and antagonism that Scarry describes in *The Body in Pain* is helpful for thinking about pain's embodiment/disembodiment in the late eighteenth century. Society as it is defined by Burke is a tapestry of attempts to imagine someone else's physical sentience, and to imagine ourselves outside of our own skins in order to do so. Yet, the attempt is always overshadowed by a regulator within itself: imagination must always remain at some distance from pain if it is not to be destroyed by it. We remember the problem David Marshall located in Marivaux: if one cannot imagine one's own pain, one is hardly in a position to imagine someone else's. Imagination and physicality are mutually dependent, but the mechanics of this dependence become tenuous when we imagine pain, an experience whose sentience occludes imaginative replication. Pain is a conscious experience that can destroy consciousness: the gibbet victim can be us, but we recognize this only if he *isn't* us, if we are safely other, observing, and imagining. Society is at once a web of imagined substitutions and a fragmented collection of individual bodies.

III

One strategy for handling this apparently irreconcilable tension is to play it not at its extremes but in the emotional middle, where Ann Radcliffe situates her emotions of terror and horror. Her now famous definition originally appeared in the *New Monthly Magazine* (vol. 7, 1826) in a dialogue essay called "On the Supernatural in Poetry." Here Radcliffe, through the character of Mr. W——, explains:

> They must be men of very cold imaginations with whom certainty is more terrible than surmise. Terror and horror are so far opposite, that the first expands the soul, and awakens the faculties to a high degree of life; the other contracts, freezes, and nearly annihilates them. I apprehend that neither Shakespeare nor Milton by their fictions, nor Mr. Burke by his reasoning, anywhere looked to positive horror as a source of the sublime, though they all agree that terror is a very high one; and where lies the great difference between terror and horror, but in uncertainty and obscurity, that accompany the first, respecting the dreader evil? (*Udolpho* ix)

In the first part of this passage, terror is that Burkean quality of experience that can lead to the sublime. It "expands the soul, and awakens the faculties to a higher degree of life," an awakening which for Burke was characteristic of the passions which lead to society. Such is Emily's experience in *The Mysteries of Udolpho*; for her, "a terror of this nature, as it occupies and expands the mind, and elevates it to high expectation, is purely sublime, and leads us, by a kind of fascination, to seek even the object, from which we appear to shrink" (248). Terror, then, is that carefully regulated aesthetic experience that can use intense feeling to seek objects in the world, objects which can include people in distress. Conversely, horror "contracts, freezes, and nearly annihilates" the passions which lead to community, and forces the horrified spectator to enclose and protect the self. "Positive horror" behaves for Radcliffe in the same way that absolute pain behaves for Burke: both render us antisocial and self-protecting. Radcliffe's distinction between terror and horror, then, is analogous to Burke's distinction between society and self-preservation. Terror situates us in the social world, the world of the outside, while horror freezes us within the self.

Significantly, Radcliffe's distinction between terror and horror is also a distinction between imagined and corporeal sentience. "Terror," the *OED* tells us, comes from the Latin *terrēre*, meaning "to frighten." As a distinctly emotional condition, it is the "state of being terrified or greatly frightened;

[of being in] intense fear, fright, or dread." In Scarry's terminology, it is the imaginal, emotional condition of fearing an object in the external world, or of the danger it potentially provides. The tentativeness of this fear, its particularly imaginative status, is what Matthew Lewis found so disappointing about Radcliffe's novels; for him, she refused to take her sensations far enough (Varma, *Flame* 145). There was in a Radcliffe novel no real pain, nothing graphic, nothing of the horrible. And by "horrible" Lewis meant the particularly physical. "Horror" proceeds from the Latin *horrēre*, meaning "to bristle [or] shudder." And in its attendant definitions, it usually refers to things corporeal: "Roughness or nauseousness of taste, such as to cause a shudder or thrill; . . . [a] shuddering or shivering, now especially (Medical) as a symptom of disease; . . . [a] painful emotion compounded of loathing and fear" (*OED*). Whereas the socializing agency of terror, by the *OED*'s definition, relies upon imaginative stimulation, the self-preserving agency of horror appeals to and exploits the sentient body. Not content with the imaginative state of terror, horror invokes the corporeal state of pain.

The mutually exclusive properties of terror and horror — Burke's society and self-preservation — become in Radcliffe's novels a continuum along which her characters move. Using the terrifying effects of imagined pain as a socializing agent, these heroines often imagine someone else's suffering in order to demonstrate their great selflessness and concern for others. In the 1791 novel *The Romance of the Forest*, Adeline de St. Pierre is being held captive by her rakish, villainous suitor, the Marquis de Montalt. As she pines for her lover and potential liberator Theodore, whom the Marquis has wounded and imprisoned, Adeline becomes sensitive to the fact that Theodore has sustained his wounds while defending *her*:

> That the very exertions which had deserved all her gratitude, and awakened all her tenderness, should be the cause of his destruction, was a circumstance so much beyond the ordinary bounds of misery, that her fortitude sunk at once before it. The idea of Theodore suffering — Theodore dying — was for ever present to her imagination, and frequently excluding the sense of her own danger, made her conscious only of his. (228)

As Burke had described it, imagined pain effects an emptying out of self that allows the imaginer to exchange places with the sufferer, and to be totally taken up with the plight of another. The *idea* of Theodore suffering — the imagined pain that Burke and Radcliffe call terror, is the social force in the novel. Indeed, it is what constitutes moral virtue.[6]

In *The Mysteries of Udolpho*, similarly, the heroine takes her fear of the wounded body to its extreme, to a fear of *murder*. Emily is so preoccupied with "the image of her aunt murdered" that she gives up all thoughts of self and self-preservation to search out Udolpho's turrets until she finds her (323). This search is not undertaken without a great deal of trepidation, but Emily is so overpowered by the "groans of [a] wounded person" (318) and a trail of blood (323) that she takes the risk numerous times. Like all Radcliffe's heroines, Adeline and Emily are motivated by the "horrid spectacle[s]" (*Udolpho* 323) that replace their own endangered bodies and become the centers of their conscious activities. But I want to stress the fact that those spectacles — those wounded, dying, or dead bodies — are *imagined*; their pain is always distanced by image, speculation and hypothesis. These painful bodies are emphasized as imaginative constructions.

These communal moments of selflessness distance the suffering or dead body in the very act of focusing on it; they narrate a terror of the wounded body without ever depicting the horror of that body. In fact, much of Radcliffe's plots center on the imaginative invocation of a mutilated body which never then seems to materialize. In *The Romance of the Forest*, for example, Adeline has a series of dreams in which she first sees a man "convulsed in the agonies of death" (108). Later she dreams of the same figure, now dead and with blood gushing from his side (109). When she awakes, she discovers in the abbey a room

> exactly like that where her dream had represented the dying person; the remembrance struck so forcibly upon her imagination, that she was in danger of fainting; and looking round the room, almost expected to see the phantom of her dream. (115)

What she finds, however, is not a convulsed and wounded body, but rather a manuscript written many years ago, a manuscript that recounts torture and pain. The characters of this manuscript are often obliterated, as is the character who wrote it: he writes, "your pity now is useless: long since have the pangs of memory ceased; the voice of complaining is passed away" (128). This, like the gibbet scene in *Udolpho*, is merely the hieroglyphics of a dreadful story. But while the pangs may long have ceased, Adeline, like all devoted readers of the Gothic, cannot put the manuscript down for long. It "awakened a dreadful interest in the fate of the writer, and called up terrific images to her mind" (128). The "wretched writer appealed directly to her heart; he spoke in the energy of truth, and, by a strong illusion of fancy, it seemed as if his past sufferings were at this moment present" (132). These sufferings, made to seem real by the force of Adeline's fancy, are of course never present; the wounded, afflicted body is always only a testament to the powers of the sensitive imagination. And those powers become all the more poignant when Adeline discovers that the author is her dead father, killed by his brother the Marquis de Montalt. The father's pained body here becomes the medium for an "anguish and horror of her mind [that] defied all control" (347). Adeline is struck by the "horror" of her father's pained body, but this body is mere imagination, record, memory (346–347) whose immediacy the novel avoids.

Similarly, *The Mysteries of Udolpho* both invokes and avoids the immediate suffering of the mutilated body. As Emily searches for her aunt, she finds a heap of bloody clothes in a room. Assuming them to be her aunt, she instead uncovers "a heap of pikes and other arms" (323). Likewise, the body behind the veil, "a human figure of ghastly paleness, stretched at its length, and dressed in the habiliments of the grave . . . , the face [that] appeared partly decayed and disfigured by worms, which were visible on the features and hands" (662), is a wax representation and not a mutilated human body at all. This representation, furthermore, Emily assumes to be the body of the "late" Laurentini, whose story Emily's father has forbidden her to hear. But instead it is yet another swerve away from the presentation of mutilation, as it is a *momento mori*, an agent of instruction, and signifies no particular person whatsoever.[7] Repeatedly, Radcliffe's novels invoke physical mutilation, suffering, and even death to stimulate great emotional activity, but to emphasize that this emotion is *imaginatively* generated. Fancy's graphic capabilities indicate their own limitations, in that their ability to imagine the pained body depends upon the distance or absence of the pained body. For all the Gothic terror, there is very little Gothic horror.

When Adeline imagined "Theodore suffering—Theodore dying," she did so by "frequently excluding the sense of her own danger." In other words, she could imagine another's pain only by absenting her *own* body from the site of suffering. The abnegation of one's own self and of one's body is itself limited in Radcliffe to the moment in which the self is threatened. Even in her dreams—moments of pure imagination without material correlative—Adeline entertains visions of Theodore in distress, "convulsed in the agonies of death" (108) or "in chains, and struggling in the grasp of ruffians" (259). But the visions terminate the moment they become too physical—the moment, in Burke's phrase, they "press too nearly." In the dream noted above, the conjured victim "suddenly stretched forth his hand, and seizing her's, grasped it with violence: she struggled in terror to disengage herself . . . [and the] effort she made to save herself . . . awoke her" (108). In a later dream, she "saw him led, amidst the dreadful preparations for execution, into the field: she saw the agony of his look and heard him repeat her name in frantic accents, till the horrors of the scene overcame her, and she awoke" (259). At precisely the moment in which imagined pain threatens to become physical—it impinges on the physicality of the imaginer rather than the imagined, and the perceiving consciousness halts its own projective capabilities—the heroine swoons or wakes up, depending on the medium of the imagined body. When consciousness comes face to face with its object, it freezes. The socializing force which constitutes the construction of community—the force R. F. Brissenden calls "virtue in distress"[8]—is halted at the moment of the perceiving subject's threatened violation and danger. And that perceived threat lies at the threshold of sympathy with the sentient, corporeal body.

That the sentient body should refuse the sympathetic sentience that Moral Philosophy and Burkean aesthetics want it to feel is only logical, since the body is moving from a state of imagined pain into one of "horror," in which "real pain" or "positive horror" is inscribed upon the body by its claims to imaginative projection. But this transference is ultimately figured not so much as an attack on the perceiver's body as a protection of it. Witness Emily in a distant turret of the castle, searching for her abducted aunt. She comes upon a curious room in which

> she perceived no furniture, except, indeed, an iron chair, fastened in the center of the chamber, immediately over which, depending on a chain from the ceiling, hung an iron ring. Having gazed upon these, for some time, with wonder and horror, she next observed iron bars below, made for the purpose of confining the feet, and on the arms of the chair were rings of the same metal. As she continued to survey them, she concluded, that they were instruments of torture, and it struck her, that some poor wretch had once been fastened in this chair, and had there been starved to death. She was chilled by the thought; but, what was her agony, when, in the next moment, it occurred to her, that her aunt might have been one of these victims, and that she herself might be the next! An acute pain seized her head, she was scarcely able to hold the lamp, and, looking round for support, was seating herself, unconsciously, in the iron chair itself; but suddenly perceiving where she was, she started from it in horror, and sprung towards a remote end of the room. (348)

Sympathy, the imagining of another's pain, claims here to be a kind of disempowerment where the subject feels the same physical intensities as the victim—hence, the weakenings, the swoonings, the falling into chairs. But in so doing this imagination severs the subject/object relationship which effected the weakening and actually *empowers* the perceiving subject; it escorts her to a remote side of the room. Similarly, near the end of *The Romance of the Forest*, disempowering sensibility actually keeps the heroine *outside* the scene of distress. Adeline has planned to visit Theodore in prison, but

> her melancholy imagination represented Theodore at the place of execution, pale and convulsed in death; she again turned her lingering eyes upon him; but fancy affected her sense, for she thought as she now gazed that his countenance changed, and assumed a ghastly hue. All her resolution vanished, and such was the anguish of her heart, that she resolved to defer her journey till the morrow. (336)

And although Adeline's moral reasoning quickly gets the better of her and she sets off to the prison, the point is clear: sensibility, as it works itself out in the Radcliffe novel, is a physical weakening to the point of disempowerment. Her sensitive characters, especially her women, are included in a community in which all sensitive characters are victims, subject to the perfidies of the villains. But that disempowerment contains the seeds of its own self-protection; Adeline's hypersensitivity here works to keep her *away* from the scene of hyperstimulation.

The kind of empowerment I am describing has implications for the kind of society Radcliffe envisions as ideal. The evil threats to the social order — Montalt, Montoni, Schedoni — are always defined by selfishness, by acting completely within their own self-interest to further their economic stature and power. The heroes and heroines, conversely, are selfless and generous: at the level of their sensitive bodies, they respond to others in the social community. But it is at the moment of physical sentience that the body's communal possibilities are destroyed. Emily, for example, responds to the bodies of other women, such as Madame Montoni, Laurentini, and the Marchioness de Villeroi. But while the novel moves toward identification among these women — indeed, at one point Emily even dresses and looks like the Marchioness — this sensitivity can only go so far. All these women die horribly, and so Emily must disassociate herself from them in order to protect herself from sharing their fate. Extreme sensitivity to another's body in pain exaggerates the heroine's reaction to such a degree that she isolates herself in a swoon, an escape, a self-preservation. Adeline's and Emily's "individuality" is the logical end of their sensitivity, enclosing their ostensibly socialized bodies within their own private spaces.

Thus we see in Radcliffe's novels a certain ideological configuration that is, in the end, political. When the imaginer of pain imagines herself into a community of others, she isolates herself by finding that imagined community impossible to sustain. In other words, she plays both sides of the solitude/society binarism that the eighteenth century was trying to negotiate. For April London, this imagination/isolation structure is essential to the novel's definition of identity. In her materialist reading of *The Mysteries of Udolpho*, London argues that the imagination in Radcliffe is limitless — indeed, Emily's father makes much the same point in his warning on excessive imagination — and so acts of human will and self-assertion are the only ways to mark the boundaries of a self that otherwise risks being diffused by a free-floating imagination ("Ann Radcliffe in Context" 46). For London, the villainous selfishness of Montoni becomes a model for defining self-presence, one which the other characters must to some degree adopt. While I agree that the novel is intent on marking the boundaries of the self, I disagree that the imagination is responsible for the erosion of those boundaries; the imagination in these novels is not limitless. In Radcliffe, as in one aspect of Burke, the imagination that claims to be limitless is bounded by the limitations of the sentient body. The moment it projects itself into pain, it finds itself incompatible with the pain being imagined. Thus, while I disagree with London's premise, I agree with her conclusion, one she shares with Mary Poovey ("Ideology"), that Radcliffe's novels are ultimately about the empowerment of the individual in a bourgeois sense. But whereas London and Poovey locate that empowerment in the maintenance of private property (i.e., Adeline inherits Montalt's estate; Emily returns to her beloved La Vallee), I would suggest that it is first affirmed at a more basic site, the one at which Locke originally located it: in the protagonist's *body* ("Two Treatises" 353–354). The body in Radcliffe is bourgeois in the sense that C. B. Macpherson speaks of it in *The Political Theory of Possessive Individualism*: property "is not only a right to enjoy or use; it is a right to dispose of, to exchange, to alienate" (215). While the Radcliffe body is private in its sentience, it is public to the degree that it exchanges its sentience with that of another. It mediates the citizen with the possessive individual.

If maintaining the privacy of the sentient body exists concurrently with the maintaining of private property at the heart of Radcliffe's novels, then Radcliffe's critique of sensibility takes on a particularly material tone.[9] Radcliffe admonishes her heroines' tendency to imagine themselves into states of unconsciousness — into states of horror — when there are *real* threats circling about them. The object of her lesson is the sensibility that weakens Emily St. Aubert as she flees from the potential rape of Count Morano, or as she faints at the feet of Bernardine, who *may* have murdered her aunt. It is the sensibility of Adeline St. Pierre as she faints from fear of her oppressors at the beginning of *The Romance of the Forest*, and thus puts herself totally at their mercy. In other words, Radcliffe attacks the sensibility that imagines immediate pain but in so doing makes the imaginer more vulnerable to the violent aggression which might cause that pain.[10] She attacks the imagination that uses pain to destroy its connection to the outside world, a world of greed, danger, and oppressive villainy. For it is this imagination, through its fascination with pain and its inability to sustain that fascination, that ultimately puts at risk the *real* private property: the corporeality of the body.

Radcliffe's validation of the body as private property is political in a general sense, but it carries overtones of partisan politics as well. At the heart of a Radcliffe novel is the contest between noble, virtuous human nature and material self-interest; between ordered stability and rapid change; between the protected security of the private estate and the usurpation of that estate by pretenders to new wealth. The terms of this contest as I have just laid them out are the same terms that Burke used in 1791 (the year of *Romance* and three years before *Udolpho*) to figure the revolution in France and its effect on England. For Burke, the revolution was a gross attempt to re-empower the middle class at the expense of aristocratic tradition and landed property. It was a demonstration of how personal greed could overwhelm a country's respect for property and propriety, and for the legitimate transfer of wealth. In Ann Radcliffe's novels, the sensitive body replays that anti-Jacobin, Tory position. The sensitive body is made vulnerable to the violence and power of the selfish pretenders, yet it ultimately returns to its protected, secluded estate, isolated from the outside world's tribulation. Moreover, the body transcends self-interest by imaginatively entering into the physical concerns of others, by becoming part of the whole; the body, in other words, becomes part of the republic. Yet, the very potency of its sensitivity keeps it from becoming too fully associated with that whole, too fully a republican. Like the Tory onlooker, the Radcliffe heroine both demonstrates human virtue and isolates that vulnerable virtue from a fallen revolutionary world.

IV

The dialectic of communal virtue and isolation that is established in Radcliffe's bourgeois Gothic is extended in Wordsworth's early poetry, for if

Ann Radcliffe is the mother of the English Gothic novel, then Wordsworth
is surely one of its children. As I mentioned earlier, Wordsworth's career
began in experimentations with the Gothic—as well as with landscape
models provided by Drayton and Milton—and many of the early works
incorporate conventional Gothic formulae. Among the clearest examples of
this influence are *The Vale of Esthwaite* (c.1787), "Fragment of a 'Gothic
Tale'" (c.1791) and *The Borderers* (1795–96). According to Paul Sheats, the
Gothic was an essential step in Wordsworth's developing conviction that
poetry had to indulge the irrational, and that reason and truth were not its
sole province (*Making* 8). And in this early praise of irrationality there is
also another Gothic fixation: the focus on the suffering body. *The Vale of
Esthwaite*, for example, transforms the traditional landscape poem into a
journey through a Gothic castle that is steeped in a history of violence and
bodily pain. The young poet is met there by a ghost who, in the fashion of a
Radcliffe heroine's dream,

> brought me to a dungeon deep,
> Then stopp'd, and thrice her head she shook,
> More pale and ghastly seem'd her look.
> [   ] shew'd
> An iron coffer mark'd with blood.
> The taper turn'd from blue to red
> Flash'd out—and with a shriek she fled.
> With arms in horror spread around
> I mov'd—a form unseen I found
> 'Twist round my hand an icy chain
> And drag me to the spot again.
> (*Poetical Works* I, ll.257–266; omission original)

This is Gothic convention as Radcliffe and her children have practiced it: it
is the representation of a horror that, in evoking images of the violently rent
body, freezes the observer to the spot. And despite the fact that the poet
then writes off this experience as the "poor and puny joys / [Of] Fond
sickly Fancy's idle toys" (ll.267–268), the experience in the castle will be
remembered in *Salisbury Plain*'s spital, and marks Wordsworth's long-time
fascination with the Gothic body.

The fascination with pain and the violently rent body in the early
poetry reflects the consciousness of pain recorded in the childhood memo-
ries of *The Prelude*. Among his earliest recollections in *The Prelude* is of
the "strong desire" to have "the Bird / Which was the captive of another's

toil / [Become] my prey" (I, ll.318–320), a plundering that results in a *Frankenstein*-like paranoia of persecution: "I heard, among the solitary hills, / Low breathings coming after me" (I, ll.322–323). Yet this supposed surveillance seems not to have curtailed his boyish crimes: he then recalls how, "when Spring had warmed the cultured Vale, / Roved we as plunderers where the Mother-bird / Had in high places built her lodge" (I, ll.326–328). The consciousness of violence and pain that informs the early poetry, moreover, is not limited to the avian or the fanciful (as in "Esthwaite"). Wordsworth's famous definition of the "spots of time" in Book XII has as it first example the gibbet scene, a memory which, according to Enid Welsford, arises out of Wordsworth's childhood fascination with the gibbet, and in the circulating stories of a murderous sailor (*Salisbury Plain* 7–8). Book V recounts the "ghastly face" and "spectre shape" of the drowned man in Esthwaite (V,l.452), and Book IV tells of the sufferings of the Discharged Soldier. In many ways, Wordsworth's early narratives read like a catalogue of suffering: his is a storehouse of images of the Gothic body.

Yet despite the early influences, Wordsworth, like Radcliffe, swerves from a representation of the pained body toward something less corporeal. His suspicion of Gothic indulgence — a suspicion he proclaims both in *The Vale of Esthwaite* and in the "Preface to *Lyrical Ballads*" — operates on the images of spectacular pain and transforms them. Regarding the attack on the birds' nests, for example, Wordsworth declares: "though mean / Our object, and inglorious, yet the end / Was not ignoble" (I,ll.328–330). It is not ignoble, he explains, because of a "dark / Inscrutable workmanship that reconciles / Discordant elements" (I,ll.341–343), and creates elevated ends out of base means:

> How strange that all
> The terrors, pains, and early miseries,
> Regrets, vexations, lassitudes, interfused
> Within my mind, should e'er have borne a part,
> And that a needful part, in making up
> The calm existence that is mine when I
> Am worthy of myself! Praise to the end! (I,ll.344–350)

This calm existence and spiritual sublime comes from Nature

> purifying thus
> The elements of feeling and of thought,

And sanctifying, by such discipline,
Both pain and fear; until we recognize
A grandeur in the beatings of the heart. (I,ll.410–414)

An interfusion of "terrors, pains, and early miseries" is sanctified through thought and feeling into what Wordsworth will call an "impressive discipline of fear" (I,l.603). Through this discipline of fear, Wordsworth is fashioning a "Sorrow that is not sorrow, but delight, / And miserable love that is not pain / To hear of" (*Prelude* XIII, ll.245–247). He is moving toward a theory of pain that will allow him to comprehend the pained body without exploiting the Gothic formula of sensational suffering. Or, to put a more cynical spin on it, he is looking for a way to contemplate bodies that are no bodies, sorrows that are not painful. He is trying to find here a way of imagining pain that is a delight in the Burkean sense—an absent pain, a corporeal horror transformed by the discipline of fear. And this transformation—one that negotiates sublime and edifying terrors without exploiting Gothic horrors—underlies the experiences of *Salisbury Plain*.

To the degree that the *Salisbury Plain* series is indebted to the Gothic, it contains those conventional Gothic images of pained bodies. In all three incarnations, it is the story of a traveler, crossing the plain near Stonehenge, who meets a poverty-stricken Female Vagrant in a deserted spital. This woman relates her story of hardship, illness, and her family's death in war-torn America, where she has been forced to follow her husband, press-ganged into service there.[11] After his and their children's deaths, she returns to England to find her city ravaged by poverty, disease, and pain, a pain that macrocosmically parallels her own. By moving through images of ancient barbarism—involving both American primitivism and Druidic sacrifice—and contemporary suffering brought on by war, the poem charts the effects of pain on human consciousness. Ultimately, it argues that the most intense suffering comes from "memory of pleasure flown" (*A Night* l.21), and that a consciousness of happiness lost is the greatest hardship one can endure. In this sense, the poems forecast a major theme of *The Prelude*, that is, that one's happiness and sorrow depend upon the imaginative states by which one understands the past and uses memory to create the future.

Despite its dealing with themes that would inform *The Prelude*, Wordsworth's adventure on Salisbury Plain is noteworthy because of its curious *departure* from the conventional forms of Wordsworthian philosophy. Paul Sheats argues that the *Salisbury Plain* poems mark a crucial period in Wordsworth's life when he temporarily abandons his interest in transcendental Nature (already established in *An Evening Walk*, 1787–89) in preference for "ordinariness," for the flesh and blood concerns of the *Lyrical Ballads* (*Making* 40–41). Moreover, says Sheats, *Salisbury Plain* displays a momentary suppression of his meditations on the self, and treats the object *as* object, and not, as Wordsworth says in "Tintern Abbey," as "something far more deeply interfused" with his own imagination (Gill, *Oxford Authors* 134, l.97). And the departures do not end there. The *Salisbury Plain* poems, like the poet's own crossing of the plain in Book XIII of *The Prelude*, contains an imaginative vision of Druidic sacrifice and tribal activity that is quite uncharacteristic of Wordsworth's visionary experience. The Druid vision is a paeon to "the power of imaginative reverie," says Alan Bewell (*Enlightenment* 43), and is uncharacteristic of an older Wordsworth who had developed a more sophisticated understanding of his relation to tradition and history (45). However, in these two departures we see a contradiction in the *kind* of imaginative vision used to tell the Vagrant's story: the poem is intensely about objects, but also about subjects; its focus is suffering, yet its focus is imagination; it depicts existing, present pain, yet it envisions early savagery long displaced by time. It registers that early Wordsworthian interfusion of pain and misery with the visionary, creative mind, yet it also refracts an individual's suffering through the mediating imagination of the onlooker.

The contradiction between the representation of someone's physical suffering and the mediation of that suffering by the imagination — a mediation we saw in Ann Radcliffe's depictions of imagined pain, and which can be traced through a whole line of critics who condemn Wordsworth's egotism[12] — takes form in the poem series as a tension between *wanting to tell* of one's suffering and *what actually gets told*. The Vagrant's story is presented as a narrative of suffering, the telling of which is medicinal both for her and for the traveler/sailor. Soon after they meet in the spital and the traveler gains her trust, she begins to speak, which brings a palpable change to the elements:

> While thus they talk the churlish storms relent;
> And round those broken walls the dying wind
> In feeble murmurs told his rage was spent.
> With sober sympathy and tranquil mind
> Gently the Woman gan her wounds unbind. (*A Night* ll.199–203)

While the "wounds" she unbinds are clearly psychological and spiritual, the Vagrant tells her story as a means of sharing her physical pain, and of inducing a "sober sympathy" in her listener. As John Williams argues, the only redemptive possibility in *Salisbury Plain* is the "instinctive response of one desolated human being for another"; only by telling and hearing the story can the interlocutors diminish their terror in a bond of compassion (*Romantic Poetry* 78–79). The traveler responds to the Vagrant with "sweet words of hope" in *Night* (l.342), and with "mutual interest" and "natural sympathy" in *Adventures* (ll.257–258). We think of Jacques Lacan here, who has argued that our "desire finds its meaning in the desire of the other, not so much because the other holds the key to the object desired, as because the first object of desire is to be recognized by the other" (*Écrits* 58). Through the medium of personal narration, the Vagrant creates a community for her suffering; she lets the traveler know how she feels.

The Vagrant's narrative reflects more than just the art of simple dramatic storytelling that Wordsworth would perfect in *Lyrical Ballads*; it also ties into Wordsworth's concern about the relationship between imagination and pain. In Ann Radcliffe, we remember, suffering was made public property through the imaginative construction of *image*, through painting a mental portrait of how someone else feels. In Wordsworth, suffering is publicized through language, through the ability to tell one's story. As Elaine Scarry has argued, language is itself an imaginative act, one that is intended to make known, among other things, our physical sentience:

> though there is ordinarily no language for pain, under the pressure of the desire to eliminate pain, an at least fragmentary means of verbalization is available both to those who are themselves in pain and to those who wish to speak on behalf of others. (*Body in Pain* 13)

The Vagrant's tale is a kind of talking cure that actually attests to the continued activity of her imagination. While she may assume that she has lost hope — she declares in *Adventures* that "I have my inner self abused" — her very speech-act indicates that the imagination continues to work on her sentient experience and to transform it into verbal image, the element of communal exchange between two subjects.

So far, so good. However, Scarry's caveat that "there is ordinarily no language for pain" raises the question of *what* the Vagrant manages to tell in her activity of telling it. As she begins to catalogue the physical ailments that befell her and her family among America's war-torn "streets of want and pain" (*A Night* l.301), she is brought up short in a significant preterition:

> "The pains and plagues that on our heads came down,
> Disease and Famine, Agony and Fear,

> In wood or wilderness, in camp or town,
> It would thy brain unsettle even to hear.
> All perished, all in one remorseless year,
> Husband and children one by one, by sword
> And scourge of fiery fever: every tear
> Dried up, despairing, desolate, on board
> A British ship I waked as from a trance restored."
>
> (*A Night* ll.316–324)

Interestingly, the moment of her described physical sufferings is presented with vagueness, strange apposition (do Disease and Agony have the same effect as Fear?), and a refusal to tell parts of the story: "It would thy brain unsettle even to hear." Her family's deaths are not distinguished: all perish by various causes in one year and, in a delirium that marks the tone of the whole stanza, the childless widow is put back on ship. She awakes from a trance that has swallowed up her consciousness of pain — both her pain and that of her family. Moreover, it has swallowed up the bulk of her story. What is most striking here is what does not get said, what remains unspeakable.

In the relating of the Vagrant's trauma, language as an imaginative act is rendered incompatible with pain as a corporeal experience. The "trance" into which she falls through pain and suffering is the abyss into which her story is hurled. (And interestingly, vis-à-vis Radcliffe, it is the state into which the Vagrant falls when the traveler enters the spital. Like Adeline and Emily, the Vagrant has been terrified by stories she had heard of the "dead house of the Plain," but when these stories actually materialize in the presence of the traveler, "Cold stony horror all her senses bound" [*A Night* l.157].) As Scarry argues, language may displace pain, but it cannot adequately communicate it.[13] In Burke's terms, pain has pressed too close. One closes off in horror; one thinks only of oneself. The moment she finishes relating (or not relating) her scene of suffering, "Here paused she of all present thought forlorn, / Living once more those hours that sealed her doom" (*A Night* ll.325–326). The "present thought" of unbinding wounds and of eliciting sympathy is given over to the private, ineffable moment of physical sentience. Like Adeline and Emily, the Vagrant is rendered silent by the intensity of her own sentience as it is re-membered in her imagination. The worlds of remembered pain and social relations are incompatible. To remember is to relive, but to relive is not to recount. Imagination — that faculty which underwrites both memory and language — is bifurcated, placing memory and language on binary poles.

The scene of remembered pain not only displaces and silences the pain it claims to remember, but it also subverts the very consciousness that experienced pain in the first place. Memory, the great Wordsworthian agency that, in *The Prelude*, transforms "terrors, pains, and early miseries" into a "calm existence," is destroyed in *Salisbury Plain* by the phenomenon of pain. The Vagrant recounts her experience as she returns to war-ravaged London:

"There, pains which nature could no more support,
With blindness linked, did on my vitals fall;
Dizzy my brain, with interruption short
Of hideous sense; I sunk, nor step could crawl,
And thence was borne away to neighbouring hospital.

"Recovery came with food: but still, my brain
Was weak, nor of the past had memory." (*Adventures* ll.482–488)

Perhaps the most interesting passage in the poem, this scene recounts how pain attacks the consciousness that registers it, deprives the victim of sense, and destroys memory. In this scene, pain is rendered incompatible not only with language, but with the memory that theoretically transforms it into something higher and more profound. Despite Wordsworth's philosophical agenda in *The Prelude*, he recognizes here that the body imposes limitations on consciousness. Like the boundaries Radcliffe draws around her heroines' imaginations — boundaries of corporeality — Wordsworth proffers his own self-critique: pain destroys imagination, rather than being healed by it.[14] As David Gervais has argued, Wordsworth was aware of how excessive passions could become anesthetizing and self-thwarting: "Too much feeling might become none" ("Suffering" 12).

The Vagrant's retreat into the privacy of silence and the abyss of the shattered memory represents the *idée fixe* of the poem series: the ineffability of suffering. The story of pain is untellable, because it is incompatible with the "lived experience" in the memory. Moreover, this private, nonverbal quality undermines the entire community of pain that the Vagrant's narrative presumably creates. As she recounts her return to England, she describes herself in the context of a city in pain, a description that clearly invites us to compare it with our own perceptions of her pain. She says:

"Of noysome hospitals the groan profound,
The mine's dire earthquake, the bomb's thunder stroke;

> Heart sickening Famine's grim despairing look;
> The midnight flames in thundering deluge spread;
> The stormed town's expiring shriek that woke
> Far round griesly phantoms of the dead,
> And pale with ghastly light the victor's human head."
>
> (*A Night* ll.363–369)

But then she adds, "'Some mighty gulf of separation passed / I seemed transported to another world'" (ll.370–371). In *Adventures* she describes further this mighty gulf as she relates hearing of her hospital neighbors' afflictions, "many things which never troubled me" (l.490). She concludes, "'These things just served to stir the torpid sense, / Nor pain nor pity in my bosom raised'" (ll.496–497). Gone is any conviction that all sufferers are bonded; gone is the Burkean optimism that we all share another's pain. Instead, the poem argues that, in pain, the self is rendered absolutely solitary and all-consumed. Pain splinters society into atoms of individual consciousness: "my only wish," admits the Vagrant, was "to shun where man might come" (l.378). And this atomism, furthermore, fragments all community in the poem by modifying the traveler as well as the Vagrant. Whereas we are told of the traveler that "He too had withered young in sorrow's deadly blight" (l.405), we are significantly never given the story of the withering. Like the Vagrant's, the traveler's narrative of pain is swallowed up in silence. It remains unspoken.

When pain's vicissitudes throw into question the possibilities of community, the result is for the poet to retreat from the depiction of the body's immediacy in pain.[15] While that retreat is begun in the early version, *A Night on Salisbury Plain*, it is much more forcefully articulated in the 1795–99 *Adventures on Salisbury Plain*, which differs from the earlier poem in a number of important ways. First, whereas the earlier poem focuses on an immediate relation of a tale of suffering, the later one displaces this immediacy by making the traveler a sailor, thereby ejecting any autobiographical suggestion that this is Wordsworth's experience on the Plain. Moreover, the "withering" that had afflicted the traveler in *A Night* is projected onto a second character, an old Soldier, whose "legs from slow disease distended" (l.4), and whose "withered arms" and "faltering knee" contrast with the "strong and stout" form of the Sailor (ll.13–14). The Soldier is introduced as a means of showing us the Sailor's kindness and sympathy, yet the sympathy is not sustained; the Soldier and his pained body are soon jettisoned in favor of a psychological profile of the Sailor, who will be the audience of the woman's tale. And while the traveler of the previous poem seemed to be a mere sounding-board for the woman's story, a sympathetic audience, the Sailor is much less ingenuous. He has murdered a man, and so the landscape, the gibbet, the painful bodies, and the reflections on justice have a particular impact on him. As his sense of guilt regulates the way he hears the story, we see what Stephen Gill argues as the main effect of the revision:

> The poem now centers, not on the Female Vagrant or on the poet's declamations, but on the sailor, on his crime and subsequent life, and the new shape is determined only by the tension between various ways of looking at the man and at his deed. On the one hand Wordsworth is concerned with man in society, with the make-up and functioning of human loyalties, sanctions, and punishments. On the other hand he is concerned with man in solitude, with the agony such a man as the sailor suffers from his own sense that he has put himself beyond human love. ("Introduction" 12–13)

Whereas the former poem was a meditation on the Vagrant's suffering, this poem is a meditation on a meditation on suffering. The Vagrant's hardship is of interest to the degree that it affects the Sailor's emotional reaction to it.

Just as *Adventures* increases its emphasis on the contemplation of suffering, so does it decrease the sociability of the body doing the suffering. Whereas the previous poem ended with a propagandistic diatribe against the politics of war and the infliction of needless pain, this poem ends with three meditations on human suffering as important pedagogical moments for the Sailor, moments that seem to have a marked insignificance for the sufferer. The first vignette depicts a father's physical abuse of his disobedient child. The scene concludes with the father gazing on the cuts and bruises he had administered, and

> Such sight the father of his wrath beguil'd;
> Relenting thoughts and self-reproach awoke;
> He kiss'd the boy, so all was reconcil'd. (ll.653–655)

Never has the reformation of a child-abuser been so easy. But more to the point, the scene reminds the Sailor of his own violent past. As he looks on the boy's head wound, he makes a train of associations that takes him back to the murder he had committed: "The head with streaming blood had dy'd the ground, / Flow'd from the spot where he that deadly wound / Had fix'd on him he murder'd" (ll.643–645). For both the father and the Sailor, the wounded body is evoked solely for the way it can engage the salvific force of an internal conscience: suffering is somehow justified if it can induce guilt.[16] Similarly, the second vignette presents a dying woman lying "spent and gone" with "wasted limbs" (ll.698,702). This woman, it turns out, is the Sailor's wife, whom he had abandoned after the murder and who has suffered in poverty ever since. The sight of her dying body, coupled with the agitation and "correspondent calm" he had felt at the sight of the abused child (l.666), induce him to make a full confession. But at her death bed, it is *he* who appears to be in the greater agony. He requests, " 'O bless me now, that thou shoulds't live / I do not wish or ask: forgive me, now forgive!' " (ll.773–774). Once again, the dying body is viewed only for what it can invoke inside the observer. And finally, in the last vignette, the Sailor is hung in a gibbet to become a spectacle for "dissolute men, unthinking and untaught" (l.820). But, we are told, we should not flinch at the pain he undergoes here any more than he sympathized with the previous victims, because some good may come of it: some potential criminal may come, "Upon his swinging corpse his eye may glance / And drop, as he once dropp'd, in miserable trance" (ll.827–828). In the spectator's "miserable trance" the criminal's pained body is invested with a redemptive potential. Indeed, all three of these added moments use the body to elicit a purification of the observer. But in so doing, the sentimental process they employ enacts a division between the body and the observer, in that the body is seen and then ignored in favor of a privileged, internal conversion. The miserable trance becomes the psychological space in which the pained body is displaced by an imaginative process whose object is itself.

In " 'That Great Stage Where Senators Perform': *Macbeth* and the Politics of Romantic Theatre," Mary Jacobus argues that, as Wordsworth's career moves toward the *Lyrical Ballads*, he puts the phenomenon of suffering — and any implications it might have — squarely within the imagination where it can be worked upon and comprehended as a subjective experience. This movement finds its clearest articulation in the third and final version of the poem, *Guilt and Sorrow; or, Incidents upon Salisbury Plain*, which Wordsworth published in 1841. Here the ending scene undergoes yet another significant revision. In this version the Sailor is again captured by the townspeople, after making a full confession. But whereas before they hung him in a gibbet as an inspiration to other criminals, this time

His fate was pitied. Him in iron case
(Reader, forgive the intolerable thought)

They hung not: — no one on *his* form or face
Could gaze, as on a show by idlers sought;
No kindred sufferer, to his death-place brought
By lawless curiosity or chance,
When into storm the evening sky is wrought,
Upon his swinging corse an eye can glance,
And drop, as he once dropped, in miserable trance.
(ll.658–666, emphasis original)

That the poet here is expounding pity over justice is unlikely: "no kindred sufferer" is to reap the benefits of this punishment by pitying the pained body. And such a pity would have been distasteful to Wordsworth by the time this poem was published: the same year that saw the publication of *Guilt and Sorrow* also produced Wordsworth's *Sonnets Upon the Punishment of Death*, in which he argued against the Whig law reforms, and advocated capital punishment in cases of treason and murder. Rather, Wordsworth seems to be shying still further away from presenting the pained body, and he is doing so, I would suggest, in order to *increase* its effect on the imagination. We are told to "forgive the intolerable thought," which assumes that we are supposed to *have* the thought in the first place; we are supposed to imagine the criminal body and the suffering it is going through. (Otherwise there would be no point in bringing up the scene of the gibbet, since, unless one has read the prior *Adventures*, one would have no reason to expect the Sailor to be hanged in the first place; without an image of the suffering body already in our imaginations, this stanza makes no sense, and is out of place.) Then, we seem to be instructed, *via negativa*, on how to respond to the body we imagine. We are supposed to fear the punished body that exists in our imaginations; we are to take a lesson from our own conscience, a lesson that exploits the pained body while at the same time avoiding the freezing, the Radcliffean horror, the "miserable trance" that an actual presentation of that body might produce.[17] The Vagrant, we remember, had fallen into such a trance at the thought of her own pain and at the threatening presence of the traveler; the Sailor in *Adventures* had also fallen into such a trance at the thought of the gibbet, as it conjured for him his own imminent pain. But here, Wordsworth seeks a different effect. In the following two chapters, I will discuss more fully the role of the imagination in state regulation and jurisprudence, and the move toward what Foucault calls the "gentle way of punishment." For now, I wish only to argue that, by removing the image of the pained body from the end of *Guilt and Sorrow*,

Wordsworth seems to want us to conjure it all the more. The "intolerable thought" seems much more tolerable — and much more effective — than an actual pained body. The "impressive discipline of fear" becomes a mode of internal regulation that depends for its power upon the ability to imagine pain, a pain that can never really be adequately imagined.

This necessity/impossibility for imagining pain has "political" implications in two senses of that word. First, it isolates the individual within a context of others, an isolation which, in Ann Radcliffe, was effected by the imagination's inability to sustain a figure of pain. However, whereas Radcliffe's heroines found it impossible to imagine the pained body — and thus to comprehend it — Wordsworth cannot comprehend the pained body *unless* it be mediated through the imagination. Thus in both authors we see a crisis of privacy and community being worked out through the pained body. Second, Wordsworth's representation of pain, like Radcliffe's, is political in that it is effected by his reaction to the carnage of the French Revolution. In 1792, just before beginning the *Salisbury Plain* series, Wordsworth returned to Paris, cheered by the thoughts that the violence had ended (*Prelude* X,l.48). But what he found in the square of the Place de Carrousel disheartened and confused him: he found a heap of dead and dying bodies, which he looked upon

> as doth a Man
> Upon a volume whose contents he knows
> Are memorable, but from him locked up,
> Being written in a tongue he cannot read;
> So that he questions the mute leaves with pain,
> And half-upbraids their silence. (X,ll.58–63)

Like the bodies in the London of *Salisbury Plain*, the victims of war here are incomprehensible, unimaginable — they resist a hermeneutic by which to understand the magnitude of the carnage. As in the earlier poem, the spectator remains outside an imaginative framework which can make sense of such pain. It is not until Wordsworth is in his hotel room, alone and at a distance, his emotion recollected in tranquillity, that he can feel anything more distinct than confusion; and this feeling is not "wholly without pleasure" (X,l.69):

> With unextinguished taper I kept watch,
> Reading at intervals; the fear gone by

Pressed on me almost like a fear to come.
I thought of those September massacres,
Divided from me by one little month,
Saw them and touched; the rest was conjured up
From tragic fictions, or true history,
Remembrances and dim admonishments. (X,ll.70–77)

The textuality of suffering and death is not new to us: we have seen it before in Adeline St. Pierre, who had read the fractured manuscript of her father's fractured body; we have seen it in Emily, who read the "plain and dreadful story" of the hieroglyphics at the gibbet site; and we have seen it in the young Wordsworth, who read the monumental letters on the heath of the Plain. But whereas, in those earlier scenes of suffering, reading gives rise to a disembodied imagining of pain, here at the Revolution embodied suffering can only be imagined if it is turned into reading. Wordsworth's experience of the Revolution required that he fictionalize the body in order to comprehend it. The strong emotion elicited from him by these dead and dying bodies is a strong emotion which he has demonstrated elsewhere he is incapable of understanding without the help of some saving intermediary. Imagination must mediate pain in order to bring it into the realm of identifiable experience.

Wordsworth's experience of the Revolution initiated in him a crucial first step in the construction of a political conservative. By exploring the limitations of the body in pain, Wordsworth was forced to *read meaning into* that body, even if it meant displacing it from its status as subject to its status as object. By becoming object, the body acts as a place for Wordsworth to begin a individualizing process which, in turn-of-the-century politics, is a conservative one. As Graham Pechey puts it,

> Wordsworth represents a moment of withdrawal in which the aesthetic is detached from the political and a new aesthetic radicalism founded upon the category of "feeling"; in the space vacated by politics a transhistorical human community is projected. (in Barker, *1789* 62)[18]

Which brings us back to Burke, and to Ann Radcliffe. When Burke argued that the pleasure of pain required a certain distancing in order to be pleasurable at all, he established an essential structural principle that would underlie his *Reflections on the Revolution in France*. For Burke, France's horrors came far too close to England for comfort, and his "aesthetic" required that they be kept at a distance. But this aesthetic is the fear embodied by a political conservative, one who is trying to valorize sympathy while protecting the imagination from foreign influence, one who recognizes yet resists identification with the suffering of the French body politic. In Ann Radcliffe's Gothic, this aesthetic took the form of a dialectic of imagination, in which one sympathetically identified with a community of sufferers in order to isolate oneself more fully from them. The degree to which the Gothic heroine imagined the pained body was the degree to which she found that pain unimaginable, so that the act of imagining pain is what simultaneously connected her to and isolated her from the possibilities of community. In Wordsworth that identification/distance is reified even more strongly, and made into an intellectual, poetic system. The sacred space which is the site of poetic genius houses both "the great social principle of life / Coercing all things into sympathy" (*Prelude* II,ll.390–391) and the mediating imagination that transforms and displaces emotionally charged suffering of the other—the other as it is so dangerously figured in the suffering French revolutionary.

3. Spectacular Pain: Politics and the Romantic Theatre

I

When Emily St. Aubert drew back the mysterious curtain in Udolpho's passageway, she beheld a wax figure that represented a human body. This representation immediately invoked the freezing effect of horror, yet later betrayed itself as a stage prop, a piece of theatre. Similarly, when Wordsworthian travelers came upon the gibbet in the *Salisbury Plain* series, they became increasingly more removed from a suffering body that might entrance them in cold, stony horror. The previously theatrical body, rendered visible in *A Night on Salisbury Plain* for its emotive, even pedagogical effects, is gradually consigned to the wings, made not to exist but in the theatre of the mind. For Wordsworth, the Gothic theatre had the same effect as the excessive sights of suffering that afflicted Emily St. Aubert. He recalls moments of theatrical spectacle from his youth:

> but when I think
> Of these I feel the imaginative Power
> Languish within me; even then it slept
> When, pressed by tragic sufferings, the heart
> Was more than full; — amid my sobs and tears
> It slept. (*Prelude* VII,ll.467–472)

Despite the effects of tragic representations of suffering — or precisely because of them — the imaginative, intellectual power is laid to sleep. Watching suffering is incompatible with thinking about it, and the suspicion of theatre is analogous to the suspicion of viewing, or even imagining, the spectacular, pained body. As Mary Jacobus argues, theatre for Wordsworth forces too much response; staged "tragic sufferings" force a numbing self-protection, or what got called in *Salisbury Plain* a "trance" ("'That Great Stage'" 354). In response, Wordsworth places the phenomenon of suffering in the imagination, where it can be processed in due time. After one failed attempt at theatrical offering (*The Borderers*), Wordsworth abandoned the stage for a less graphic, more internal program.

Wordsworth was certainly not alone in his disillusionment with the stage. Coleridge, after a momentary hope of making a living by dramatic composition, had to admit that "I have no genius that way" (quoted in Doughty, *Perturbed Spirit* 123), and did not honestly expect his playwrighting to be a success. In a letter to John Thelwall of 16 October 1797, Coleridge christened his new play, *Osorio*: "Oh, my Tragedy! it is finished, transcribed, and to be sent off today, but I have no hope of its success, or even of its being acted" (*Letters* 231). (Coleridge was not disappointed: *Osorio* was rejected by Drury Lane and not produced until 1813, when it resurfaced as the revised *Remorse*.) But his decision to abandon theatre is more than sour grapes: as Julie Carlson has demonstrated, for Coleridge "the contemporary stage fails to live up to his theoretical expectations; it impedes rather than facilitates the workings of imagination" ("An Active Imagination" 23). Thus Coleridge turned with vitriol against the ideology of stage drama as it was being practiced in turn-of-the-century England. And Lord Byron had even fewer pretensions to theatrical production. In the "Preface" to his *Marino Faliero, Doge of Venice*, he claimed, "I have had no view to the stage; in its present state it is, perhaps, not a very exalted object of ambition" (*Poetical Works* 408). On 23 August 1821, he wrote to John Murray about his joint publication of *Sardanapalus* and *The Two Foscari*,

> I admire the old English dramatists — but this is quite another field — & has nothing to do with theirs. — I want to make a *regular* English drama — no matter whether for the Stage or not — which is not my object — but a *mental theatre* — (*Letters* Vol. VIII, 186–187; emphasis original)

Byron does not explain what he means by a "regular" drama, but he clearly does want it to exist internally, to be read in the closet and to be performed, like the Wordsworthian experience, on the stage of the mind. Spectacle is not his interest, except as it pertains to imagined activity.

Wordsworth, Coleridge, and Byron's lack of design on the theatre comes out of their disdain for the state of the stage at the present time. With the success of bloody Gothic melodramas like Matthew Lewis's *The Castle Spectre (1798)* and Charles Robert Maturin's *Bertram; or, The Castle of Aldobrand* (which Byron actually liked,[1] but Coleridge panned), the stage had become the site of excessive violence, fevered emotion, and special effect.[2]

In Lewis's *The Castle Spectre*, for example, a ghost is haunting the castle to avenge her murderer. And with the taste for the graphic which Lewis loved to indulge, her murdered body appears on stage to increase the shock of the crimes committed against her. The stage direction reads:

> The folding-doors unclose, and the Oratory is seen illuminated. In its centre stands a tall female figure, her white and flowing garments spotted with blood; her veil is thrown back, and discovers a pale and melancholy countenance; her eyes are lifted upwards, her arms extended toward heaven, and a large wound appears on her bosom. (79)

This ostentatious display of the wounded body occurs again when, at the concluding and climactic scene, the ingenuous heroine Angela dispatches the villain. She "springs suddenly forwards, and plunges her dagger in Osmond's bosom, who falls with a loud groan" (98). Similarly, Bertram and Aldobrand, the rival characters in Maturin's *Bertram*, both die on stage, each succumbing to a thrust of the poniard and expiring in a pool of his own blood. These dramas seem to express a nostalgia for the days of Jacobean drama in which the staging of bloody murders was commonplace, days before Restoration tragedians like Dryden and Otway cleaned up all traces of excess from the stage. But more to the point, Gothic dramatists like Lewis and Maturin always had their eye on the main chance: stage violence was immensely popular in both Covent Garden and Drury Lane. As Peter Brooks points out, both the term and the genre of "melodrama" were French in origin, and "were written for a public that extended from the lower classes, especially artisans and shopkeepers, through all sectors of the middle class, and even embraced members of the aristocracy" (*Melodramatic* xii). In England, melodrama became immensely popular with the lower classes who came in droves to see the spectacle of pain, violence, and special effect. Thus the packed houses would net a playwright like Lewis an impressive £18,000 for *The Castle Spectre*'s three-month run ("'Introduction to *Castle Spectre*'" n.p.).

But while the Romantics expressed distaste for the current state of theatre, they often saw theatrical production as essential to their own poetic agendas. Percy Bysshe Shelley's *The Cenci*, for example, was "expressly written for theatrical exhibition," as he wrote to his publisher Charles Ollier on 13 March 1820; and despite its rejection by Drury Lane, "I believe it singularly fitted for the stage" (*Complete Works* Vol.X,151; emphasis original).[3] By being "fitted for the stage," Shelley meant that *The Cenci*, unlike the first three acts of *Prometheus Unbound* that preceded it in 1819, was to represent characters as they "really were" (*Complete Works* Vol.X,61). He wanted to present in Beatrice's story a "sad reality," "that which has been," with a realism unlike his previous, more idealistic works ("visions which impersonate my own apprehensions of the beautiful and the just" ["Dedication," *Poetry and Prose* 237]). Yet, Shelley too was suspicious of the Gothic theatre. He sought in *The Cenci* to "increase the ideal, and diminish the actual horror of the events," so that the pleasure of the poetry might "mitigate the pain of the contemplation of the moral deformity from which they spring" ("Preface," *Poetry and Prose* 239–240). From this mitigation, he hoped to make the "Imagination . . . [an] immortal God which should assume flesh for the redemption of mortal passion" ("Preface" 241). Shelley's problem is one of presenting acts of extreme violence — in this case, rape and parricide — without succumbing to the Gothic excess which characterized the stage in the early nineteenth century. The theatre is to assume flesh, to represent material, bodily fact, but only in order to transcend that materiality, and to elevate human passion into Shelleyan idealism.

If we take Shelley's challenge as paradigmatic of the early nineteenth-century stage, the phrase "Romantic theatre" becomes somewhat oxymoronic. When Shelley, Coleridge, and Byron take their places on — or off — the stage, they choose as their subject matter extreme and volatile situations: political revolution, murder, rape, torture — tyrannies both political and domestic. But they choose these subjects with a conviction not to contribute to the popular Gothic theatre that defined public taste.[4] For Shelley, the mitigation of pain and horror was intended to teach "the human heart, through its sympathies and antipathies, the knowledge of itself" ("Preface" 240). Coleridge hoped in *Osorio* to capitalize on "the anguish and disquietude arising from the self-contradiction introduced to the soul by guilt, a feeling which is good or bad according as the will makes use of it" (*Letters* Vol.II, 607–608). And finally, "What I seek to show in 'the Foscari's'," wrote Byron, "is the *suppressed* passions — rather than the rant of the present day" (*Letters* Vol.VIII,218). In all cases, these Romantic playwrights seek to move the excess of spectacle off-stage and make the real site of theatre a more internalized, mental, pedagogical one.[5] Like Wordsworth in his "impressive discipline of fear," the Romantic theatre banished from the stage the image of violence because it sought to relegate it to the imagination, where it could be formed and controlled within the solitary imagination.

Just as the dynamics of imagined pain in Wordsworth and Radcliffe betray political foundations, so does the Romantics' suspicion of theatrical excess illuminate political ambivalences. On the one hand, theatre is the most embodied of literary art forms. As Shelley's Preface indicates, in the theatre the imagination assumes flesh, a flesh that lives, breathes, and is subject to political forces, oppressions, and pains. But on the other hand, this embodiment carries with it the possibility of ideological, rhetorical force. I noted in Chapter one that the presentation of pained bodies could induce sympathy, either for Wordsworth's hunger-bitten girl or for Burke's Louis XVI, depending on one's prior political allegiances. Moreover, that rhetorical force could itself be a form of tyranny. Shelley dedicated *The Cenci* to Leigh Hunt because of the latter's "patient and irreconcilable enmity with domestic and political tyranny and imposture" (238). Strictly speaking, "imposture" is a feigned representation of self which is then enforced upon other people; it is an act of theatre. For Shelley, it is also an act of political tyranny: it is the assumption of false authority, as the tyrant claims a power to which he has no legitimate claim. As Jonas Barish suggests in his discussion of the "antitheatrical prejudice," theatre represents the ambiguous boundaries of legitimate self-representation, in which one can present "the facts" or in which one can impose upon those facts an ideological agenda. The "imposture" of theatre, then, can either expose *or* replicate the imposture of a tyrant like Francesco Cenci. These problems in representation not only inform the work of Romantic playwrights, but also bring into sharp focus the problem of spectacle's rhetorical effects in that most prominent of theatrical tyrannies, the French Revolution.

II

As John David Moore points out, drama in the early nineteenth century came to be seen "in terms of an opposition between a high art blessed by tradition and a vulgar popular art" (444). This "popular" art, as Foucault, Paulson, and Brooks have demonstrated, was associated with popular political movements and, albeit in a fantastical way, represented the struggles of the middle-class hero over the aristocratic tyrant, the *nouveau* over the *ancien régime* (Foucault *Discipline* 68; Paulson *Representations*). For a writer such as Coleridge (in his later, conservative years, after 1797), popular theatre was "identified with Jacobinism, which rose up from below and threatened the life of the more dignified tradition" (Moore 444). In a letter published in the second part of *The Friend*, Coleridge lashes out at Gothic and sentimental playwrights who make it their business to transform moralists into villains, criminals into heroes, the poor into the rich, and the rich into the poor:

> the whole System of your Drama is a moral and intellectual *Jacobinism* of the most dangerous kind, and those common-place rants of Loyalty are no better than hypocrisy. . . . For the whole secret of dramatic popularity with you, consists in the confusion and subversion of the natural order of things in their causes and effects, in the excitement of surprize, by representing the qualities of liberality, refined feeling, and a nice sense of honour (those things rather, which pass among you for such) in persons and in classes of life where experience teaches us least to expect them; and by rewarding with all the sympathies that are the dues of virtue, those criminals whom Law, Reason, and Religion, have excommunicated from our esteem! (*Collected Works* Vol. 4, pt.II 220)

By "representing" — or rather "misrepresenting" — virtue, Gothic theatre enacts for Coleridge a destruction of the moral order. The theatrical is always political, and the Gothic, to Coleridge, subversive.

Conversely, the political is also theatrical. At the end of the eighteenth and beginning of the nineteenth centuries, says Moore, the "events of the French Revolution, that period's prototype of social upheaval, were described and analyzed by Tory and Jacobin alike in terms of a stage drama. The Revolution was theatre" (446; see also Butwin "French Revolution"). For Edmund Burke, the storming of Versailles on 6 October 1789 was an "atrocious spectacle" (*Reflections* 175), what Moore calls a "tragedy succeeded by the hideous burlesque acted by the populace" (446). As Burke describes it in *Reflections on the Revolution in France*, the Revolution has all the characteristics of the Gothic theatre that the Romantics profoundly loathed. In his famous attack on Richard Price, whose speech at the Old Jewry helped to crystallize the Jacobin movement in England, Burke equates Jacobin enthusiasm with the Gothic theatre:

> Plots, massacres, assassinations, seem to some people a trivial price for obtaining a revolution. A cheap, bloodless reformation, a guiltless liberty, appear flat and vapid to their taste. There must be a great change of scene; there must be magnificent stage effect; there must be a grand spectacle to rouze the imagination, grown torpid with the lazy enjoyment of sixty years security, and the still unanimating repose of public prosperity. The Preacher [Price] found them all in the French revolution. This inspires a juvenile warmth through his whole frame. His enthusiasm kindles as he advances; and when he arrives at his peroration, it is in full blaze. (156–157)

Burke's antitheatrical prejudice here is one he shares with Rousseau, whose *Letter to M. d'Alembert on the Theatre* argues that the theatre is nothing but an attempt to fill an otherwise empty life with amusement (16). But it is not just any theatre that Burke condemns here: it is the theatre of excess, of violent assassinations and massacres, spectacular pain which comprises "magnificent stage effect" and "grand spectacle." Burke notes with horror how, following the raid on the bedchamber, two of the King's gentlemen, "with all the parade of an execution of justice, were cruelly and publickly dragged to the block, and beheaded in the great court of the palace. Their heads were stuck upon spears, and led the procession" (164–165). The theatre of revolution here is detestable because it is extreme, violent, and public. Revolutionary sympathy, Burke implies, proceeds from the same bad taste that buys tickets to Matthew Lewis — the taste, dulled to torpidity, that can only be excited by excessive, bloody spectacle.

Burke's disdain for the public spectacle of violence is, at another level, a disdain for the public spectacle of the body. Civilization, he argues, is a tasteful clothing of society in proper behavior and sentiment, but in the Revolution, "All the decent drapery of life is to be rudely torn off" (171). Burke's fear that the "decent drapery" be violently removed is most clearly expressed in his treatment of Marie Antoinette who is, for him, the victim in this Gothic spectacle. When he had first seen her sixteen years prior, she had presented herself in a kind of theatrical glory: "I saw her just above the horizon," he writes, "decorating and cheering the elevated sphere she just began to move in, — glittering like the morningstar, full of life, and splendor, and joy" (169). Here the Queen's body was draped, adorned, and, moreover, distanced, bathing in the glory of a spectacle as she moved above the crowd. But in the Gothic spectacle of the Revolution her body is denuded and rendered immediate. As the bedchamber is invaded,

> this persecuted woman had but just time to fly almost naked, and through ways unknown to the murderers had escaped to seek refuge at the feet of a king and husband, not secure of his own life for a moment. (164)

For Burke, the crime here is that Marie Antoinette's body is rendered both visible and vulnerable. She is threatened with becoming that female figure which Matthew Lewis would stage so successfully, the figure whose veil is thrown back, whose arms are extended in display and supplication, and who shows a large wound upon her bosom. Gothic spectacle, by indulging its love of the gratuitously violent and spectacular body, strips the Queen of human decency. That ain't no way to treat a lady.

Against the Gothic love of spectacular effects Burke proposes a different reading of the raid on Versailles. Rather than beholding the assaults on the Queen with the cheering of a Yahoo, Burke wants us to feel "*natural*" and "melancholy sentiments" regarding "the unstable condition of mortal prosperity, and the tremendous uncertainty of human greatness." In the fall, he says,

> we learn great lessons; because in events like these our passions instruct our reason; because when kings are hurl'd from their thrones by the Supreme Director of this great drama, and become the objects of insult to the base, and of pity to the good, we behold such disasters in the moral, as we should behold a miracle in the physical order of things. We are alarmed into reflection; our minds (as it has long since been observed) are purified by terror and pity; our weak unthinking pride is humbled, under the dispensations of a mysterious wisdom. (175)

Burke's ideal spectator here is one who feels pity, fear, and intellectual engagement, one who eschews the spectacle of horror for its own sake, and educes from it a more subtle and delicate sensibility. The ideal spectator would reclothe the naked body and soften the horror of the scene. He would provide "All the super-added ideas, furnished from the wardrobe of a moral imagination, which the heart owns, and the understanding ratifies, as necessary to cover the defects of our naked, shivering nature, and to raise it to dignity in our estimation" (171). Burke's conservative response to the Revolution argues a restrained reclothing of the afflicted body over the Gothic indulgence of the naked one. The "aesthetic" theatre of the mind is evoked in preference to that other, intensely threatening aesthetic: the glorification of the vulnerable body made into a theatre-piece.

Burke's vision of the Gothic theatre as the model for Jacobin conduct, and his return to delicate sentiment as its corrective, are criticized by his adversary, Thomas Paine. In his response to Burke's *Reflections*, Paine's 1791–92 *Rights of Man* demystifies Burke's interpretation of the events of the Revolution. One of those interpretations is the theatre of violence as Burke depicts it. For Paine, Burke's *Reflections* is itself nothing more than "a dramatic performance; and he must, I think, have considered it in the same light himself, by the poetical liberties he has taken of omitting some facts, distorting others, and making the whole machinery bend to produce a stage effect" (59). Burke had accused his enemy of producing a stage effect which would cause the spectator to forget the real victim, but Burke himself, Paine charges, has produced the same show,[6] only the problem is that Burke assumes the *natural* response to be sympathy with the aristocrat. The tears which Burke would educe by his classical representation of Louis and Marie

Antoinette affect him, in Paine's words, "not . . . by the reality of distress touching his heart, but by the showy resemblance of it striking his imagination. He pities the plumage, but forgets the dying bird" (51). By Burke's reasoning, argues Paine, we would end up pitying Othello for his downfall, rather than condemning him for killing Desdemona. In other words, Paine shares with Burke the disdain for a theatre that promotes sympathy for criminals, but he also uses that disdain against the criminal; for Paine, it is the aristocrat, and not the revolutionary, who is the criminal.

From such admonishment Paine concludes, "Mr. Burke should recollect that he is writing History, and not *Plays*; and that his readers will expect truth, and not the spouting rant of high-toned exclamation" (50; emphasis original). To write History, for Paine, means *not* to order events according to rules of classical decorum and neoclassical sentiment, but to show everything as it is, with a realism that underlies a Jacobin novel like Godwin's *Caleb Williams; or Things As They Are*. Paine writes:

> It is to be observed throughout Mr. Burke's book, that he never speaks of plots *against* the Revolution; and it is from those plots that all the mischiefs have arisen. It suits his purpose to exhibit the consequences without their causes. It is one of the arts of the drama to do so. If the crimes of men were exhibited with their sufferings, stage effect would sometimes be lost, and the audience would be inclined to approve where it was intended they should commiserate. (60, emphasis original)

Although Paine continues a strain of antitheatricality here, he himself draws on spectacle for rhetorical strategy: atrocities and tyrannies, he argues, should be *exhibited*. The drama of the French Revolution is to be staged in its entirety if it is to be staged at all. And such exhibition would do two things: first, it would destroy the "stage effect" of Burke's delicate sentiment (pity and fear for the tragic hero) by stripping away the false feeling we should have for the King and Queen of France. And second, such display would exploit the spectacle of suffering to demonstrate who is the victim in the drama and who is the villain. Whereas Burke advocated clothing the body in order to minimize the potential for sympathy for the commoner, Paine advocates its display. Despite his suspicion of theatre, Paine does not argue for the destruction of theatrical representation here (as had Rousseau) so much as he advocates the representation of *everything*, of both the causes *and* effects of tyranny. The truth of politics depends upon presenting crimes and their attendant pains, and by reading the bodies that Burke would have shrouded in decorum.

This representational theatre, furthermore, is made analogous to representational or representative government. Representational government, says Paine,

> possesses a perpetual stamina, as well of body as of mind, and presents itself on the open theatre of the world in a fair and manly manner. Whatever are its excellences and defects, they are visible to all. It exists not by fraud and mystery; it deals not in cant and sophistry; but inspires a language, that, passing from heart to heart, is felt and understood. (182)

Paine's desire for an open theatre harks back to the great directors of the French Revolution itself. As Joseph Butwin notes, Maximilien Robespierre attempted to stage the National Assembly in a theatre, which required finding a space large enough to accommodate "'the entire nation.'" Butwin quotes Robespierre:

> "A vast and majestic edifice, open to 12,000 spectators, should be the meeting place of the legislature. Under the eyes {*sous les yeux*} of so many witnesses neither corruption, intrigue nor perfidy would dare show itself; the general will {*la volonté générale*} would then be consulted, the voice of reason and the public interest would then be heard." (145, braces in original)[7]

In Burke's theatre and politics, representation should be veiled, selective, and discrete; by avoiding excessive, uncontrollable emotion and gratuitous spectacles of pain, it should affirm human sentiment and pity for the fallen. In Paine's production of history, on the other hand, *everything* must be brought on stage. Politics, like theatre, is comprised of excessive, tyrannical powers that operate under the veils of secrecy. The only way to combat these powers is to see them, and to commit them to the public gaze.

To see or not to see: that is the question that underlies Romantic drama, both in the political representation of the French Revolution and in the playwrights' designs for drama. In the dialogue between Burke and Paine, we see the tension that Byron, Coleridge, and Shelley will inscribe in their writings about their plays. On the one hand, their "aesthetic" sensibilities demanded that they avoid Gothic excess, that the ideal and the delicate, the intellectual and the mental be cast in the principal role, one that upstages the horror of political tyranny and violent physical pain. But on the other hand, the dedication to a Painite, Jacobin vision of things as they are — a dedication to representing the politically downtrodden by representing the condemnably tyrannical — constantly tempted Romantic playwrights to stage their violence, and to explore the politics of this spectacle.

To return to Shelley's *The Cenci* for a moment, we find that the original story of the Cenci tragedy was wrapped up in secrecy. "The Papal government," writes Shelley, "formerly took the most extraordinary precautions against the publicity of facts which offer so tragical a demonstration of its own wickedness and weakness; so that the communication of the MS. had become, until very lately, a matter of some difficulty" ("Preface" 239n). Here the Catholic Church (itself a representative of theatre and theatrical imposture in the English Protestant imagination) hides the facts of the story in a cover-up which implicates it in an act of tyranny. Through the imposture of its own self-dramatization as innocent, the Church commits another imposture, that of hiding the "true story" of Beatrice's sufferings and crimes, a story that Shelley wants to uncover, expose, and represent on stage. Given this ambivalence, Byron's *Marino Faliero*, Coleridge's *Osorio* (as well as its later version, *Remorse*), and Shelley's *The Cenci* register an interesting problem: while the playwrights preferred the sentiments of Burke's disembodied, aesthetic drama, their political allegiance to Paine's representational government continually drew them toward the presentation of the aesthetic in its physical, empirical sense. Burke's and Paine's aesthetics reflect Burke's and Paine's politics, and their political differences center on the distinctions in the meaning of the "aesthetic": Burke's aesthetic is a disembodied intellectualism, while Paine's is a political materialism. And so, Romantic playwrights must grapple with a mode of representation that avoids the Gothic excess of bodily immediacy, yet also avoids the conservative Burkean distortions of the real.

III

Marino Faliero, Doge of Venice charts the same treacherous landscape that Byron himself was always trying to traverse — the landscape of aristocratic privilege and the subversion of that privilege. Written in 1820, published in 1821, and produced at Drury Lane that same year (despite Byron's wishes to the contrary),[8] *Marino Faliero* concerns the Doge, himself a member of the ruling class, conspiring against the ruling class for freedom. Faliero is outraged by Michael Steno, a naughty nobleman who has carved on the ducal throne some lascivious wisecrack (which we never get to hear) about the Doge's wife. Steno is reprimanded by the Senate, who sentence him to a mere one-month house arrest. Faliero, who had hoped for the death penalty, quickly transfers his rage for Steno onto the Senate who have allowed him and his wife to be "tainted by the accursing breath / Of calumny and scorn" without proper retribution (I,ii,189–190). Faliero joins with Israel Bertuccio and a band of plebeian rebels to massacre the Senate, but the plot fails when Bertram, one of the band, weakens in his resolve and warns a Senatorial friend to flee for his life. The band is captured, the plebeians are executed in full view of the assembled crowd, and Faliero is decapitated in a private execution. Ultimately, Byron's play presents the failure of a revolution, and explores the possible reasons for that failure with the ambivalence of an aristocrat advocating republican empowerment.

Integral to this revolutionary failure is the inevitable inflicting of pain and murder, and the construction of a Gothic spectacle. When Faliero commits himself to the revolution, he is willing to destroy the amorphous body of Senators, to "strike, and suddenly, / Full to the Hydra's heart" (III,ii,237–238). However, when theory becomes practice and he must imagine the attack on individual bodies, he expresses a reluctance to see the bloody business through:

> All these men were my friends: I loved them, they
> Requited honourably my regards;
> We served and fought; we smiled and wept in concert;
> We revell'd or we sorrow'd side by side:
> We made alliances of blood and marriage;
> We grew in years and honours fairly, — till
> Their own desire, not my ambition, made
> Them choose me for their prince, and then farewell!
> Farewell all social memory! all thoughts
> In common! (III,ii,319–328)

Faliero, the man who would not be doge, cannot fully shake off his allegiances to his former aristocratic circle, even though they have shaken theirs to him. His response to the thoughts of revolution is, as Burke would have it, to move from an abstract political vision to a personal, individual pity: Faliero is alarmed into reflection by the imagined physical suffering of his old friends. He asks, "can I see them dabbled o'er with blood? / Each stab to them will seem my suicide" (III,ii,471–472). As Carl Woodring has argued, Faliero is a man of feeling, not of action, and therein lies his tragedy (*Politics* 183). Faliero prepares to inflict pain and suffering, but is plagued by aristocratic, sentimental vestiges of his past.

Spectacular pain, such as the revolution will produce, generates in the erstwhile aristocrat those humane sentiments of which Burke was so enamoured. These are the same humane sentiments that motivated the characters of Burke's student, Ann Radcliffe, as they found it impossible to imagine another's pain without making it their own: "each stab to them will seem my suicide." However, as Burke suggests, these sentiments need not—and must not—be the sole property of the old order (although that order naturally has them by heredity), but must also be the moral guardian of the plebian, or the sans-culotte. The democratizing of this sentiment is embodied in the play by Bertram. Bertram is the sympathetic soldier, the man of sensibility for whom the spectacle of pain is intense and moving. In Bertram, says Calendaro,

> There is a hesitating softness, fatal
> To enterprise like ours: I've seen that man
> Weep like an infant o'er the misery
> Of others, heedless of his own, though greater;
> And in a recent quarrel I beheld him
> Turn sick at the sight of blood, although a villain's. (II,ii,68–73)

By his own admission, Bertram has "not / Yet learn'd to think of indiscriminate murder / Without some sense of shuddering; and the sight / Of blood which spouts through hoary scalps is not / To me a thing of triumph" (III,ii,64–68). In a way, Bertram is a study in Romantic heroism and sensitive pacifism: like Faliero, and Byron's Sardanapalus, he refuses to inflict pain where it is unnecessary, or to indulge in horror for its own sake; like Wordsworth, he has moulded the thought of pain and "indiscriminate murder" into a discipline of fear that keeps him humane and well-behaved; like Faliero, he is the sympathetic spectator as defined by Burke, the spectator for whom the spectacle of pain leads to a contemplation of the tragedy of human greatness and the fragility of life. In Bertram, then, Byron enfranchises the lower classes with a Burkean reverence for authority, order, and the dignity of the private human body, but by doing so Byron also plants the seed for the revolution's failure.

Bertram's dilemma is similar to Faliero's in that both men are troubled by sympathy for the individual bodies they intend to destroy. But while this sympathy is the undoing of the revolution (because it makes Bertram a stool pigeon), it is also the central force that *empowers* the lower-class rebels and, paradoxically, furthers the revolutionary cause. This empowerment comes through Byron's treatment of the debate waged by Burke and Paine over victimization in the Revolution. When Burke had argued that the spectacle of suffering, if tastefully presented, would induce a moral sympathy from his audience, he had in mind the particular sufferings of Louis XVI and Marie Antoinette. In so doing, Burke cast the oppressors in the role of the oppressed. But if to see is to sympathize with the victim of oppression, then *any victim* whose pain is made visible is potentially worthy of sympathy. This is an important point for Paine's attack on the *Reflections*, and provides the means by which Byron moves sympathy from the Burkean aristocracy to the Painite commoner. Faliero's sensibility makes him not only the ideal conservative aristocrat, but, as Israel Bertucci describes, the ideal rebel. Faliero is

> so full of certain passions,
> That if once stirr'd and baffled, as he has been
> Upon the tenderest points, there is no Fury
> In Grecian story like to that which wrings
> His vitals with her burning hands, till he
> Grows capable of all things for revenge;
> And add too, that his mind is liberal,
> *He sees and feels the people are oppress'd*
> *And shares their sufferings.* (II,ii,168–176, emphasis added)

Faliero will be a revolutionary because the spectacle of suffering makes him sympathize with the oppressed — and in Venice, the oppressed is not the Senate, but the commoner. What Byron picks up on here is the flaw in Burke's logic that opened up the space for rebellious sentiment: any kind of tragedy is capable of inspiring pity, and so it is difficult to regulate how and to whom the spectator will respond.[9] Faliero is a tragic hero in that he recognizes his allegiance to an old order which must pass away, but he is a revolutionary hero in his willingness to die while destroying that order.

In an attempt to reduce the possibility of sympathizing with the wrong person, Burke (like Wordsworth) ran Gothic spectacle — and its depictions of violence against criminals — off the stage and into the imagination; he reclothed the vulnerable, naked body in decorous draperies, and held it at a distance from revolutionary violence. Gory spectacle, he wrote, was to be rejected on the modern as it was on the classical stage (176), and "personated tyrants" demanding sympathy were to be censored. In Byron's positioning within the debate over what can and cannot be shown, such censorship is itself a form of tyranny. The Senate has ordered the execution of the plebeian rebels to take place "upon the balcony / . . . in the place of judgment, / To the full view of the assembled people!" (V,i,92–97). However, this public display of bodies is not to be made without precautions: Benintende, the Chief of the Ten, decrees, "lest they should essay / To stir up the distracted multitude— / Guards! let their mouths be gagg'd even in the act / Of execution" (V,i,100–103). Moreover, Faliero's execution is to be kept completely out of the public eye and away from the public ear. As he is led away to the chopping block, Faliero is warned, "Think not to speak unto the people; they / Are now by thousands swarming at the gates, / But these are closed" (V,i,550–552). As Jerome Christensen argues, "Faliero is tried and executed within the palace, where there is no possibility that his words or demeanour could incite the volatile populace" ("Fault" 320). Like Burke, the Senate recognizes the dangers inherent in publicizing one's pain, and like Burke, it does all in its power to keep suffering off-stage.

That Faliero should be executed "in private" indicates forcefully the Senate's tyrannical hold on the city. For Byron, as for Thomas Paine, political tyranny is defined by what goes on off-stage, outside the view of the public. He creates this feeling through an accretion of images of privacy. As the play opens, Faliero is waiting for some indication of the Senate's decision on Steno's sentence, but none can be had: "you know," says Vincenzo, "The secret custom of the courts of Venice" (I,ii,24–25). This "secret custom" surrounds the Senate, whose dealings are never made known to the public, and in which the public has never had input. Byron's condemnation of this secrecy is made even more evident in *The Two Foscari*, where "The Ten"—the select, executive group of government—performs with such discretion that one of the Senators complains: "the secrets / Of yon terrific chamber are as hidden / From us, the premier nobles of the state, / As from the people"; "men know as little / Of the state's real acts," says the Senator, "as of the grave's / Unfathom'd mysteries" (*Complete* I,178–181 and 184–186). This secrecy is akin to what Foucault calls the "gentle way of punishment" in the eighteenth century in which the forms of intimidation moved out of the public gaze (that is, away from the spectacle of the scaffold) and into the threatening private punitive spaces behind closed doors (*Discipline* 104–131). Like Paine, for whom a representative government had the responsibility of exposing its acts to the public for accountability, Byron condemns the aristocratic conservative tendency to conduct its business in secret. The play exposes the secrets of government to public view, and reclaims a Painite openness for the political theatre of Venice.

This Senatorial secrecy, however, is more than just an obvious tactic of deviousness. For Foucault, moving punishment behind closed doors was an effective means of public regulation not because of the way secrecy allowed the ill-treatment of bodies in prisons and asylums, but because it made the public at large wonder what really went on in these places. In short, the "gentle way of punishment" transferred the site of regulation from the body to the imagination, what I identified in Wordsworth as "the impressive discipline of fear." That very site which, for Burke, was capable of feeling all the pangs of fallen grandeur was also, for radicals sceptical of the monarchist cause, the faculty most prone to the insidious manipulations of aristocratic ideology. Given this paradoxical function of the sensitive imagination, Byron's reclamation of the public gaze appears to be more than simply an expression of allegiance to Paine and Robespierre's "open theatre" of politics. He is as well reclaiming the epistemological assumptions that open theatre makes. When Faliero is criticized for his periodic sympathies for the soon-to-be-murdered aristocrats, he explains,

> It was ever thus
> With me; the hour of agitation came
> In the first glimmerings of a purpose, when
> Passion had too much room to sway; but in
> The hour of action I have stood as calm
> As were the dead who lay around me. (IV,ii,93–98)

The further he is from the spectacle of pain the weaker he is in his resolve. Whereas Wordsworth needed the distance of a hotel room to calm his troubled mind over the carnage in Paris, Byron makes that distantiation its own source of disturbance. The imagination, that space associated both with Burke's theatre and with aristocratic tyranny, is in Faliero the site of doubt and weakness — the source of the sentimental tears one would shed for the tyrant. To get the revolution under way, one must be strong, Stoic, ready for the spectacle of pain, and not weakened by it.

In the final scene of the play, the political power invested in spectacle is wrested from the Senatorial tyrants and given to the Painite revolutionaries. Whereas the aristocrats hitherto had paralysed the city by their "spies, the eyes / Of the patricians dubious of their slaves" (III,ii,234–235), they now accede to the public "gazers" who, Faliero brags, will crowd around his tomb to read his epitaph. But before they get to reading gravestones, they are far more interested in the execution. I indicated earlier that Faliero's execution occurs off-stage in order not to incite public feeling. But it isn't quite that simple. The stage direction for the final scene of *Marino Faliero* shows us "people in crowds gathered round the grated gates of the Ducal Palace, which are shut" (V,iv). They have come to get a glimpse of the suffering, or to "hear at least, since sight / Is thus prohibited unto the people" (V,iv,4–5), or perchance even to "catch the sound" (V,iv,14) — of what we aren't told, but presumably the axe. At one level, this is probably Byron's critique of the Gothic audience and its taste for spectacle. Like theatrical spectators straining their necks to catch a full view, the towns-people await — and even hope — for violence. But at another level, this prurience is not for its own sake. As one spectator reports seeing the deed done, the entire spectacle takes on a political directive:

> *Third Cit.* Then they have murder'd him who would have freed us.
> *Fourth Cit.* He was a kind man to the commons ever.
> *Fifth Cit.* Wisely they did to keep their portals barr'd.
> Would we had known the work they were preparing
> Ere we were summon'd here — we would have brought
> Weapons, and forced them! (V,iv,21–26)

Despite the Senate's best attempts to hide the murder, despite their best attempts to keep the violence off-stage, the spectacle is given to a public which, when made aware of the Senate's business, indicates its harsh disapproval of it. As the curtain lowers, Byron destabilizes senatorial power by using spectacle to engage public anger. The plebian masses here are given an open view of aristocratic tyranny, and they vow to fight that tyranny. We are left with a vision of the open theatre of politics, one that empowers the republican cause.

But the presentation of public power here is, at best, ambivalent. I began my discussion of Byron by noting that his political landscape was always made treacherous by mixed allegiances.[10] And so it is here. Byron's revolutionaries have seen it all, but they have seen it too late. They can only speak in the conditional tense of what they would have done, had they seen this execution in time. The power which is granted them by the spectacle of violence is, at the same time, rendered impotent by the Senate which committed the violence, and their political threats now sound like bluster.[11] Moreover, this is only one of a series of degradations of the entire rebellion. After all, Marino Faliero's noble revolutionary sentiments are often up-staged by his petulant desire to avenge a slight to his pride. His entire place in the revolution begins in response to a schoolboy prank against his wife Angelina who has long since forgotten the matter, and for whom Steno's loss of public respect is punishment enough. And finally, the text gives us numerous examples of the generosity and benevolence of the aristocrats (indeed, their crime against Faliero is that of being too kind to Steno). The revolution may have failed, but it also may not have been worth fighting in the first place. Byron's supposed sympathy for the plebians is undercut by his suspicion of their very cause.

The ambiguity that underlies the commoners' spectatorship at the end of the play is also, to some degree, ours as readers and members of an audience. Even though the crowd is given the spectacle — the very staging of which carries potentially enormous political weight — the theatre audience is not. In the printed text — perhaps the only representation Byron wanted us to see — we see the power of the open theatre being tentatively affirmed in the service of revolution. But at the level of stage spectacle, we are made acutely aware that this open theatre, in which all is seen, is not ours. We merely watch the crowd watching the violence. If seeing empowers the revolution, even minimally, then it is significant that we do not get to see. Despite Byron's suspicious dislike of the conservative Wordsworth, he too throws us back to the imagined, rather than the spectacular, body. As we have seen in Wordsworth's "hunger-bitten girl" or his gibbeted prisoner, spectacle often awakens a political energy, but that energy can be misplaced or, like Wordsworth's in the previous chapter, incomprehensible. In Byron's apparent desire not to have us sympathize wholeheartedly with the revolution, he draws the boundaries around his political theatre, boundaries that seem not to go beyond the wings of his own stage.

IV

The ambivalence that Byron explores in his representation of open theatre is presented more fully by Samuel Taylor Coleridge. Although Coleridge's *Osorio*, like *Marino Faliero*, does not deal directly with the French Revolution, its subject matter is still both intensely political and theatrical.[12] The play is set during the "reign of Philip II., just at the close of the civil wars against the Moors, and during the heat of the persecution which raged against them" (*Complete Poetical Works* Vol.II, 519). Coleridge's sympathies with this persecution centre most clearly on the character of Alhadra. The obvious revolutionary force in the play (Moore 453), Alhadra, a Spanish

Moor, has been cruelly imprisoned by the Christian church (in the guise of the Dominican Inquisitor Francesco, but represented also by Osorio). And like the victims of the Senate in Byron's play, Alhadra is locked up in secrecy, kept out of the public view:

> They cast me, then a young and nursing mother,
> Into a dungeon of their prison house.
> There was no bed, no fire, no ray of light,
> No touch, no sound of comfort! The black air,
> It was a toil to breathe it! I have seen
> The gaoler's lamp, the moment that he enter'd,
> How the flame sunk at once down to the socket.
> O miserable, by the lamp to see
> My infant quarrelling with the coarse hard bread
> Brought daily. (I,208–217)

As a result of this imprisonment, Alhadra wants revenge and, like a true Jacobin, she attempts to incite the ingenuous Maria to similar acts of revenge: "Know you not / What Nature makes you mourn, she bids you heal? / Great evils ask great passions to redress them" (I,229–231). At this point Alhadra commands our sympathy. She is the innocent victim, the object of tyrannical abuses of power. In her Coleridge gives voice to the last vestiges of Jacobin sympathy of which he was capable in 1797, the year of wrote *Osorio* (Watkins, "'In That New World'" 495).

Alhadra's prison, without light, sound, or human contact, is like Paine's and Byron's monarchy: it exercises its tyranny in secret, outside the public view. This secrecy, furthermore, characterizes the climactic act of violence and tyranny in the play, Osorio's murder of Ferdinand. Osorio lures the Moor to a dark, isolated cave, one that has a chasm which "never thirsty pilgrim blest, which never / A living thing came near" (IV,45–46). They fight, and Osorio throws him into the chasm, remarking how the secrecy of the place enables him to murder: "Now — this was luck! No bloodstains, no dead body!" (IV,150). Like Byron's Senate, and like the tyrant in Paine's vision of the French Revolution, Osorio acts in secrecy here, capitalizing on the lack of public spectacle that might otherwise testify against him. Once again, secrecy promotes tyranny.

It is part of Coleridge's republican agenda in this play that such tyranny be exposed to public accountability. Osorio's faith in his good luck, for example, is unjustified, because he *is* seen entering the cave. Alhadra, who first watched Ferdinand go in "the mouth of yonder cavern," then "saw the son of Velez [that is, Osorio] / Rush by with flaring torch; he likewise entered" (IV,387–389). After Osorio leaves, she says, "I crept into the cavern" and "I look'd far down the pit":

> My sight was bounded by a jutting fragment,
> And it was stain'd with blood! Then first I shriek'd!
> My eyeballs burnt! my brain grew hot as fire!
> And all the hanging drops of the wet roof
> Turn'd into blood. I saw them turn to blood!
> And I was leaping wildly down the chasm
> When on the further brink I saw his sword,
> And it said, Vengeance! (IV,414–422)

Here, Osorio's tyranny has left just enough telltale signs to inform Alhadra of what has happened. In response, she wants a revenge which itself takes the form of public demonstration. As the representative of Coleridge's Jacobin sympathies, she wants to expose tyranny to public accountability: "none shall die" she declares, "Till I have seen his blood!" (V,98–99). And it is this quest for blood, this desire to expose Osorio's guilt, that constitutes the final act of the play, in which Osorio is killed. He is brought into a public forum where everything is open to be seen. To the degree that the play engages a revolutionary sympathy, one that Coleridge shared in the early 1790s, it demonstrates that public accountability and justice depend on what Paine called the "open" representation of things as they have happened.

When Alhadra sees the tell-tale signs of Ferdinand's murder, she not only affirms Coleridge's revolutionary conviction that murder will out, but she also demonstrates the effects of violence on the imagination. Like Emily St. Aubert and the young Wordsworth, she sees fragments of a story of murder, hieroglyphics that tell a plain and dreadful story. Bloodstains, an abandoned sword, a groan—these mere hints provide enough sensory stimulation for her to know what has happened and to act on it. Whereas for the conservative Radcliffe heroine, the thought of a loved one suffering and dying induced a cold and stony trance, here the partial spectacle of pain engenders political revolution: "my brain grew hot as fire! / . . . And it said, Vengeance!" Imagining pain may cause a closing off of self in the political conservative, but spectacular pain, even incomplete spectacle, opens up in the political radical the desire to avenge the wounded body. Coleridge demonstrates here the possible infectiousness of pain, the way the spectator can be moved to violence by violence perpetrated on another.

However, the infectiousness of pain—the "great passion" for revenge that calls to see Osorio's blood—borders on a hyperbolic excess, one that Coleridge, with his own anti-Jacobin ambivalence, clearly fears. To articulate that fear, Coleridge does not indulge the violent spectacle which Alhadra had imagined. Rather, at the play's close, Alhadra orders that Osorio be led away from the delicate Maria to be murdered, because "Why should this innocent maid / Behold the ugliness of death?" (V,301–302). Like Marino Faliero, Osorio is escorted off-stage, where he will be murdered and Ferdinand avenged. And, instead of violent climax, Alhadra is given the last word, a word on justice:

> I thank thee, Heaven! thou hast ordain'd it wisely,
> That still extremes bring their own cure. That point
> In misery which makes the oppressed man
> Regardless of his own life, makes him too
> Lord of the oppressor's! Knew I an hundred men
> Despairing, but not palsied by despair,
> This arm should shake the kingdoms of this world;
> The deep foundations of iniquity
> Should sink away, earth groaning from beneath them. (V,307–315)

Coleridge's hopes for the revolution, like Byron's, are dubious at best: miserable, despairing people become so unconcerned about their own lives that they have nothing to lose by rising up against their oppressors. Nothing remains but pain and suffering. Yet there is some revolutionary hope here: out of the ashes of fallen tyranny, Alhadra prophesies, "the spirit of life / [Sings] a new song to him who had gone forth / Conquering and still to conquer" (V,19–22). And what hope there may be in transforming the desolate and despairing world into something beautiful is embodied in Maria. It is she who was spared the spectacle of misery and violence; it is she who remains untainted by murder's rhetorical effects. Unlike Radcliffe and Wordsworth, for whom society depends upon the spectacle of suffering, Coleridge fears spectacular violence as infectious and destructive. Thus the play allows the possibility of a new world order, as long as it is based on innocence as well as justice, on keeping the site of state-induced pain outside the public view.

What seems clear from this treatment of the Jacobin cause is the playwright's marked restraint in depicting the spectacle of suffering, a restraint that affects the audience as much as it affects Maria. While Alhadra — and presumably any Jacobins in the audience — wanted to see Osorio's blood, and have it be seen as part of the poetic justice due the tyrant, Coleridge withdraws the privilege. He does not allow the radicals in his audience the vicious glory of feasting upon Osorio's blood. But neither does he cater to decorous good taste. To indulge the spectacle of a blood-bath would be to sully his revolutionaries and to open them up to a conservative condemnation of barbarity. Osorio's violent death would invite a misguided sympathy in the way that Louis XVI was sympathetic, regardless of his cruelties; consequently, to stage Osorio's death would be to undermine the Jacobin cause. Coleridge avoids dramatizing the ghastly punishment inflicted on Osorio so that we will maintain the proper response (here, a response of Burkean sympathy) for Alhadra. Despite the Painite sympathies which the play espouses, Coleridge adheres to a Burkean theatrical sentiment, one that keeps Jacobin violence and Gothic excess off-stage. And the result is the kind of restrained, intellectual theatre that the Romantics so strongly wanted.

If Coleridge appears to be resisting Alhadra's and Paine's revolutionary program by resisting the Gothic spectacle that is its medium, he makes that resistance even more clear in the character of Albert. Like Alhadra, Albert too is a victim in the play: he is attacked by his brother Osorio and presumed dead, so that the evil brother can have his wife, Maria. But unlike the Moresco Mohammedan Alhadra, Albert is a white Christian, a symbol of aristocratic goodness and order. Thus it is not surprising that while Alhadra wants blood publicly to flow, Albert wants to induce a more internal, non-violent revolution in the conscience of Osorio.[13] In disguise, Albert recounts to Maria and Alhadra a dream in which he had been given over by a "friend" and an "idolized maid" for assassination. Having escaped, he sought no revenge, but rather "Pray'd that Remorse might fasten on their hearts, / And cling, with poisonous tooth, inextricable / As the gored lion's bite!" (I,319–321). As Carl Woodring has argued, Albert counters Alhadra in that he represents the play's private, metaphysical purpose — the internal sentiment or "impressive discipline" of remorse as a revolutionary force — over the more public, Jacobin issue of the opposition to tyranny (*Poetry of Coleridge* 204). The trajectory from Alhadra to Albert, like that from Paine to Burke, represents the trajectory from where Coleridge had been, as a Jacobin, to where Coleridge was going as a Christian and a metaphysician: toward an interest in the revolution of the mind.[14]

Osorio resembles the later *Marino Faliero*, then, in the privilege it accords aristocratic goodness, despite its professed allegiances to plebian or republican revolution. Moreover, the two plays are similar in the ambivalence they betray in regard to the visible pained body. It is interesting that while Albert is the Burkean propounder of sentiment, he is also the Gothic dramatist *par excellence*. He hopes to induce the all-important remorse in Osorio by means of a spectacle—a spectacle of suffering. For some reason—psychotherapy perhaps—Albert has painted a picture for his friend Maurice of his own assassination at the hands of Osorio's henchmen. During a seance requested by Osorio to conjure his dead brother (and thereby prove to the reluctant Maria that Albert is indeed dead), Albert intends to conjure smoke, music, and theatrical paraphernalia, at the end of which he will expose the portrait as the "soul" of the deceased Albert. In so doing, he hopes to induce in Osorio the guilt that will convert him:

> That worst bad man shall find
> A picture which shall wake the hell within him,
> And rouse a fiery whirlwind in his conscience! (II,ii,323–325)

Now *this* is a Gothic spectacle if ever there was one. This is exactly the kind of thing Burke hated: special effects, violence, excess, melodrama. Moreover, Albert conjures images of a "cold corse . . . / With many a stab from many a murderer's poniard" (III,i,81–82), an image that greatly moves Osorio prior to Albert's presenting of the portrait. Like Paine, Albert hopes to "uncover all concealed things" (III,i,9) and, by use of the Gothic spectacle of the pained body, to expose tyranny and to bring the tyrant to account for himself. But unfortunately, Osorio is too stupified by all the Gothic stage business to notice the portrait at all. He is struck by a "lazy chilliness" (III,i,120), a stony trance that numbs him to spectacle's effects. Whereas images of pain had thrown the Wordsworthian Sailor into a guilt-ridden trance, and eventually into self-transformation, images of pain in Coleridge distract the villain from himself and the implications of pain. There is no internal transformation at all. The spectacle fails miserably and with it, Paine's theatre of politics is turned upon itself: Gothic excess induces no change of heart, but rather is destroyed by its own gimmicks. This moment is representative, I believe, of what Julie Carlson describes as Coleridge's mandate for dramatic restraint:

> When [theatre's] circumstantial qualities overpower its ideal qualities, drama fails to achieve its proper ends and ceases to exist. This is exactly the state of the

contemporary stage, which Coleridge condemns for its rage for spectacle, exaggerated acting style, and substitution of the sentimental for the tragic muse. ("An Active Imagination" 28)

And this condemnation is, of course, political: as Coleridge explores the antirevolutionary aspect of his play, he undermines both Jacobinism and the efficacies of Gothic theatre.

If *Osorio* registers Coleridge's political ambivalence in 1797, his later dramatic work is far more unambiguously conservative. In the few years preceding 1807, when a revised *Osorio* was staged at Drury Lane as *Remorse*, Coleridge's anti-Jacobin sentiments hardened into a firm Tory position, one that Coleridge advocated with a fierceness bordering on self-delusion.[15] Thus, there are significant changes to *Osorio* in Coleridge's later dramatic offering, changes that reflect a more anti-Jacobin agenda. Unlike *Osorio*, *Remorse* does not give the final word to the oppressed Jacobin rebel. Rather, Alhadra is eclipsed in the final scene by Alvar (Albert in *Osorio*), who gives the closing speech. And rather than espousing a theory of political *justice*, which Alhadra had delivered as a kind of teleological justification for violence, Alvar apostrophizes the *conscience* as the real site of political change:

> In these strange dread events
> Just Heaven instructs us with an awful voice,
> That Conscience rules us e'en against our choice.
> Our inward Monitress to guide or warn,
> If listened to; but if repelled with scorn,
> At length as dire Remorse, she reappears,
> Works in our guilty hopes, and selfish fears!
> Still bids, Remember! and still cries, Too late!
> And while she scares us, goads us to our fate.
> (*Complete Poetical Works* Vol. II,V,286–294)

Here we see the intellectual project of Coleridge and indeed all Romantic drama, despite its political allegiance: to move from the body to the mind; to make us think rather than see; to make the theatre a site for mental drama that validates the conscience and the mind, rather than gory stage spectacle, as the real site of politics. Thus Coleridge arrests the "rootedness, short-sightedness, and enslavement to sense" that, as Carlson says, he associated with both graphic theatre and the English theatre-going mob, and "seeks to transcend by advocating an elevation from immediate circumstances," the circumstances of Gothic spectacle ("An Active Imagination" 32). The internalized, mental position that Albert advocated in *Osorio*, but which was countered by the play's sympathy for Alhadra, here metamorphoses into an implicit condemnation of Gothic excesses, excesses that are identified with Jacobin ideology.

However, the ambivalence that spectacle produced in *Osorio* shows up, under a different guise, in *Remorse*: the revision may be more Burkean in its politics, but conversely, it is more Painite in its spectacle. In this version, Ordonio (Osorio in the original) is killed *on stage*. Having just reconciled himself to his wronged brother Alvar and having proclaimed the everlasting majesty of conscience and remorse, Ordonio is then murdered. This murder we are to see, and to see as senseless and unnecessary. Staging the murder, I would suggest, does two things: first, it pleases the crowd by catering to the very taste for stage-violence that Coleridge abhorred (and does so successfully: *Remorse* ran for twenty-eight nights and netted at least £300, whereas *Osorio* was never produced); and second, it uses Paine's desire for spectacle to condemn Paine's own apostle, Alhadra. When Alhadra hustled the violence off-stage in *Osorio*, she not only prevented Maria from exposure to a horrific spectacle, but also made us less likely to condemn her by giving us no direct image of her barbarity. By watching Alhadra commit violence in *Remorse*, we *know* we are to condemn her. At the end of the play, Ordonio is plagued by everlasting remorse (and Coleridge knew what punishment that could be), and so he hardly needs further punitive measures. Alhadra's (and the play's) violence is gratuitous and therefore condemnable. Thus, the Burkean conservatism which more clearly underwrites this play damns Painite politics, but to do so it uses the very Gothic excesses which it hates, and which Paine's theatre demands.

In Coleridge's dramas, the spectacle of violence evokes a certain ideological allegiance: by seeing acts of violence, we are asked to align our sympathies with the victim of that violence. In this way, Coleridge picks up the debate waged by Paine and Burke. For Paine, as for Foucault, the lower classes are always the oppressed, the aristocracy always the oppressor, and staging the pain of that oppression offers a clear political directive for where our sympathies should lie; for Burke, conversely, it is the aristocracy that should command our sympathy. But while Paine and Burke have opposing views on who was the victim in the French Revolution, Coleridge is much more anxious about keeping distinct the categories of victim and tyrant. Coleridge's attempts at drama are attempts to align himself with one political-theatrical position, only to be plagued by the *other* (the Jacobin *Osorio* required Burkean restraint, whereas the Burkean *Remorse* found it necessary to make violence into spectacle).[16] The obfuscation of political allegiance here is due, in part, to the dynamics of observed, spectacular pain. At the same time that the spectacle of violence is being ejected from the stage (squelched by Burke in the theatre of politics and by the Romantics in the politics of theatre), Coleridge resurrects it as a form of political instruction. His visible violence, however, may do more than situate us within a certain ideological position; it may also testify to its own ability to invade our consciousnesses and force us to adopt sympathetic positions, no matter how reluctantly. For Coleridge, the Gothic body was a detestable stage show, but it was also political in precisely the ways he hoped it wouldn't be.[17]

V

While Shelley never abandoned his sympathy for the oppressed, he too, like Coleridge, understood how insidious theatrical representation could be. As we have already seen, *The Cenci* was Shelley's attempt to portray "the impartial development of such characters as it is possible the persons represented really were, together with the greatest degree of popular effect to be produced by such a development" (*Letters* Vol.X, 61). This was not to be "a mirror which makes beautiful that which is distorted" (as is the function of poetry in "A Defence of Poetry," *Poetry and Prose* 485), but rather a theatre of realism, a demonstration of the "perfect mirror of pure innocence / . . . Shivered to dust" (V,iv,130–132).[18] However, in that realistic theatre, Shelley wanted to employ the imagination to "mitigate the pain" of Beatrice's life story. We are to pity her, but we are to avoid "the restless and anatomizing casuistry with which men seek the justification of Beatrice" in the murder of her father ("Preface" 240). Shelley tells us in *Prometheus Unbound*, "the deep truth is imageless" (*Poetry and Prose* II,iv,116); in *The Cenci*, pain seems to be as well. *The Cenci* is about rape, parricide, and torture, all of which occur off-stage. Like Coleridge's *Osorio*, we are constantly denied images of the suffering body in an attempt to understand more fully the suffering body.

Shelley's reliance on an ideal and idealizing imagination sounds a troublesome chord in the Romantic theatre as I have discussed it to this point. Shelley, like Wordsworth, privileges the imagination as the real site of drama and poetic truth but, in so doing, conjures the spectres of conservatism that we have already seen in Burke, Byron's Senate, and Coleridge's "conscience." If imagination is that "last place of refuge, my own soul," as Wordsworth called it in *The Prelude*, it is also the site of tyranny in the Romantic theatre; it is the secretive and the impostured, as opposed to the public, the visible, the accountable. Imagination itself is part of a binarism of internality/externality that promulgates the "impressive discipline of fear," that conservative force of self-maintenance and self-regulation exploited by Byron's Senate and made into Foucault's "gaze" of (self-) surveillance. But what is even more disturbing is that, as Coleridge has shown, the imagination cannot be sealed off from the spectacle of violence; the post-revolutionary utopias of a Maria are often unimaginable in the spectacular realities of an Alhadra. Thus Shelley writes in a tradition that not only pits the mental drama against the spectacle of pain (with disturbing ideological importance), but also questions whether such a distinction can really be maintained.

That the spectacle of pain might invade and sully the purity of the imagination is most clearly expressed in Shelley's representation of Francesco Cenci.[19] In Cenci we face the same problem as we did with Coleridge's Osorio: we are clearly meant to condemn him, but we are not so sure that we should want to kill him. In Shelley's depiction, Cenci is sympathetic to the degree that he is a victim of violence. Olimpio and Marzio, his murderers, express this tenuous sympathy as they describe hovering over his deathbed, unable to kill him. Olimpio says,

> We dare not kill an old and sleeping man;
> His thin grey hair, his stern and reverent brow,
> His veined hands crossed on his heaving breast,
> And the calm, innocent sleep in which he lay,
> Quelled me. Indeed, indeed, I cannot do it. (IV,iii,9–13)

To this Marzio adds,

> And now my knife
> Touched the loose wrinkled throat, when the old man
> Stirred in his sleep, and said, "God! hear, O, hear,
> A father's curse! What, art thou not our father?"

And then he laughed. I knew it was the ghost
Of my dead father speaking through his lips,
And could not kill him. (IV,iii,16–22)

Like Byron's Faliero and Bertram, Shelley's cutthroats find abstract tyranny easy to kill (especially for money), but real bodies, especially paternal ones, are another matter. The sight of Cenci's Duncan-like vulnerability[20] is enough to soften the resolve of the most hardened criminals, who are willing to spare Cenci despite his villainy. This temporary reluctance introduces us to the possibility of a sympathy for Cenci, one that would be heightened to dangerous levels if his murder were to appear on stage. After all, if hardened criminals are hesitant to kill the body that lies before them, then how should a sensitive audience respond? Cenci's spectacular murder, while perhaps "just," would undermine our desire to assume him guilty. We just might pity the plumage and forget the dying bird.

The same critical distance is used to keep us from the spectacular effects of Beatrice's pain. Shelley has stated clearly in the Preface the "pernicious effects" of justifying Beatrice, of privileging her violent revenge over idealism and imaginative transcendence. If we were to witness the rape and violent abuses perpetrated on Beatrice, our sympathy would increase with her markedly through the direct visual image of her suffering. We would react with the same incensed horror that motivated Burke in his account of the attack on the Queen. Thus, like Burke, might we fall prey to what Shelley fears, "the restless and anatomizing casuistry" that numbs the salvific imagination and valorizes the infliction of pain. In Thomas Paine's open theatre, representations of violence demonstrated through clear cause and effect who was tyrant and who was victim. But for Shelley, such representations of violence might dangerously obfuscate that distinction all the more.

Shelley's reluctance to stage the play's violence indicates his sense of the ideal imagination's vulnerability, in that an observer can be easily manipulated or swayed by the staging of pain. Yet, like Byron and Coleridge, Shelley is also aware that a refusal to make tyranny visible carries with it its own political prices. Like Byron and Coleridge's villains, Count Cenci operates in *secret*: his power proceeds from his unpredictability, the invisibility of his violence, and his unaccountability to public sanction. At the most obvious level, secrecy promotes tyranny as Cenci decides that the rape must take place in the remote castle of Petrella, as opposed to the public city of Rome. This secrecy, moreover, has empowered Cenci throughout his career. In the opening lines of the play, we see Cenci's power established by keeping his deeds off-stage: "That matter of the murder is *hushed up*," Cardinal Camillo tells him, "If you consent to yield his Holiness / Your fief that lies beyond the Pincian gate" (I,i,1–3, emphasis added). The last time "that matter" had been discussed, an architect in the employ of the Pope's bastard son had seen "the deed" and so Cenci vows, "Henceforth, no witness — not the lamp — shall see / That which the vassal threatened to divulge / Whose throat is now choked with dust for his reward" (I,i,21–23). Finally, as his guests rail over the announcement that the sons are dead, he counsels, "Beware! For my revenge / Is as the sealed commission of a king / That kills, and none dare name the murderer" (I,iii,96–98). This secrecy proceeds not only from a fear of the public gaze (from witnesses who might tell the Pope what the tyrant is doing, or "name the murderer"), but also from what Paine described as the medium of aristocratic tyranny: by not being exposed to public accountability, by not making a spectacle of himself, the tyrant can exploit and fulfill his own desires at others' expense. Thus, while Shelley on the one hand keeps violent excesses off stage, in the private, secret space of the imagination, he seems on the other to argue that secrecy and discretion are themselves agents of tyranny. Like Byron and Coleridge, Shelley makes problematic the holy space of the secret as the potential site of barbarism and cruelty.

However, while Byron emphasized the manipulative effects of fear that proceeded from a power operating in secret, Shelley, like Coleridge in *Remorse*, is aware of the degree to which tyranny can also exploit the public forum. Shelley not only associates tyranny with privacy but, like Burke, also sees gratuitous violent spectacle as a medium of despotic power. Early in the play, Cenci defines human nature thus:

> All men delight in sensual luxury,
> All men enjoy revenge; and most exalt
> Over the tortures they can never feel —
> Flattering their secret peace with others' pain.
> But I delight in nothing else. I love
> The sight of agony, and the sense of joy,
> When this shall be another's, and that mine. (I,i,77–83)[21]

If human nature loves to see agony in order to triumph over it, then the slight on lovers of the Gothic theatre could hardly have gone unfelt here. But tyranny is not simply limited to sadistic (or Addisonian, for that matter) delight in seeing someone else suffer. Tyranny actually uses the public status of theatre to increase its own effects. Cenci is repeatedly represented as reveling in the public gaze: Cardinal Camillo tells him that the Pope is aware of the manifold and hideous "deeds / Which you scarce hide from men's revolted eyes" (I,i,13–14). Moreover, when Cenci wishes to announce the death of his sons Rocco and Christofano, he throws a banquet, invites his friends (?!) and kinsmen, provides entertainment, food, and raiment—in short, constructs an entire spectacle to make himself look carefree and benevolent—only to announce that he has murdered his own children. Cenci uses theatre to heighten the impact of his announcement, and thereby to increase the fear he induces in his family and guests. As he intimates later, theatrical spectacle increases publicity, and increased publicity means increased power over a world which is "Loud, light, suspicious, full of eyes and ears" (II,i,179). Rather than avoiding the public gaze, as Paine and Byron had argued tyrants do, Cenci revels in it as a medium of power. And this desire for publicity is the final torture he can inflict on Beatrice:

> I will drag her, step by step,
> Through infamies unheard of among men:
> She shall stand shelterless in the broad noon
> Of public scorn, for acts blazoned abroad. (IV,i,80–83)

Cenci's power not only enjoys spectacle, it is bolstered by spectacle. In Shelley's depiction of tyranny, "imposture" (in the sense of a theatrical appropriation of unearned authority) cuts across both the political and the theatrical, as theatre itself becomes an agent of abuse.

Cenci's power, then, proceeds from the public indulgence of violence, a visibility that is necessary to the fear he generates in others. By rendering both off-stage violence and spectacular violence as endemic to the strategies of tyranny, Shelley is actually addressing the site at which tyranny is most directly understood: the spectator's imagination. He is suggesting that, in the operation of despotism on the innocent observer or victim, there may be no significant distinction between private terrorism and public display. This destruction of the private/public distinction is Cenci's legacy to Beatrice. Before she is raped, the beginnings of madness express themselves in her contemplation, in her imagining of Cenci's tyranny:

> He comes;
> The door is opening now; I see his face;

He frowns on others, but he smiles on me,
Even as he did after the feast last night. (II,ii,18–21)

And moments later, Beatrice says,

> Oh! He has trampled me
> Under his feet, and made the blood stream down
> My pallid cheeks. And he has given us all
> Ditch water, and the fever-stricken flesh
> Of buffaloes, and bade us eat or starve,
> And we have eaten. — He has made me look
> On my beloved Bernardo, when the rust
> Of heavy chains has gangrened his sweet limbs,
> And I have never yet despaired — but now! (II,ii,64–72)

None of this, of course, has really happened, and yet all of it has happened. As is commonplace in criticism of the play, Beatrice eventually becomes what her father cursed her to be; her internal self comes to imitate his tyranny.[22] By the logic of the play, Beatrice's imagination joins with the body to experience degradation and tyranny. Her incipient madness here, that which will finally lead her to kill her father, is a product both of the pain of rape and of an imagination that becomes unable to recognize a difference between external stimulation and internal, imaginative constructions. Whether Beatrice actually saw Bernardo chained and gangrenous (which she didn't; Bernardo's is the only body in the Cenci family to remain unscarred) makes no difference to her experience of the horror she perceives in Cenci. The impact of the play, and the tragedy it invokes, come from Shelley's depiction of the imagination as penetrable, rendible, corruptible. Whereas Burke had privileged the imagination over the degrading effects of spectacle, Shelley makes spectacle an internal phenomenon: he depicts it as product of the active, sensitive imagination. Nothing exists but as it is perceived.[23] In Romantic imaging, the distinction between the two is collapsed (Wordsworth and Radcliffe notwithstanding), and the infectious degradation of spectacle becomes imaginative and self-generated by its victim.[24]

By collapsing the distinction between the imaginative inside and the spectacular outside, the play ultimately obscures the boundaries between privacy and publicity, between what we imagine ourselves to be and what others see us as being. Because of this obfuscation, Beatrice can no longer distinguish between what is happening to her physically and what is conjured imaginatively. And with no distinction between the inside and the outside, she is unable to find a refuge from her affliction: she can retreat neither to a private world cut off from the tortures of the outside nor to a communal sharing of her pains. She is trapped by a psychological catch-22: on the one hand, her health and sanity depend upon naming the crime of rape, of representing it publicly, to herself and others, in order to be able to control and understand it:

> If I could find a word that might make known
> The crime of my destroyer; and that done
> My tongue should like a knife tear out the secret
> Which cankers my heart's core. (III,i,154–157)

But, on the other hand, to speak the crime, to make it a matter of public understanding outside the privacy of the self, to let someone know how she feels, is to make the experience of the crime even worse: "If I try to speak / I shall go mad" (III,i,84–85).[25] Besides, she argues to Lucretia, "What are the words which you would have me speak? / I, who can feign no image in my mind / Of that which has transformed me" (III,i,107–109). Just as the Female Vagrant of Wordsworth's *Salisbury Plain* needed to find a language to relate her suffering, so must Beatrice represent the painful experience of violence. This she is unable to do, not only because there is no language for pain, but also because to find such a language would be to replay on the body what the imagination remembers through words.

Ultimately, Beatrice's need to "feign [an] image in my mind / Of that which has transformed me" is to represent herself to herself in an act of theatre. However, to perform such theatre is to distance one's body from one's imaginative powers; it is to become someone else, to replicate rather than to inhabit corporeality. Self-theatricalization is tantamount to self-annihilation, because to make the rape known is to destroy the self that experienced the violation; yet, at the same time, expression is necessary for distancing herself from pain, for giving her some framework to understand, process, and control it. The private world and the world of spectacle are indivisible, and yet irreconcilable. While Shelley's idealism asserts that the deep truth is imageless, it also *demands* an image, a theatricalized expression of pain. David Marshall argues that the eighteenth-century convention of theatricalizing the self was a way of negotiating the demands of bourgeois citizenship: by constructing oneself as theatre-piece, one hid one's true "self" from the gaze of the world at the same time that one performed one's duties in the *theatrum mundi* (*Figure of Theatre*). However, in the Romantic theatre of cruelty, such a distinction upon which the self can be predicated is no longer tenable. Pain destroys the mind/body division and, like a "[scorpion] ringed with fire" (II,ii,70), the self (mind *and* body) destroys itself.

In Shelley, then, we find the clearest articulation of an anxiety that has been running through each of the plays I have discussed. Early in this chapter, I noted Mary Jacobus's point that the Romantics ran violence off the stage in order to consign it to the imagination where it could be controlled and worked upon. But while the imagination may be a private theatre, a Wordsworthian space where the playwright might control the rhetorical implications of spectacular pain more fully, the Romantic dramatist also feared it as a potential space for the very violence he sought to control. Thomas Paine had written with a naive optimism that "It is the faculty of the human mind to become what it contemplates, and to act in unison with its object" (*Rights* 109).[26] For Radcliffe and Wordsworth, the imagination was a space where one could safely contemplate one's community with the pained body, all the while affirming one's distance from that body. Yet, as Charles Maturin eloquently puts it, "The drama of terror has the irresistible power of converting its audience into its victims" (*Melmoth* 345). Byron, Coleridge, and Shelley all contemplate the effects of violent revolution on the mind, and in such contemplation, realize how images of pain may infect and destroy one's private, imaginative space. For Byron, such an invasion was initially necessary to the thwarting of government tyranny, yet was always plagued by self-delusion, by the possibility that a republic's liberation was never wholly desirable or controllable. For Coleridge, mental revolution could never be trusted to effect the kind of social change he thought was necessary: public displays of violence are still the most effective means of social control. And for Shelley, the mental revolution did not so much replace the public one as it risked becoming like the public one; for him, the spectacle of violence is itself an imagined act, one that destroys the boundaries between public and private. Violence renders the salvific imagination itself a political stage, one whose vestiges of revolution frequently allow spectacular violence to invade and destroy it.

Intermezzo

"The origins of melodrama," writes Peter Brooks, "can be accurately located within the context of the French Revolution and its aftermath. This is the epistemological moment which it illustrates and to which it contributes: the moment that symbolically, and really, marks the final liquidation of the traditional Sacred and its representative institutions" (*Melodramatic* 14–15). Melodrama, for Brooks, is a victory over the repression instituted by tradition: "The desire to express all seems a fundamental characteristic of the melodramatic mode. Nothing is spared because nothing is left unsaid" (4), a total disclosure that informs discourses from Rousseau's *Confessions* to the Marquis de Sade. With this impulse toward total expression, *tout dire*, comes the attempt to assuage the fears engendered by the fall of the old order. Visibility becomes the new god. Brooks writes:

> Melodrama does not simply represent a "fall" from tragedy, but a response to the loss of the tragic vision. It comes into being in a world where the traditional imperatives of truth and ethics have been violently thrown into question, yet where the promulgation of truth and ethics, their instauration as a way of life, is of immediate, daily, political concern. (15)

Thus, while Charles Lamb would bemoan that the Gothic stage has "materialised and brought down a fine vision to the standard of flesh and blood" (*Poems* 222; also quoted in Richardson, *Mental* 2–3), playwrights like Byron and Shelley would see as morally and politically imperative the representation of "things as they really were," the demonstration of the "truth and ethics" of their heroes' flesh and blood.

The tendency toward *tout dire* that Brooks locates in melodrama placed contradictory demands on the human body as a spectacle. On the one hand, this body was expected to tell all: it was to telegraph its internal emotions (cf. Radcliffe); it was to register sympathy with another (cf. Wordsworth's traveler); it was to engage its audience in political allegiance, even if that allegiance required a body like Marino Faliero's to be inscribed and displayed in pain. But on the other hand, the pain that the melodramatic imagination often inscribed on the spectacular body concealed all in the very act of display: bodies were violated, but not on stage; these violations were often parodically represented (Faliero's public, Albert's self-portrait), their pain undercut by excessive staginess; and most important, such violations and their political gestures were often, as in the case of Beatrice Cenci, presented within a context of personal isolation and impenetrable subjectivity. Beatrice's pain may in some ways be spectacular and political, but it is also ineffable, undemonstrable, insignificant in the sense that her pain cannot be given a language. To the degree that the melodramatic or Gothic imagination tells all, it tells of what cannot be told. By telling all, it tells nothing, except that the pain it makes spectacular is a pain whose representation it does not trust. If Shelley is close to the mark at all, pain occurs in the interstices of expression — between our need to tell and our inability to do so.

If I am correct in assuming that spectacular pain is itself an epistemological problem, then the tendency to total revelation in Rousseau, Paine, Sade, Robespierre, and the Gothic answers what Brooks identifies as its epistemological crisis by providing another: its inability to understand the signification it demands of the body in pain. These epistemological crises are less the product of the French Revolution (as Brooks suggests) than they are brought to their clearest moment by the Revolution. The crises in body knowledge and body language inscribe themselves from at least the 1750s in the discourses of sentimentalism. Moreover, they are not limited to an imagination we can define as melodramatic or Gothic, if such imagination is limited to the literary and theatrical. The Gothic imagination — or anti-Gothic, given its resistance to telling and showing all — is culturally widespread, informing more theatres than the ones at Covent Garden and Drury Lane. I want to shift gears slightly now and discuss three other significant theatres in which the epistemological crisis betrays itself: the theatre of the scaffold, the operating theatre, and what Norman Schwarzkopf has so lucidly defined for us as the theatre of war. As Peter Brooks argues, melodramatic spectacle (what I am calling the Gothic body) not only arises out of a particular history but also contributes to it. At the end of the eighteenth and beginning of the nineteenth centuries, the history of pain was being written (as it was being unwritten) on the body in the judicial, medical, and military theatres of Europe. And a good place to start reading this body language is on the victim of torture.

4. The Epistemology of the Tortured Body

I

A young boy has been murdered. His lacerated body has been discovered near his home, the Castle Frankheim. The suspect: a ne'er-do-well from the rival house of Orrenburg, presumed to be operating under instructions from his boss. But the suspect, once apprehended, is reluctant to confess; the proper means must be taken to extort a confession. When Osbright, the victim's brother, learns that the "proper means" are the rack, and that until Frankheim "had recourse to torture, not a syllable would [the suspect] utter, but assertions of his own and his master's innocence," he is outraged. For Brother Peter, who had watched the scene and who now relates the details to Osbright, this was a moment of great sympathetic inspiration — he heartily pities the suspect. But for Osbright this is an enraging judicial stupidity. Osbright had been relieved by the belief that Gustavus, Count of Orrenburg was responsible for the young brother's death, but now

> That belief grew weaker with every question, which he put to brother Peter; he found, that while in possession of his strength and faculties the supposed culprit had most strenuously denied all knowledge of the crime; that the excess of torture alone had forced from him the declaration, that Gustavus of Orrenburg had any concern in it; that the name of Gustavus had been suggested by the prejudices of the suspicious and already exasperated father; and that the whole confession was comprised in the mere pronouncing that name, when the speaker was seduced into uttering it by the certainty of immediate release from tortures most excruciating. (Lewis, *Romantic Tales* 44–46)

Osbright's doubt is prudent. The tortured victim *had* lied. Young Joscelyn was accidentally killed by a wolf. The extorted confession was simply what the torturers wanted to hear and so the confession proves nothing. And the moral of the story: "Of all the defects of the human heart, there is none more encroaching, more insidious, more dangerous than mistrust: viewed through her distorted optics, there is no action so innocent, no every-day occurrence so insignificant, that does not assume the appearance of offence" (57).

When Osbright rejects the evidence gathered under pain of the question, he indicates the ludicrousness of torture as a means of inquiry. And he is not alone in his outrage. In the last chapter, I discussed how violence was run off the stage of the Romantic theatre and was made the property of the imagination. At another venue, the same is true for the stage of the scaffold, and for public execution. As Edward Peters explains, by the late eighteenth century the use of torture was being abandoned by the courts of Europe as a remnant of the *ancien régime*. The use of torture — or the refusal to use it — became a symptom by which a nation could diagnose the state of its moral health (*Torture* 74). Foucault has an even more interesting way of putting it: "At the end of the eighteenth century, torture was to be denounced as a survival of the barbarities of another age: the mark of a savagery that was denounced as 'Gothic'" (*Discipline* 39). But such Gothic denunciation is more than a self-satisfying belief in the progress of European society: it registers an epistemological crisis that novels at the end of the eighteenth century had to explore.

Matthew Lewis's 1808 *Romantic Tales* articulates an outrage against torture, and for two reasons. The first is the problem of *uncertainty*: as Osbright knows, judicial torture proves nothing; it simply uses torture to affirm "the prejudices of the suspicious and already exasperated father." While attempting to gather information, torture actually points to epistemological breakdown. Torture had always been in some way associated with the search for truth, ever since it was defined by Ulpian, a third-century jurist, as "'the torment and suffering of the body in order to elicit the truth'" (Peters, *Torture* 1). And even though Cicero had known that torture is a self-contesting mode of inquiry, that did not stop European courts from reaping the benefits of coerced confession. Throughout medieval jurisprudence, the tortured body was considered to offer direct access to guilt, and consequently to truth: *tormentum* (to torture) is even etymologically linked to *torquens mentum* — the "twisting of the mind" to wring out the truth. Elizabeth Hanson has analyzed how, in the Renaissance, Cartesian dualism wreaked havoc on the social institution of legal inquiry by reifying the schism between interior motivation — the "real" site of guilt — and the body that displayed this guilt.[1] Renaissance torture displayed not only a crisis in inquiry, in that the body could no longer be counted on to speak the truth, but also a crisis in epistemology, in that it constructed the internal subjective space that it then could not violate (38). The body could no longer be invested with the certainty it had been granted by, say, England's Star Chamber or the Holy Inquisition (two notorious agents of torture), and had to be distanced from the legal procedure it was once so necessary to. And since recourse to torture was always a last resort in reaching a judicial conclusion, torture could only be used after all other time-consuming methods had been tried, and after the courts had been tied up for too long in costly litigation. Thus, some two hundred years later, Lewis's Osbright could take as commonplace the inefficacy of torture as a mode of inquiry.

But the tale objects to something other than the practical inefficacies of torture. When the family of Gustavus Orrenburg avenges the slander perpetrated on their master, they kill Frankheim's herald and nail his head to the gate. Gustavus is as outraged at this act as Osbright had been at the torture, but for a different reason: "has my Castle indeed been polluted by so horrible an outrage?" he demands (75). Whereas Osbright objects on judicial grounds to the persecution of the body, Gustavus responds to the debasement and suffering of the victim. And while, strictly speaking, the castle Orrenburg has not committed torture, it has undertaken a willful intrusion into the private human body. Such an invasion represents the kind of violation that Enlightenment judicial reformers lobbied so strongly to eliminate. Since the publication of Cesare Beccaria's extremely influential *An Essay on Crimes and Punishments* in 1764, the question of torture became less a judicial and more a humane one. The rational concern for the judicial use — or uselessness — of torture that so clearly plagued the Renaissance lawmakers in Hanson's discussion was gradually replaced by what Pieter Spierenburg calls a "critical threshold of sensibility" (*Spectacle* x), a sense that the spectators of torture actually identified with and shared the pain of the accused undergoing the question. This emphatic sensibility played down the phenomenon of torture as a judicial, epistemological question and elevated it as a moral one, thereby privileging sensitivity over rationality, identification over disengagement, and in a larger sense, the inside over the outside. These binarisms arise in Beccaria's *On Crimes and Punishments*[2] but, as I hope to show, are unstable and problematic to the reformist task. Beccaria's essay is indeed the most influential text in judicial reform, but its curious mixture of rationality and sensitivity becomes a problem that writers of fiction — such as Matthew Lewis, Percy Bysshe Shelley, and William Godwin — will have to face.[3]

II

As the frequent citations in Blackstone's *Commentaries* demonstrate, Cesare Beccaria became the primary spokesperson for the enlightened eradication of torture from the courts. In an address to the reader in the second edition of *An Essay on Crimes and Punishments*, Beccaria asserts that his study of torture is "designed to ward off the unenlightened and excitable masses" from imitating the laws, those "dregs of utterly barbarous centuries," by which countries have sanctioned the use of torture (4).[4] There can be no room in jurisprudence for irrational and unbridled passions. Beccaria sought to replace these highly superstitious models with an enlightened judicial procedure that would be thoroughly rational: all penalties should be evaluated on purely utilitarian grounds. Punishments must be useful, necessary, just, and effective (10). Only through this rationality would legal reform ensure "the greatest happiness shared by the greatest number" (8), a slogan the British associate with Jeremy Bentham but which Bentham probably first read in Beccaria. The linchpin of Beccaria's logic, one that goes as far back as Cicero, is the conflict of interest to which torture submits the body:

> it tends to confound all relations to require that a man be at the same time accuser and accused, that pain be made the crucible of truth, as if its criterion lay in the sinews of the wretch. (31)

Nineteen years later, Sir William Blackstone would footnote Beccaria and repeat the same charge, that it is ridiculous to rate "a man's virtue by the hardiness of his constitution, and his guilt by the sensibility of his nerves!" (*Commentaries* Vol.IV,326). Ultimately, the problem with torture is that it confounds the mastery of reason over the senses. For Descartes, such a mastery is necessary for any kind of epistemological certainty. In a Cartesian universe, rational judiciary process must be based on evidences that are demonstrably true through pure reason, rather than through unquestioned sensual stimulation. Torture reverses the relationship of reason to sensation, says Beccaria, by privileging sensations over the master-mind:

> Every act of our will is invariably proportioned to the force of the sensory impression which is its source; and the sensory capacity of every man is limited. Thus the impression of pain may become so great that, filling the entire sensory capacity of the tortured person, it leaves him free only to choose what for the moment is the shortest escape from pain. (32)

Hence the suspect's confession in Matthew Lewis's tale.

The privilege that Beccaria affords to logical truths extends to his radical assertion that the law should not concern itself with the accused's *motives*: rather, it must only judge the suitability of his actions to the larger community (15). But Beccaria's attempt to remain outside the accused's subjective space is then somewhat undermined by a segue from the rational into the sentimental. In a passage worthy of Godwin's *Caleb Williams*, Beccaria identifies what *should* be the motivation of law reformers:

> the groans of the weak, sacrificed to cruel ignorance and to opulent indolence; the barbarous torments, multiplied with lavish and useless severity, for crimes either not proved or wholly imaginary; the filth and horrors of the prison, intensified by that cruellest tormentor of the miserable, uncertainty — all these ought to have roused that breed of magistrates who direct the opinions of men. (9)

This appeal is problematic in that it allows the body to demonstrate an internal space of emotion and sentiment that Beccaria argued must be kept tightly closed. In other words, Beccaria advocates that pity rush in where reason has feared to tread, that the eradication of torture should be founded in sympathetic identification rather than detached logic. For Alessandro Manzoni, the Italian novelist whose novel *The Betrothed* is a fictional illustration of his grandfather Beccaria's reform tract, the passage marks the elder's characteristic "overflow of spontaneous inspiration" that masquerades as "a work of premeditated study" (quoted in Introduction to Beccaria xxii). For Henry Paolucci, a recent translator of the *Essay*, outbreaks like this one are a convoluted attempt to cover for Beccaria's marked ignorance of judicial history (including his apparent misinformation regarding the actual state of affairs in the courts, that is, that even prior to his publication, torture was dead or dying in most European courts [Introduction xxiii]). But Beccaria's Romantic outburst is not simple idiosyncrasy. Charles Taylor agues that, as confidence in the Deistic order of the universe waned in the eighteenth century, radical Enlightenment thinkers had to maintain the belief in the primacy of human benevolence in order to provide for themselves some moral foundation for their enterprise (*Sources* 331). Feeling, which they tried to make coterminous with scientific logic, was the origin of all reformist and enlightened thought. And, as we have seen in the dramatic representation of tyrannicide, feeling presents problems. One of Beccaria's opening premises had been that "no lasting advantage is to be hoped for from political morality if it is not founded on the ineradicable feelings of mankind" (10), but it is precisely these feelings that are else-where described as "the tenderest feelings and most violent passions" that play "on men's hearts like musicians on instruments" (41). In essence, Beccaria has worked himself into a corner: reason is dependent upon ineradicable feelings, but such feelings can manipulate and pervert reason. He has posited a thoroughly rational, syllogistic treatment of the body, but then he has advocated an emotional awareness of and response to that body. Rational distantiation is replaced by sentimental identification. Thus Beccaria undermines the distance/identification paradigm upon which his judicial theory rests, and demonstrates what Jürgen Habermas would call a legitimation crisis, that is, for an ideological order to "claim to be recognized as right and just," while its very demand "highlights the fact that legitimacy is a contestable validity claim" (*Communication* 178). In Beccaria's text, jurisprudence is defined by the agencies of sentimentalism, yet those same agencies undermine its claim to validity.

By the "agencies of sentimentalism" producing a judicial "legitimation crisis," I am referring to that tendency of authors like Radcliffe and Edmund Burke to collapse (however partially) the distance Descartes had placed between bodies and souls. As John Mullan notes, eighteenth-century sensibility obscured the distinction between one's moral, sensible relation to *external* stimuli and one's *internal* physiological reaction (*Sentiment* 201); all the swooning and collapsing into chairs, we remember, was the physical manifestation of a psychological state. With sentimentalism, the body once again became a demonstrable space that could emphasize the internal, affective life of the soul in a way similar to the medieval correspondence between vice and physical deformity. The legal implication of this return — at least for Gothic fiction — is a nostalgia for the body as an unmediated testimony of vice or virtue. Often we see in the physiognomies of Gothic characters an easily readable guilt or innocence: good guys are beautiful and bad guys are ugly. This easy correspondence was belied in, say, *Lear*'s Edmund or the Restoration's handsome rake-villain, whose bodies mapped that separation that Cartesian dualism had created. Such bodies successfully hid their internal spiritual state. (And this ability to hide — or to *lie* — brings us back to judicial reform: it is what renders torture useless as inquiry.) However, with the attempt to redress the social and epistemological implications of dualism came the renewed attention to the body as a possible site of the spirit.

This (partial) collapse of Cartesian dualism in the subject engendered the (partial) collapse of a second Cartesian division — the division between subjects that Descartes had predicated on the isolation of the soul. As we saw in Radcliffe, sentimentalism invited the subject to feel what the other person was feeling, and to construct a dialogic community between subjects. Yet, in Radcliffe's representation of that connection, the perceiving subject was always isolated by the paralytic agency of horror. One never truly knew how another one felt. Moreover, the spectacle of the highly pained body, as it appeared on the theatrical stage, engaged the spectator in manipulation and control: its "sympathy" is so much political rhetoric, rather than unmediated, humane response. Given these failures in the discernment of bodily "truth," we find a crisis in law that runs through Beccaria's text and gets picked up in the Gothic: the body in pain is highly charged in its emotional moral appeal, yet untrustworthy all the same. In a curious paradox, the body—held sacred by a post-Lockean tradition of private property—becomes the greatest enemy to a judiciary trying to secure its protection. Rationalist jurisprudence and emotive sentimentalism, both of which underwrite Lewis's tale, seem to be mutually exclusive epistemologies when one is viewing the body.

Beccaria's response to the threat that a sensitive body poses for a rationalist judiciary is to fashion punishment that works as a gentle deterrent rather than as a barbarous demonstration of punitive power. The more torture is used, he reasons, the less effect it will have, because people will grow used to the idea of it (43). Rather,

> It is not the intensity of punishment that has the greatest effect on the human spirit, but its duration, for our sensibility is more easily and more perfectly affected by slight but repeated impressions than by a powerful and momentary action. (46–47)

Punishment should be *threatening*, omnipresent but rarely enacted, imagined rather than exercised, existing mostly in the future tense. Whereas earlier in the tract, Beccaria had called uncertainty "that cruellest tormentor of the miserable," here uncertainty becomes a most useful criminal deterrent. For Spierenburg, such a move demonstrates the increased sensibility that wanted to remove grotesquerie and torture from public view because the spectators could actually feel the tortured victim's pain (*Spectacle* 184–185). (And in this sense the eradication of torture markedly parallels the eradication of stage violence that I discussed in the previous chapter.) Subjected to Foucault's hermeneutic of suspicion, the move to gentler modes of correction simply recast the semiotics of state power as they were exercised upon the body, and empowered various state apparatuses—the prison, medicine, psychology, religion — to define their specialized states of "normalcy" to which they could then submit the body. Gentler correction, to Foucault, merely helped to fix the causal relationship of crime and punishment within the *mind* of the public, so that torture need no longer be used. In either case, what Beccaria is articulating here is a way of maintaining social control without resorting to the immediacy of the body and all its vicissitudes. In other words, Beccaria uses a strategy to get rid of or to compartmentalize the sensitive body in order to diminish the possible contradictions or underminings it presents to the rationalist elements of its program. This strategy, which had shown up in Wordsworth's *Guilt and Sorrow* as an absent body made present only by a "disciplined" imagination, also informs the scene of torture in turn-of-the-century literature. But whereas Wordsworth would invoke the body by keeping it absent, these literary scenes of torture attempt to displace the sentimental body altogether.

III

One such example of physical displacement comes from Percy Bysshe Shelley, whose literary career virtually begins with torture. His early novel *Zastrozzi*, written in 1805 when Shelley was eighteen, relates the convoluted revenge plot of its titular villain who attempts to murder the hapless Verezzi, the son of his mother's seducer. Zastrozzi, like many a Gothic villain, is exposed for his crimes at the end of the novel and dragged away by the Inquisition — to a dungeon, once again out of the public view — to endure the rack. But what is curious here is that the inquiry-by-torture comes *after* he has made a full confession. By now the Inquisition knows that Zastrozzi is guilty and that he acted with an accomplice (Matilda), and so it has nothing to enquire or discover. Thus its infliction of pain becomes a metaphorical *quid pro quo*, administering punishment for crime in a strictly causal relationship, rather than using torture as a means to obtain information. By a judicial sleight-of-hand, the novel transforms torture from inquiry into punishment and, in so doing, indulges its Gothic sensation without allowing it to be plagued by the judicial problem of torture as useless inquiry.

At an obvious level, Shelley is drawing on a popular novelistic convention that was flooding the popular presses in the early nineteenth century (and that would appeal to a teenager looking for instant fame). But the use of torture here is not only sensationalism. The implications of inflicting pain on Zastrozzi's body, and proclaiming the truth of his guilt, reverse the general treatment of his body throughout the novel. Whereas the first chapter foregrounds the immediacy of Verezzi's body — he is forcefully abducted, shackled in a dungeon, and forced to suffer reptiles slithering over him — our first sight of Zastrozzi is no sight at all: he is masked, elusive, and moving about in the dark (5). When we finally *do* see his face and figure, we learn little more than does the bewildered Verezzi, who has no idea why he has been kidnapped. Zastrozzi's body is unreadable; it *conceals* an inner truth. As he tells Matilda,

> My maxim . . . through life has been, wherever I am, whatever passions shake my inmost soul, at least to *appear* collected. I generally am; for, by suffering no common events, no fortuitous casuality to disturb me, my soul becomes steeled to more interesting trials. I have a spirit, ardent, impetuous as thine; but acquaintance with the world has induced me to veil it, though it still continues to burn within my bosom. (47; emphasis original)

Characterized by its dualism, Zastrozzi's body is a shield, an impediment to the truth, as opposed to the sentimental hero whose body broadcasts an internal state. Given this configuration in which the body hides the soul, torture is used to "get inside," and to get at the truth. It externalizes the internal, and makes the body the site of proclaimed guilt. Shelley gets around the Cartesian body-problem here by simply ignoring it, or by returning to a vision of the body as it existed before Descartes, in which the flesh could telecast the state of the soul. In this way, his early Gothic novel documents that conservative morality for which the Gothic, *pace* Sade, is famous.[5] Torture here is both poetic and criminal justice: by reuniting the body with the soul, the state reads the guilt written on the body, and thereby circumvents the epistemological problem that torture had always evoked. Without the text's slightest allowance for uncertainty or the moral ambivalence that accompanies it, *Zastrozzi*'s torture is unquestionably effective.

The case gets more complicated in Shelley's later Gothic work, *The Cenci*, in that the moral question of torture begins to emerge. Like the state apparatus in *Zastrozzi*, legal investigators in *The Cenci* do their torturing offstage. I argued in the previous chapter that the body provided problems for Shelley's idealistic project in *The Cenci*, in that its vulnerability and fragility could inspire sympathy for a tyrant like Cenci. The same is true for the torture of Marzio: to administer the question on stage is to invite a sympathetic response to him, and to make his body more potently charged than any other on stage. Since Shelley's project in this play is to present the trials of Beatrice, and to have the audience focus on *her*, he must eliminate any victimization that might detract from her. If the ultimate aim of the drama is to teach "the human heart, through its sympathies and antipathies, the knowledge of itself" ("Preface" 240), then such an idealistic internalized project cannot afford to be compromised by a cheap scene of bloody spectacle. Shelley demonstrates an awareness of the problem that Beccaria faced in the highly charged sentimental body. Torture can invite a sympathy for the devil (Cenci, Marzio). And that sympathy, and the excessive out rage it can provoke, can detract the spectator from an awareness of his or her own responses, the knowledge of his or her own heart. In the case of *The Cenci*, then, didactic idealism necessitates that the tortured body be kept from public view.

Moreover, while *Zastrozzi* transforms torture from inquiry into punishment, *The Cenci* unquestioningly utilizes torture to "solve" the mystery of who murdered Count Cenci. The assassin Marzio, "with lips yet white from the rack's kiss" (V,ii,9), confesses that he killed the Count who lay sleeping in the castle of Petrella. Furthermore, he admits, he was urged to the crime by Cenci's

> own son Giacomo, and the young prelate
> Orsino sent me to Petrella; there
> The ladies Beatrice and Lucretia
> Tempted me with a thousand crowns, and I
> And my companion forthwith murdered him.
> Now let me die. (V,ii,14–19)

Here torture adequately performs the state's legal business: it exposes both criminal and accomplices without the slightest recognition that such exposure may not be trustworthy. Even when Marzio repeats, "I have told it all; / For pity's sake lead me away to death" (V,ii,110–111), the Judge and detectives do not suspect that he might be trying to avoid further examination and torture. As I argued earlier, *The Cenci* explores Shelley's fear of pain's ability to collapse the distinction between one's internal life and one's external affliction, and it is this distinction upon which the question of "truth" is founded, not only for Descartes, but for Beatrice as well. (With the collapse of the inside/outside boundary, she loses her perception of what is happening to her, and even of who she is.) But in the minor character of Marzio, Shelley seems to be working at cross-purposes. The collapse of the inside/outside distinction, although horrible for Beatrice, effects in Marzio a convenient circumvention of the judicial problem of torture. Inflicted pain turns his inside out; it delivers the truth the state needs to hear and thereby empowers the state whose benevolence the play does not question. (Indeed, the irony of the play is that Savella, the Pope's legate, arrives with a warrant for Cenci's arrest just moments after Beatrice has had her father killed.) In Marzio, torture becomes not a judicial stupidity but rather a means of substantiating state power and justice. In *The Cenci*, cruelty is truth and truth cruelty: that is all the state needs to know.

IV

If Shelley's play hints at a contradiction between sympathy for the private, individual body and the utility of state apparatus in torture, such a problem is central to his father-in-law, William Godwin, who was working out the same problems ten years earlier. For Godwin, the mutual exclusivity of rationality and sentimentalism, and their relation to judicial inquiry, are crucial to the development of his political philosophy. In the 1793 *Enquiry Concerning Political Justice*, which would exert great influence on Shelley, Godwin tells us that the "subject of punishment is perhaps the most fundamental in the science of politics" (631) because it proceeds directly from the social contract; that is, it defines the rights and limitations that protect one citizen from the violent forces of another. Judicial law is fundamental to a definition of individualism (a definition that is the ultimate project of the *Enquiry*) because it demarcates the powers by which all social institutions may potentially compromise the individual.

But it is this whole emphasis on individualism that opens up the epistemological problem for Godwin. On the one hand, he shares with Beccaria (whom he quotes copiously) the conviction that punishment must always be determined by a just and rational process of inquiry. For Godwin, there is no such thing as a freely committed crime: "The assassin cannot help the murder he commits" (633). Rather, he is the victim of Necessity, of the inevitable chain of circumstances that forced him to commit it. And so, reason dictates the eradication of those circumstances that will, in turn, eradicate the need to commit crime. But on the other hand, reason must allow that the heinousness of a crime is often necessarily determined by motives: first-degree murder must meet with sharper punishment than involuntary manslaughter, the crucial difference being the offender's motivation or intention. It is precisely the identification of this motive that troubles Godwin. He argues that

> Man . . . may, in a certain sense, be affirmed to consist of two parts, the external and the internal. The form which his actions assume is one thing; the principle from which they flow is another. With the former it is possible we should be acquainted; respecting the latter there is no species of evidence that can adequately inform us. (649)

Thus the "inscrutability of intention" (650) poses an epistemological problem, a "mystery" (653) that we can never adequately penetrate. We may "reasonably enquire first into [the accused's] intention, but when we have found this, our task is but begun" (654). And that task, as Godwin outlines it, moves away from internal motivation and into the dismantling of social circumstances that cause crime. Whereas Shelley's conventional Gothicism will get around the "inscrutability of intention" by equating the internal with the external in torture, Godwin remains aware of the problems it poses. The internal/external dualism is both essential and antagonistic to criminal justice as Godwin outlines it in the *Enquiry*.

The inside/outside distinction, which both establishes and threatens the very foundations of criminal justice, is a particularly acute problem for Godwin as a political philosopher and novelist. Since Leslie Stephen's influential analysis in 1902, many Godwin critics have seen an antagonism between his rationalist project in the *Enquiry* and the more personalized emotional and psychological histories of his later novels. Godwin himself characterizes the *Inquiry* as an attempt to reason as "an impartial spectator of human concerns" (76), whereas *Caleb Williams* purports to appeal directly to "a very powerful interest" (xxv). Hence it is a commonplace in Godwin criticism that he moves from rationalist-anarchist political philosopher to emotional, sympathetic novelist, a move usually located between the first and second editions of the *Enquiry*. Mitzi Myers attributes this change to the death of Mary Wollstonecraft, Godwin's writing of her biography, and his reconsideration of the importance of domestic affections contained therein. Myers quotes Godwin from *Thoughts on Man* as she argues that he came late in life to see sympathy as "the epistemological ground of all philosophy, the 'only reality of which we are susceptible . . . our heart of hearts'" ("Godwin's *Memoirs*" 305). Here, the internal life is given a privileged space that was carefully closed off in the earlier work, and it is a space that, I hope to demonstrate, magnifies the problems of a rational jurisprudence with a human face in much the same way that it did for Beccaria.

While Godwin may applaud the incorporation of domestic affections into the rationalist (perhaps masculinist) agenda of the *Enquiry*, this progression is not without its difficulties. In his preface to the 1799 novel *Travels of St. Leon*, Godwin discusses the changes in his thinking since the first publication of *Political Justice* in 1793:

> Some readers of my graver productions will perhaps, in pursuing these little volumes, accuse me of inconsistency; the affections and charities of private life being every where in this publication a topic of warmest eulogium, while in the Enquiry concerning Political Justice they seemed to be treated with no great degree of indulgence and favour. In answer to this objection, all I think it necessary to say on the present occasion is, that for more than four years, I have been anxious for the opportunity and leisure to modify some of the earlier chapters of that work in conformity to the sentiments inculcated in this. Not that I see cause to make any change respecting the principle of justice, or any thing else fundamental to the system there delivered; but that I apprehend domestic and private affections inseparable from the nature of man, and from what may be styled the culture of the heart, and am fully persuaded that they are not incompatible with a profound and active sense of justice in the mind of him that cherishes them. (ix–x)

Here Godwin argues that there is no need to change the principles of justice; public policy still requires rational utility. However, principles of justice must be tempered with affection in anyone who reverences sufficiently the very idea of justice. In other words, characters must display the proper motives. With this proviso Godwin does not so much achieve a great union of affections and justice, as Myers argues, but rather sets up the conditions for keeping "affections" and "justice" separate. By declaiming that affections bond with rational justice only "in the mind of him that cherishes them," he allows for the possibility of a certain social policy that remains distinct from the domestic, affectionate one: in other words, those who do not cherish affections may be treated under the rubric of utilitarian rationalism.

Such a separation of affection and justice is central to the 1805 novel, *Fleetwood; or The New Man of Feeling*, in which the protagonist is plagued by the conflict between passion and reason — both in his domestic affections and in matters of law and public policy. The novel squarely sets affections and emotions against a rationalist program to demonstrate that affections and rationality are always intertwined, mutually defining, and mutually problematic. This interrelationship employs the binarisms that have structured our consideration of pain thus far — rationality / sensitivity, distance / identification, outside / inside — and demonstrates them to be both necessary to and estranged from a "proper" mode of inquiry. Furthermore, Godwin sets the whole question within a framework of judicial inquiry, punishment, and torture. Fleetwood uses the model of judicial inquiry and punishment to try to sort out his domestic problems, but with that model comes the problem of how one reads motivation in general and the body in particular. What we see in *Fleetwood* is the same legitimation crisis that tormented Cesare Beccaria, where the body is the site of both sympathy and deception. The novel carries this crisis into the domestic realm in an attempt to reconcile Godwin's internal, emotional impulses with his disengaged, utilitarian rationalism.

V

Throughout most of *Fleetwood*, the eponymous Casimir is a misanthrope, and it is the project of the book to document the stages of that misanthropy. As the narrator, Fleetwood traces the development of his misanthropy from the young Wordsworthian solitaire, through the distanced and disillusioned Oxford student, to the misanthropic adult. Like Falkland in *Caleb Williams*, Fleetwood hates humanity because of the circumstances he has encountered: cruelties among his university mates, deceptive women, pretentious wealth, and corrupt government. The central plot centers on his marriage to the pure and innocent Mary who, thanks to the evil deceptions of Fleetwood's nephew Gifford, appears to have been unfaithful to Fleetwood. (She hasn't been, of course.) He leaves her and travels to Italy, where he decides he will cut her off from his money and sue her for adultery. While in Italy, he sends for some of Mary's clothes, out of which he constructs life-sized mannequins of her and Kenrick, the supposed correspondent. These he proceeds to torture and "vivisect." On his return to England, he is attacked by highwaymen who attempt to murder him, but is quickly rescued by an unidentified savior, who turns out to be Kenrick. When he discovers that Gifford staged the adultery and attempted the murder — for which Gifford is hanged at a public execution — Fleetwood returns to his life with Mary and the domestic affection for which Mitzi Myers had such great hope. But Fleetwood's marriage is always shadowed by the tensions of disbelief and paranoia: we get the sense that he will never really be sure that Mary is totally trustworthy. In fact, Fleetwood's problem throughout the novel, as we shall see, is that he can never really be *sure* of anything. It is because of this uncertainty, and its relation to inquiry, justice, and domestic affections, that Godwin's novel will take the sentimental premises of its namesake, Mackenzie's *Man of Feeling*, and explore the epistemological problems of sentimentalism as they inscribe themselves on the judicial body.

The problem of sentimentalism in legal inquiry becomes a primary focus when, near the beginning of the novel, Fleetwood recounts a practical joke from his days at Oxford. The joke involves Withers, a would-be tragedian who fashions his taste and intellect as superior to those of his peers, Fleetwood's friends. These friends arrange a mock-reading of Withers's play, at which the playwright becomes drunk and riotous. He is summarily called upon to stand trial before a "judge" who is nothing more than a life-sized doll made for the occasion (a doll that prefigures the ones Fleetwood will construct later on). At the trial Withers finally realizes the degree to which he is being ridiculed, and, out of humiliation, kills himself. For Fleetwood, the whole sordid scene is reducible to a moral lesson, as he expresses his sympathy for Withers:

> It is suffering only that can inspire us with true sympathy, that can render us alive to those trifles which constitute so large a portion of earthly misery or happiness, that can give us a feeling of that anguish, which, sometimes in human beings, as most evidently in the brute creation, works inwardly, consuming the very principle of life, but has no tongue, not the smallest sound, to signify its excess, and demand our pity. (38–39)

These sentiments of course echo a tradition of Moral Sense Philosophers to which I alluded in the first two chapters, philosophers such as Adam Smith, for whom the imagination puts us in the place of the sufferer: "we conceive ourselves enduring all the same torments, we enter as it were into his body, and become in some measure the same person with him, and thence form some idea of his sensations" (*Moral Sentiments* 9). This is the Man of Feeling as he comes to us in Mackenzie. While Smith does base his statement on the premise that "we can have no immediate experience of what other men feel," he does envision a sensibility-as-moral-community, one that blurs the division between self and other and replaces it with a single dialogic "inside." As in the sentimental Radcliffe heroine, the philosophy of observed suffering in Fleetwood ostensibly proclaims "I know how you feel."

While Fleetwood may have found in sentimental doctrine an easy and satisfactory summation to this whole unpleasant incident, his behavior throughout the scene is much more complicated. His declaration that sympathy creates a community of subjects loses its force when juxtaposed with his equally forceful defense that *he* was certainly never involved in the taunting, or if he was, he didn't enjoy it much. His is a bad faith that will become more important at the end of the novel: "For myself . . . I had no relish for this amusement. Once or twice, inconsiderately and precipitately, I yielded to the importunity of my companions, and became entangled in such adventures; but I presently abjured every thing of that sort" (38). In his interpretation, the whole incident was *really* Withers's fault: "He had given himself up passively from the beginning to the ideas which his deluders wished to excite in him" (36). Thus, as Fleetwood puts on trial his own moral worth and the behavior of Withers, he righteously claims a sympathetic community with the victim while actually rationalizing himself into a position of guiltlessness. This entire scene, and the way it prefigures the climactic trial and inquiry of Gifford at the end of the novel, establish a dual discourse in Fleetwood: he is both a sympathetic man of feeling, like Mackenzie's Harley, and a disengaged individualist, like the logician of the *Enquiry*. It maintains a division between self and other, between inside and outside, that undermines its more benevolent claim.

What unites these two discourses is the suspicious role that perception plays in Fleetwood's affairs. This perception is a Romantic, creative consciousness through which Fleetwood perceives the world and which leaves him bitterly disillusioned. As he leaves Oxford and travels to France, he falls in love with a "faithless" woman who deceives him or, more accurately, demonstrates to him that he has deceived himself. He concludes from this that when an imaginative spectator watches objects in the empirical world, he sees not "the things themselves . . . [but] the growth and painting of his own mind" (56). Nothing exists but as it is perceived, and would that he and Withers before him had realized this in time. Moreover, this construction of the world directly relates to the sentient body, to the mechanics of judicial inquiry, and to the formulation of an epistemology. Above, Fleetwood used the notion of suffering as a medium for constructing community: I know how you feel. But when he pursues the medium further, to the point of using torture and physical pain as a metaphor for creating this community, we find a confusion in who is feeling what, or whom:

> I do not wish to stand alone, but to consider myself as part only of a whole. If that which produces sensation in me, produces sensation no where else, I am substantially alone. If the lash inflicted on *me* will, being inflicted on *another*, be attended with a similar effect, I then know that there is a being of the same species or genus with myself. (179; emphasis added)

When Ann Radcliffe's heroines imagined a painful body, they experienced a sympathetic sharing of that pain to the point of appropriating it: they knew how someone felt to the degree that they dialectically imitated and isolated that pain. In Fleetwood, the knowledge of someone else's pain is less dialectical than tautological: we are a community not because I feel your pain, but because I think you feel mine. Your feeling, the experience of your sentient body, becomes nothing more than the growth and painting of my own mind. The victim's sentimental body, wishfully a decentralized and dialogic site of subject relations, becomes inscribed as object, as other, the repository of the perceiving subject's interests. As the Marquis de Sade well knew, sentimentalism provides a communal body that destroys its own potential for community.

The attempt to know the other's body — an attempt that communal sentimentalism invites but which is then destroyed by it — is at the heart of Fleetwood's psychological problems in the novel. For his psychological problem is also an epistemological one: he never knows for sure what is happening inside another person. Thus, like Wordsworth in Paris, he is forced to *read* someone else's body, and to interpret the inside by reading the outside. In the terms set up by the *Enquiry*, Godwin's protagonist has to read *motive*, an act in which he places little trust. As he focuses on the physiognomy of Gifford, he compares it to that of Mary and Kenrick as an exercise in body reading:

> Under the olive-tinctured skin of Gifford, beneath his scowling brow, and among the lines which time and climate have indented there, hypocrisy might hide herself; but, in the other two, there is no opacity or discoloration to intercept the passage of a thought, there is not a furrow in their cheeks for treachery to lurk in. Mary, Heaven has moulded its own image in thy features: if thou art false, oh, then Heaven mocks itself! (292)

Like a modern advertisement for acne creams, this passage suggests that a clear complexion is enough for an astute reader to read through its trans-

parent signification to the goodness therein. But Fleetwood does not con-
sistently trust his ability to read the body. Moments after this encomium,
when Gifford fashions another lie, Fleetwood is just as willing to believe it
as he had been to believe in Mary's guilelessness. And the most convincing
proof that Gifford can offer is not the objective, factual "evidence" of
adultery (read: manufactured illusions), but rather the signification of his
body: "His visage was colourless; his eyes averted with a mournful air; his
hands hung down, as languid and incapable of motion. . . . 'I need not ask
you'" for particulars, says Fleetwood. "'I read it all in your countenance'"
(297). Fleetwood's overarching problem here and generally, I would suggest, is his desire to read the body as a site of unmediated truth as a way of
settling these disturbing questions. Undetermined motivations and impenetrable, mysterious hearts are profoundly unsettling, as the *Enquiry* well
knows. However, as Fleetwood also knows from his reading of Gifford's
"olive-tinctured skin," and from his own paranoia, answers cannot be found
on the body; this supposedly readable site *can* conceal hypocrisy. The body
cannot be trusted. In response to a critical breakdown in epistemology,
Fleetwood must insist on a naive belief—which to a degree he *knows* is
naive—that the sentimental body offers a sound hermeneutics, that it can
ground an epistemology of motives even though that epistemology is
contradicted by rational evidence.

This hermeneutic is similar to that in Beccaria, who threw into crisis
the agencies of sentimentalism and rationalism as contradictory grounds for
jurisprudence. In Godwin, the crisis lies at the intersection of the rationally
empirical   what one *sees*   and the affectively experienced   what one *feels*;
for him, you can't believe everything you see *or* feel. It is a crisis founded on
the tenuous distinction between inside and outside, in which the inside
colors and creates the outside. Fleetwood's response to this crisis is to
envision an outside—which he will adopt as the public, judicial body—that
can still be legitimately separated from the private, domestic body. Remain-
ing true to the unchanged principles of justice, he must leave the judicial
body *outside* the obfuscating agencies of sentimentalism. This vision, I want
to argue, constitutes the latter section of the novel, and is established by two
scenes of torture, scenes that carve out very different and mutually exclusive
possibilities for the sentimental body.

By the middle of the novel, Fleetwood has received sufficient information (all lies) from his nephew Gifford to prove that Mary is guilty of
adultery. And Hell hath no fury like a husband cuckolded. His reaction is to
want physical violence, to extract a confession from her with "red-hot

pincers" (325). As Elaine Scarry explains in *The Body in Pain*, we tend, in the most profound moments of doubt, to turn to "the sheer material of the human body" for some sort of confirmation (14). Fleetwood seeks punishment, rather than inquiry, in the same way that Percy Shelley and many other Gothic novelists transform the ambiguous inquiry of torture into a confirmed and sure punishment. But since he can't extract such a confession, he constructs wax dolls resembling Mary and Kenrick and, making his preparations with a "tormenting pleasure," proceeds thus:

> I gazed at the figure of Mary; I thought it was, and it was not, Mary. With mad and idle action, I put some provisions on her plate; I bowed to her in mockery, and invited her to eat. Then again I grew serious and vehement; I addressed her with inward and convulsive accents, in the language of reproach; I declaimed, with uncommon flow of words, upon her abandoned and infernal deceit; all the tropes that imagination ever supplied to the tongue of man, seemed to be at my command. . . . But, while I was still speaking, I saw her move — if I live, I saw it. She turned her eyes this way and that; she grinned and chattered at me. I looked from her to the other figure; that grinned and chattered too. Instantly a full and proper madness seized me. . . . I rent the child-bed linen, and tore it with my teeth. I dragged the clothes which Mary had worn, from off the figure that represented her, and rent them into long strips and shreds. I struck the figures vehemently with the chairs and other furniture of the room, till they were broken in pieces. (334–335)

The spectacle of suffering here is markedly different from Fleetwood's experience with Withers or indeed, with the judicial infliction of torture in general. Clearly, Fleetwood's private search for some understanding of his domestic situation is not the same thing as the state's terrorist mechanism of torture. But what Fleetwood's action here has in common with the scene of torture is its imaginative projection of what Fleetwood wants Mary to be: the torturer *creates* the truth he wants to hear. Fleetwood imagines the wax figure to be Mary and for the purposes of his own desires, wishing makes it so. She moves; she chatters; she is alive. And because she is alive, she can be tortured and made to feel pain. But interestingly, it is only the imaginatively constructed Mary that is alive and potentially capable of sentience. The moment he makes contact with her and inflicts pain on her, she becomes "the figure that had represented her," a distanced object, a puppet on a stage. When Fleetwood encounters a body as a sentient, alive other, that body becomes an object and not Mary herself. The scene is a paradigm of imaginative projection where the other in the object world becomes completely defined by the paintings of the subject's mind; it stands as pointed allegory of the process of imagination that I had discussed in Radcliffe and Wordsworth's imaginings of victimization. In Fleetwood's creative consciousness, "Mary" is both a living, sentient being and an insentient figure, both animate subject and inanimate object.[6] And the dividing line, that which separates the animate from the inanimate, is the sentient body, a body that simultaneously invokes sympathetic knowledge and precludes it.

While the scene emphasizes the limitations of what can be known about the other's body, it also registers the desire for a kind of "body language" in the torturer. The act of inflicting torture, says Scarry, demonstrates the knowledge of what is painful. It articulates the usually unarticulated experience of pain, in which the "I" expresses presence by orchestrating pain in another's body. Godwin says as much in the *Enquiry*, when he defines torture as a demonstration of "my power to inflict . . . being placed in my joints and my sinews" (641). Obviously, then, the effigy scene is intended not only to rid Fleetwood of bottled-up hostilities but to give him a sense of power, of the individual autonomy that B. J. Tysdahl argues is so important to Godwin's characters (*William Godwin* 116) and which the sentimental body jeopardizes. This power is granted in the way the scene constructs a concept of "Mary" that is immediately rendered object: the torturer turns the sentient body into something incapable of sentience, or, at least, a sentience to which he can respond. This insentient object-body is incapable of both autonomy (it is, after all, only a puppet, mine to do with as I please) and the communality that the earlier sentimental body had implied (since it is insentient, I need feel no emotion for it). In the effigy scene, Fleetwood constructs an objective correlative of the Gothic body as we have seen it to this point: a body whose sentience is constructed and destroyed by the Romantic consciousness.

The individuating powers of torture effect not only Fleetwood's sentient response to Mary, but also the language in which such sentience can be expressed. Torture actually gives Fleetwood a language, a way of expressing the impotence he has secretly been fearing. Unleashed violence results in unleashed eloquence, the "uncommon flow of words . . . [and] tropes that imagination ever supplied to the tongue of man." The sympathy he had felt for Withers had "no tongue, not the smallest sound to signify its excess," because clearly the pain was not his. And such silence, moreover, parallels the ineffability of pain in the Gothic texts we have considered so far: the Radcliffe heroine, the Female Vagrant, Beatrice Cenci. But torture, as Scarry argues, *makes* as well as unmakes: Fleetwood finds a voice. In the infliction of individualized and voiceless pain comes an individualized and vocal power.

The isolating qualities of pain go even further than a mere proclamation of power. When Fleetwood has finished abusing the wax figures, he staggers into a chair with the following:

> I am firmly persuaded that, in the last hour or two, I suffered tortures, not inferior to those which North American savages inflict on their victims; and, like those victims, when the apparatus of torture was suspended, I sunk into immediate insensibility. (335)

As Fleetwood assumes for himself the role of victim, we are given pause by a sudden reversal in the torturer-victim relationship. The confusion we feel is the same confusion felt by the reader of *Caleb Williams*, where, at the end of the novel, we are unsure who is the victim and who is the tyrant. This confusion results from overturning the sentimental paradigm in which the spectator enters into the victim's pain. Like his earlier sentimental self, Fleetwood projects himself into the body in pain. But the Oxford student's claim to sympathy — to the engagement of fellow-feeling that connects subject and object — is reversed by the adult's fantasy of subjection. He claims a monopoly of victimization that centers pain solely in himself and obliterates the object with which he had claimed to identify. In effect, the effigy scene enacts a series of bodily displacements: the effigy first replaces Mary's body, but *it is then replaced by Fleetwood's*. He becomes the victim in the torture he has executed. He transforms the sentimental potential of the tortured body from "I know how you feel" to "This hurts me more than it hurts you." His point is not, we remember, that the lash is inflicted on another, but that the lash is inflicted on the self; it is the self whose experiences are central here. And since hurting is, according to Elaine Scarry, a totally individual and centripetal experience, Fleetwood's pain centers him fully within himself. By assuming the status of victim, Fleetwood indicates that the real victim's interiority — feelings, affections, *motives* — can never be known. They can only be projected creations, the deluded paintings that he shared with Withers earlier on.[7]

It is at this point that Fleetwood loses his resemblance to the state torturer and becomes more like the sympathetic spectator or reformist thinker. But in the transition, he demonstrates the limitations of that "critical threshold of sensibility" that Spierenburg presents. In Chapter two I outlined Scarry's argument that, in acts of imagining, we are taken outside our bodies; we create an external referent that is not ourselves, but rather an imagined materiality outside ourselves that cannot feel pain. (This was also the basic structure of theatricality underlying David Marshall's discussion of sympathy in the late eighteenth century.) Yet, given that sentimentalism fosters the illusion that pain *can* be shared, and given that pain is, to a great degree, defined by one's consciousness or recognition of it, pain can to some extent be said to exist in the sentimental spectator, as it did in Ann Radcliffe's sentimental women.[8] However, Radcliffe and Wordsworth sounded an epistemological crisis in their fictions: if one could never know how another felt, then one must retreat from community into the holy privacy of manor houses or individualized imaginations. Godwin, conversely, used the scene of torture to sound an epistemological *confirmation*. By becoming the inflicter of pain, Fleetwood finds himself a sentience he can appropriate and a language he can use to represent himself. Whereas Beatrice Cenci would go mad without language, Fleetwood can find that language, one that gives him what Maturin called that "glorious impenetrability," an actual feeling of *triumph* over those who suffer, rather than a sympathetic sharing with them. And whereas imagined pain began a destruction of Beatrice that would culminate in her physical violation and madness, imagined pain shores up in Fleetwood a sense of his own power, agency, and effectiveness; in short, pain gives Fleetwood identity.

Fleetwood's individuation, his empowerment through another's pain, provides the rubric by which we can interpret the final scenes of the novel, and Godwin's problematic treatment of the legitimation crisis he shares with Beccaria. Gifford's identity as Fleetwood's would-be assassin is discovered by pain of torture. Fleetwood gets this information from his benevolent nurse Martha: "They have given the valet the boots, they call it —a contrivance the French have to squeeze the truth out of a man—and he has confessed that Gifford was at the bottom of all" (343).[9] While Martha unquestioningly trusts this confession, Fleetwood will have no part of its findings. Rather, he demands:

> Now, Martha, learn from me, and blush for what you have said! Can you, a Briton, believe, that torture makes a man speak the truth? that, when he writhes with agony, and feels himself debased below a brute, his words are to be regarded as oracles? Would not a man then say any thing, to put an end to what he suffers? (343)

Fleetwood's response has that same ambivalence we saw in Lewis's story: torture is epistemologically unsound *and* morally reprehensible, debasing the creature below a brute. But while Fleetwood objects to the mode of extraction, he quickly accepts the truth of Gifford's guilt: he willingly suspends his disbelief in coerced confession if it helps with his own project of inquiry. Similarly, his reaction to Gifford's hanging is a blend of utilitarian logic and emotionally charged revenge:

> I shed no tear upon the bier of Gifford. . . . I have always regarded with horror those sanguinary laws which, under the name of justice, strike at the life of a man. For his sake I was willing to admit of one exception. . . . What discipline, or penitentiary confinement, could rationally be expected to inspire him with one touch of human nature? Die then, poor wretch, and let the earth, which labours with thy depravity, be relieved! (371)

We hear in this speech the earlier Godwin, the man who wrote in the *Enquiry* that he would "inflict suffering, in every case where it can be clearly shown that such infliction will produce an over-abundance of good" (635). While suffering may inspire pity and demand sympathy, it can never truly reveal what is inside; pity must not get in the way of the larger public good. The criminal and judicial body must always and only be a site for the discourses of reason, even if those discourses conceal a personal, selfish, impassioned agenda. If sentimentality were allowed to intrude, if we allow for "one touch of human nature," then the judicial process is undermined. The sentimental body must be kept *out* of judicial proceedings, in favor of a reconstructed, albeit fallacious, critical distance.

And yet, while Gifford's trial gives the lie to sentimental knowledge of the inside, it is also critical of disengaged, empiricist inquiry. The courts had found Mary and Kenrick guilty of adultery "upon the most demonstrative evidence" (346), but that evidence turns out to be the product of manipulation, corruption, and bribed testimony. Gifford, it seems, was a "mastervillain, whose task it has been to paint every thing in false colours, and to obstruct all the glimpses of truth and virtue" (347). This conclusion, I believe, smacks of bad faith. True, Gifford did arrange all appearances, but to conclude that he acted alone is to assume that Fleetwood had a pristine, unbiased vision before meeting him. This is patently untrue. The image of painting in false colors is precisely the one Fleetwood had used earlier to criticize his own deceptive perceptions, although he conveniently forgets that here. Furthermore, a simple empirical explanation of all the facts that Gifford had obstructed does not exonerate Fleetwood from guilt or Mary from suspicion. Rather, they are always tainted by internal fears, secrets, *feelings* that should unite them:

> It seemed as if, now that what the vulgar mind would call the obstacles to our re-union were removed, we were more certainly divided than ever. . . . Now we were separated by sentiments, that must for ever twine themselves with the

vitals of every honourable individual, and that can only be exterminated by the blow which lays the head that has conceived them in the dust. (368)

Logical, empiricist inquiry, then, is never pure; it always reaffirms the heart's impenetrability. Moreover, sentiments do not collapse the distance so much as they separate subjects — and subjects' emotionally charged bodies — into isolated individualism. As Tysdahl has argued, the sentimentalist premises of *The Man of Feeling* are transmogrified into an individualism that is both empowering and frustrating. Both inquiry and affection yield no truth: rather, they point to the inability to overcome the inside/outside division.

In a sense, then, Fleetwood gets nowhere. By the last page of the novel he is still plagued by the solitude he demonstrated in his relations with Withers, and he still has no way to enter into and identify with someone else's subjectivity. The legitimation crisis of how to read the body has settled nothing, either by reason or by sentiment. It is in response to this familiar situation that Fleetwood undertakes yet another reading of physiognomy. After a protracted separation, he and Mary come together in the same room, and he declares:

> Mary never looked half so beautiful, half so radiant, as now. Innocence is nothing, if it is merely innocence. It is guileless nature, when impleaded at a stern and inhuman bar, when dragged out to contumely and punishment, when lifting up its head in conscious honour, when Heaven itself seems to interpose to confound the malice of men, and declares, "This is the virtue that I approve!" there, there is presented to us the most ravishing spectacle that earth can boast. I never till now was sensible of half the merits of my wife. (370–371)

Here is the sentimental fallacy: unlike the judicial body of Gifford, Mary's domestic body externalizes the internal, and exposes the hidden. But what has preceded this in the novel should make us sceptical. Given the desperation by which Fleetwood has always seen what he *wanted* to see, given the novel's fascination with the problem of reading the body, given the disbelief in the outside as an unmediated testimony of the inside, this final flourish in not convincing as a reconciliation. What it *does* illustrate is the epistemology of the tortured body as it runs throughout the novel. Mary is deemed innocent because she *looks* innocent, but that very innocence requires for its extraction "contumely and punishment." Torture, as we have seen, is the invasion of a body whose interiority can never really be known by a reliable epistemological model. The only way to make that invasion reliable is to sympathize with it while at the same time hurting it. It has been necessary that Fleetwood make Mary suffer, not so that he can sympathize with that suffering, as Spierenburg would have it, but so that he can usurp it and make it part of his hermeneutic for reading the body. Inquiry cannot make him a fitting husband; nor can sentiment. Only through her pain which he assumes and supplants can he come to accept her innocence.

Painted by the false colors of the creative imagination, Mary's pain is the means by which Fleetwood can carve out a subjectivity and identity for himself. And despite Godwin's praise of domestic affections in his later years, this individualist isolation must not be compromised by marriage. True, Fleetwood does return to domesticity, but the relationship carries with it the vestiges of his solipsism and petulance. If there is a sentimentality and praise of domestic affection here, it is perverse and twisted. Hypostatized by the spectacle of pain, sentimentality charts the transference from the sentient body of the other to that of the self. But this sentimentality, this "knowing how you feel," transfers the masochistic pleasure of appropriating another's pain into the sadistic pleasure of causing it. Godwin's domesticity here is similar to that of Oscar Wilde's jailmate at Reading: "each man kills the thing he loves" (*Complete Plays* 823).

When Martha informed Fleetwood that Gifford had been tortured, she unleashed in him a philosophical diatribe. That diatribe ultimately outlined Fleetwood's protectionist individualism, which remained immune to the politically tortured body: he felt *no* sympathy, *no* outrage. But Martha's information also did something else. Torture by the boots, as she relates it, is a "contrivance the *French* have to squeeze the truth out of a man" (emphasis added). In Martha's account it is France that tortures, and France that is deemed barbarous. The assignation that torture is a French — or at least, Catholic — practice is common Gothic stock, as I have already indicated: indeed, the French torture Gifford here, Fleetwood tortures the dolls while he is in Italy, the French torture Jean D'Aunoy in Radcliffe's *The Romance of the Forest*, the Spanish torture Ambrosio in *The Monk*, and the Italians torture Schedoni in Radcliffe's *The Italian* and Marzio in *The Cenci*. But what this heyday of literary torture suggests is not simply a facile condemnation of Catholic countries in general, and France in this particular case; nor is it merely an ironic projection onto Catholic countries of England's fondness for its own pillory and the spectacle of the Tyburn scaffold, which, as I noted in Chapter one, was a highly visible and highly active site of torture and persecution (of sodomites, as a particular example). Literary torture as I have outlined it above replays at the political level what Fleetwood experiences at the personal: it invites an English audience to sympathize, but only so that, in sympathetic pain, it can return to its own protected, private, empowered body; it affirms for the spectator a kind of solitary confinement. Like so many other young radicals at the turn of the nineteenth century, Godwin lost faith in the French Revolution, and began to fear its influence. His depiction of torture argues a kind of aesthetic protection against a creeping Catholic, francophile influence. We may not know much from the act of torture, but we know that only the barbaric would practice it. And in that very knowledge we exclude ourselves from such condemnation. By utilizing torture as a convention, the Gothic capitalizes on its epistemological vicissitudes to re-enclose the threatened English body.

Thus, in *Fleetwood*, the stage of the scaffold is the theatre in which we meet someone else's pain, realize that it is not ours, appropriate it all the same, and use that appropriation to sacralize our own power and sense of identity. The stage of the scaffold, like the stage of the Romantic imagination in Wordsworth and Radcliffe, epitomizes the distance between the victim of pain and the onlooker; its audience is given no tongue to express pity. Yet, like the stage of the Gothic theatre, the scaffold exploits the infectiousness of pain; pain can easily become part of the audience experience at some level of ideological, sentient manipulation. Whereas Romantic theatre critics like Wordsworth, Coleridge, and Byron feared such infectiousness as breeding chaos, Godwin's utilitarian judiciary capitalizes on that infectiousness to shore up the sense of self by allowing it to *feel*, and to gain an ontological conformation from that feeling. I hurt, therefore I am. In this way, criminal barbarity—be it the barbarity of a Gifford or of a revolutionary France—conveniently provided the disrespect for the body that an English public could define itself against, not because it was incapable of barbarism, but because it could appropriate the "tormenting pleasures" of barbarism to establish its own identity as non-barbaric. The tormenting pleasures of torture are as much about feeling as they are about inflicting, and the delights of pain, *pace* Burke and Radcliffe, are heightened by proximity rather than destroyed by it. The self in Romantic fiction, then, can be defined not only in its isolation from another's pain, but also in the degree to which it feels that pain.

5. Aesthetics and Anesthetics at the Revolution

I

The theatre of the scaffold as it is represented by Godwin bridges the gap between the specularized victim of state repression and the (un)sentimental audience member watching the cruelties perpetrated on that victim. Under the guise of horror at barbarity, Godwin delineates the subjective pleasure of feeling the lash, a pleasure in placing oneself in both a community of sufferers and the sure space of one's own corporeality. Yet, Fleetwood's "pleasure" in feeling the suffering he inflicts on his stage props is coterminous with the pleasure of ending that suffering: "Like those victims, when the apparatus of torture was suspended," he remembers, "I fell into immediate insensibility" (*Fleetwood* 335). It would seem here that the Godwinian "self" is constructed in the schism between feeling and numbness, sensibility and insensibility. The theatre of one's own corporeality, like the theatre of the scaffold, both calls the body onto the stage of sentient consciousness and pulls the curtain on it: for the body in pain, opening and closing night is the same thing.

The spectacle of suffering on the late eighteenth-century scaffold provides us with terms to discuss the spectacle of suffering in the late eighteenth-century self as this self was being produced (and was producing) a new medical body. I noted in Chapter one the affinity between humane punishment and medicine, in that the "guillotine" was used both as a judicial and a surgical instrument: it removed diseased members of the body (like the uvula) as well as diseased members of the body politic (Louis XVI, Marie Antoinette, and company). But what is more interesting here is the way the sensibility/insensibility paradigm constructs both the judicial subject and the medical subject, for in both cases the definition of health rests on a proper negotiation of feeling and insensibility. Moreover, the judicial/medical sentience one is to feel in one's own body has a political context, in that it synecdochically represents what one is to feel in the larger *theatrum mundi*. At the end of the eighteenth and the beginning of the nineteenth centuries, the epistemological questions circulating around the body of the judicial subject — questions of feeling and numbness, pain and appropriation — were even more forcefully defining the medical body as it moved through a vale of tears. Let us first turn to Byron to make the case.

In Canto X of *Don Juan*, our hero is taken ill at Catherine the Great's court. Fearing he may die, Catherine summons a physician who applies rigorous doses of purgatives and emetics. The narrator reflects on this treatment as follows:

> This is the way physicians mend or end us,
> > *Secundum artem*. But although we sneer
> In health, when ill we call them to attend us
> > Without the least propensity to jeer. (X,42,ll.1–4)

As Byron well knew, we are as distrustful of physicians as we are of lawyers and the judiciary process. The medical care Juan undergoes, like the treatment Byron received at Missolonghi, almost kills him. But Byron points to a further problem here: we *need* the physician, and are forced to trust him, during times of ill-health. Sickness and its attendant pains disempower us, and the only hope for re-empowerment is to submit ourselves — not only bodily but intellectually as well — to the "expert" in bodily matters. In other words, physical re-empowerment necessitates a further disempowerment, as we resign control of ourselves to the hands of another.

Questions of empowerment are ultimately political questions, and the resignation of the individual to the physician has the overtones of a kind of tyranny. But as this passage from *Don Juan* points out, such resignation is potentially liberating, and ultimately for our own good. At the end of the eighteenth century, medicine's liberating potential was trumpeting its developments in the theory and technology of healing and promising a *nouveau régime* of personal and political empowerment through health, what Foucault would call a "master discourse." To ensure this new regime, doctors began to work together with governments to promote higher health standards, stricter regulations for care, and more humane surgical procedures,[1] methods akin to the kinder, gentler ways of punishment in the courts and prisons. But whereas courts were finding more humane ways of restricting liberty, medicine was taking upon itself the ultimate task of liberty, as it sought to free us from the most immediate of all tyrannies: our own pain. That liberation, as Byron well knew, puts us in the ambiguous position of surrender—a doctor's Scylla to pain's Charybdis. Such ambivalence—the ownership of a painful body versus its resignation to medicine—constitutes a discomfort that pulses through the body at the turn of the century, and structures the way the western world has come to see its own pain in a post-Romantic age.

II

To frame this understanding of our intimate, personal relationship to sentience, we can paradoxically return to the discourses of war, perhaps that least personal of human events. In *The Birth of the Clinic*, Foucault suggests an analogy between the medical revolution in France and the great Revolution of 1789, in that both movements looked toward the formulation of a perfect, pristine, healthy body—the individual body in the case of medicine, and the body politic in the case of France (38). In *The Body and the French Revolution*, Dorinda Outram explores this analogy further, seeing changes in the medical system as a necessary precondition for the events of 1789. Outram discusses how a changing conception of health attempted to wrest the image of the body from the monopoly that the monarchy had held over it (in the iconography of the sovereign body) and to center it instead in the bodies of the middle class (47). Rather than concerning itself with the saving of souls, as the *ancien régime* had advocated in order to regulate public behavior, medicine began to look at saving bodies, bodies with an innate dignity regardless of class.[2] (Obviously, the switch in emphasis from the King's body to the commoner's provided the master trope by which the sans-culottes tried to empower the middle classes at the expense of monarchical rule.) With this restructuring of medical demographics came an emphatic dictum to assume *personal* responsibility for health, an exhortation to tend one's own garden through a regime of proper diet, exercise, temperance, and abstinence. For Foucault this regime was ultimately part of a capitalist strategy to police the circulation of foods, goods, utilities, and persons—anything that might spread disease and compromise personal/public health (25). But for Outram this policing goes further than market power struggles or the professionalization of health and its assumption of powers: for her it is a move toward the articulation of an entirely new, post-revolutionary citizen, one who managed his own affairs autonomously and individually, and whose physicality constructed a clear boundary around the self, yet who was also a "citizen," and whose personal health habits reflected and magnified a larger constitutional or contractual community. The concept of health, she argues, "entailed a reflexive idea of the individualized body: person, body, health and self-management were welded indissolubly together in a way which separated each body from any other body" and in so doing, constituted the body politic (48). This individuated citizen, this *homo clausus*, became the revolutionary ideal that embodied the contradictory needs of individual freedom and public identity (67).

Both Foucault and Outram are interested in (but not confined to) the social implications of this new bodily iconography, and how its audience came to view the body through revolutionary ideals. But, as I discussed in Chapter one and as Outram points out, there is also a democratizing going on "inside" the body in the way the entire nervous system was being remapped. The secularization of the body, she notes, changed the medical community's conception of how the human body received and responded to physical stimuli. I argued in Chapter one that Robert Whytt's "sentient principle" democratized the individual body by wresting it from Cartesian theories of sentience. For Whytt (and others like him, including John Hunter and Theophile de Bordeu, in Montpellier, France[3]), all parts of the body contributed to one's sentient experience — be it pleasure or pain. By the end of the eighteenth century, the sentient principle had replaced — or seriously challenged — the hierarchically structured image of the body as a mechanistic reflex, the model that Descartes had propounded. This sentience, moreover, was part of a large-scale movement to validate the "aesthetic" as that complex of physical sensations by which we move in and know the world. The aesthetic, what Alexander Baumgarten first named the myriad of physical responses we call experience, became the declaration of each person's connection to the material world. With the universal connection to the aesthetic came a universal dignity, in that each person had a *natural* relation to nature, to others, and to the self, a relation defined in the sinews of the body. With this sentient democratization, with this validation of aesthetics, the late eighteenth century effected at the individual level what the French Revolution would attempt to do at the political.

However, the medical community, like the philosophical, theatrical, and judicial communities already discussed, recognized that within the liberating potential of bodily sensation was also a potential tyranny. Sentience, we remember, exists on a continuum: it need only be exaggerated a bit before it produces *pain*, the logical extension of sense perception. And this continuum creates a contradiction. On the one hand, as we witnessed in Casimir Fleetwood, pain is the most powerful confirmation of our existence we can imagine; as Elaine Scarry argues, pain is the most "aesthetic" experience possible, if we take aesthetic in its original sense (4). But on the other hand, Fleetwood's collapse into insensibility reminds us that pain breeds the monster that destroys itself; it threatens to destroy our awareness of it in the way that Radcliffe and Burke have demonstrated. Intense pain often becomes numbness (as in the shock that often follows a serious wound or violence) or induces unconsciousness. This continuum — or contradiction — in the nature of pain tends to confuse the heightened sense perception of *aesthetics* with the unperceiving state of *anesthetics*. The two risk becoming the same thing. And at the end of the eighteenth century, the age of the aesthetic par excellence, this confused relation became all the more acute.

It is not surprising, then, that with the validation of aesthetics and the individuation of feeling in the late eighteenth century came a concerted movement on the part of physicians to control the medical experience of pain. Medicine employed the binarisms I have already discussed — sentience/insentience, feeling/numbness, terror/horror — and casts them in terms of aesthetics and anesthetics. As surgical practices became more sophisticated and more widespread, so did physicians' and surgeons' sensitivity to the pain they were inflicting on their patients. By the 1750s, the man of feeling had truly entered the operating theatre.[4] And with him came the development of anesthetics. When Joseph Priestley discovered in 1776 that gaseous nitrous oxide could be absorbed immediately into the lungs, rather than being ingested through the stomach, he paved the way for Humphrey Davy to suggest in 1800 that this "laughing gas" could be an effective anesthetic (Robinson, *Victory* 55).[5] Until Priestley's discovery, opium had been the major analgesic in surgery. But opium is ineffective, addictive, and nauseating in large doses, as Coleridge and Thomas De Quincey knew all too well. In fact, opium became so discredited as a pain killer that it soon became associated with quackery, witchcraft, and black magic (Robinson, *Victory* 40).[6] Nitrous oxide, finally used in 1844, reduced the unpleasant effects of narcotics at the same time that it reduced pain, and thereby replaced morphine, first used in 1803, as the most popular form of anesthesia (Fülop-Miller, *Triumph* 72). This tenuous experimentation with anesthetics reflected a change in the entire definition of "anesthetics" throughout the eighteenth century. In the early 1700s, "anesthesia" had meant a *defect* or *lack* of feeling, following its direct translation "without feeling"

(*OED*). However, by the early years of the nineteenth century, "anesthetic" came to take on the sense of a positive medical *relieving* of feeling, a blessing rather than a defect. This connotative shift reflected the curious change in the status of physical sentience I have been emphasizing throughout this study: feeling in the late eighteenth century is validated and attacked at the same time. And this contradictory status is documented in the fictions of pain.

If sentience is indissolubly associated with revolutionary freedom, yet is at the same time feared and suppressed, then anesthesia also becomes an ambivalent agent. It can either be a condemnable suppression of liberating aesthetics, or a liberation from the tyranny of pain. In the discussion that follows, I want to suggest that the revolutionary discourses of the late eighteenth and early nineteenth centuries employ the metaphor of anesthesia to signal a complex of attitudes relating not only to political bodies but to one's own pain. Edmund Burke's *Reflections on the Revolution in France*, Matthew Lewis's *The Monk*, and Byron's comic-epic *Don Juan*, all use the image of the anesthetized body to discuss revolution, and in this discussion, they present the paradox of the liberated, unfettered self whose political materiality is compromised by the experience of anesthesia. Throughout these texts runs a definition of the healthy body that exists somewhere between feeling and numbness, a body whose political significance recapitulates the ambivalence of pain and anesthesia.

III

The clearest articulation of ambivalence regarding feeling and anesthesia comes from Priestley's famous adversary Edmund Burke, in the *Reflections on the Revolution in France*. Here, Burke uses the image of the body to refer to its familiar metaphorical analogue, the body politic. According to David George Hale, the image of the body politic had moved from the premodern symbol of organic unity and wholeness through the Civil War to being synonymous with the state, a group of individuals bound together by social contract (*Body Politic* 7–8). In a way, this development is precisely the one that troubles Burke. In the *Reflections*, Burke tells his French correspondent de Pont that France is "bound, in all honest policy, to provide a permanent body, in which that spirit [of rational liberty] may reside, and an effectual organ, by which it may act" (85). But liberty for Burke must be circumscribed and controlled, because "liberty, when men act in bodies, is *power*" (91; emphasis original), and it is precisely the usurpation and misuse of power that Burke attacks in the French Revolution. The need for a strong political body, yet the fear of what this body can do (and *will* do, given that Burke's *Reflections* actually predicts the regicide and Reign of Terror to follow) lead him to nostalgia for an organic body politic, "a permanent body composed of transitory parts" (120), one that allows for evolving differences in class, political opinion, and economic policy, but that respects the overall stability of tradition, property, and religion. Both in the *Reflections* and in the *Letter to a Member of the National Assembly*, Burke emphasizes the importance of political *wholeness*, and of the constituent parts submitting to a larger unifying principle. In other words, Burke envisions an ideal body politic as vigorous, healthy, and active in all its parts, but like the earlier ideal, one that is ruled by the mind, that unites its discord into the concord of a central, monarchical reason.[7]

But for Burke, the French body is not behaving as it should. Its members have assumed a power for themselves that contradicts the central authority of the mind. The body of France is diseased. As James T. Boulton has pointed out, Burke figures revolutionary power as illness: the body of France has been attacked by a virulent, infectious disease that Burke fears will spread to England through an "epidemical fanaticism" (*Language of Politics* 117). Confusion in France, Burke says, is "like a palsy, [which] has attacked the fountain of life itself" (137); it is a "plague" (185), a "disease" or "distemper" (116). While Gary Kelly reads this distemper as a literal dis/temper, a lack of psychological balance that results in madness, it is also distemper in the sense of physical disorder, of disease. And like an animal distemper, this disease is contagious:

> Formerly your affairs were your own concern only. . . . [Now they] are part of our [that is, British] interest; so far at least as to keep at a distance your panacea, or your plague. If it be a panacea, we do not want it. We know the consequences of unnecessary physic. If it be a plague; it is such a plague, that the precautions of the most severe quarantine ought to be established against it. (185)

Leaving aside momentarily Burke's interesting conflation of "panacea" and "plague," I want to emphasize the contribution this passage makes to the fear of physicality in the *Reflections*. For the English conservative, France's efforts at democracy have evinced an entire collapse of humanism's structuring principle: they have privileged the irrational and unwieldy parts of the body, the "moral and almost physical inaptitude" of the incompetent revolutionaries (134) over the divinely ordained principle of reason. The body — through its disease — has stormed the bastion of reason, overturned the monarchy, and imprisoned the soul.

While Burke abhors the disease that has attacked France, he detests more its methods, and the ways in which it justifies itself. For Burke, the medical management of its condition is an even greater travesty than the disease. This management continues the strain of what I am calling the anti-medical prejudice in the eighteenth century and beyond. In Burke's early following of events in France,[8] he was surprised to find that a great proportion of the National Assembly were "practitioners in the law," but "the inferior, unlearned, mechanical, merely instrumental members of the profession" (129–130). Now if this weren't bad enough, this "handful of country clowns" (131) had taken up with a group of lower-level physicians: "To the faculty of law was joined a pretty considerable proportion of the faculty of medicine" (131–132). And this is a prescription for disaster. In a line that anticipates Nietzsche's *Genealogy of Morals*, Burke complains that "the sides of sick beds are not the academies for forming statesmen and legislators" (132). By promising a "constitution" and "natural rights," France has privileged the diseased body over the monarchical one. And in so doing, France's leaders "have seen the medicine of the state corrupted into its poison" (126). Like the famous *pharmakon* in Derrida's analysis of Plato's *Timaeus* (*Disseminations*), the poison and the cure are collapsed into each other through France's specious political policies. The hopeful panacea has become indistinguishable from the plague.

Promoting the status of physicians and disease over the wisdom of high-born elder statesmen has dire political consequences. Burke writes:

> I never liked this continual talk of resistance and revolution, or the practice of making the extreme medicine of the constitution its daily bread. It renders the habit of society dangerously valetudinary: it is taking periodical doses of mercury sublimate, and swallowing down repeated provocatives of canthar-ides to our love of liberty.
>
> This distemper of remedy, grown habitual, relaxes and wears out, by a vulgar and prostituted use, the spring of that spirit which is to be exerted on great occasions. (154)

Burke's pharmacology here is complex. Mercury sublimate was a purgative used to promote the flow of bile as well as to treat infection and syphilis. Cantharides were made from an extract of the Spanish fly, and we know what *that* promotes. Both drugs are stimulants, meant to excite the patient — in this case, French revolutionaries and Jacobin sympathizers — into high levels of physiological and metabolic activity. Indeed in Burke's passage, this activity is sexual as well as medicinal. But the effect, Burke reasons, is quite the opposite. Aphrodisiacs are a vulgar, prostituted use of sexual energy, and all that arousing and purging is ultimately exhausting. By invoking too much excitement, too much stimulation, France risks relaxing and wearing out the spirit of reason and prudence that it needs to manage its affairs properly. And having worn out this spirit through overuse, revolutionary France is in the position of being no longer able to diagnose its own condition; it does not know how sick it really is. In effect, excessive stimulation leads to a kind of numbing. Stimulants become anesthetics.[9]

The problem with France, then, is that too much feeling often creates too little. Moreover, this tendency for stimulation to anesthetize itself is not a mere symptom of the disease, it is one of its causes. By dousing itself with drugs, France is *perpetuating* its illness. The promise of democratic reform may be the spoonful of sugar that helps the medicine go down, but for Burke, "The anodyne draught of oblivion, thus drugged, is well calculated to preserve a galling wakefulness, and to feed the living ulcer of a corroding memory" (163). Excitement, stimulation, an excess of the revolutionary aesthetic produce anesthesia, and beneath the numbness of the diseased body an ulcerous illness continues to rage. For Burke, joining medicine to the National Assembly is a sure way to destroy the moral order. The relief from pain which characterized the democratic movement in medicine — and upon which a whole new medical discourse of freedom was based — is here a dangerous sedative that makes the patient worse instead of better.

Burke's critique of anesthetics implicitly suggests that pain can be an effective teaching tool, that there is a diagnostic value in the ability to hurt. That value, of course, is in the ability of the physician (in this case, the Tory parliamentarian) to isolate and identify exactly what the illness is, so that he can treat it more effectively. In a situation where there seems to be no hope for improvement, where the future is as bleak as the past — "in that lamentable condition," Burke writes, "the nature of the disease is to indicate the remedy to those whom nature has qualified to administer in extremities this critical, ambiguous, bitter portion to a distempered state" (116). Elsewhere in the *Reflections*, those whom nature has qualified are those who "are not repelled through a fastidious delicacy . . . from the medicinal attention to [the] mental blotches and running sores" of the ignorant pagans or the swinish multitude (200–201). We must meet illness head on, without the obfuscation of pain-killers or stimulants. Thus in Burke's own way he necessitates the presence and privilege of the diseased and painful body over the anesthetized one, because *that* is the only body that can be treated directly and effectively; in the terms of contemporary health discourse, no pain, no gain. And so, there is a crowning irony in the praise of one of Burke's greatest supporters, Edward Gibbon, who called Burke's conservatism (under the guise of "chivalry") a "most admirable medicine against the French disease" (quoted in Watson, "Burke's Conservative Revolution" 94). In describing the medicinal value of the *Reflections*, Gibbon uses as encomium the image Burke seems most to suspect. And, as we shall see in the Gothicism of Matthew Lewis, Burke *could* have had the effect of inoculating the English public against French influence, but by the time Byron addresses the issue, Burke's prescription takes on a medicinal value in exactly the way he hoped it wouldn't.

IV

The privileging of anesthetics in the late eighteenth century brought with it not only blessed relief from pain but suspicion as well. Such suspicion is inscribed near the end of Matthew Lewis's *The Monk*, when the distressed damsel Antonia reports seeing her mother's ghost. A physician is consulted regarding her health, and gives the following diagnosis:

> He said, that to keep her quiet was all that was necessary; and He ordered a medicine to be prepared which would tranquillize her nerves, and procure her that repose, which at present She much wanted. (326)

Unknown to the physician, his tranquillizing medicine is being supplemented by a "soporific draught" administered by Ambrosio, the novel's villain (329). With designs of carrying her off to a dungeon for his sexual pleasure, Ambrosio secretly gives her the "juice extracted from certain herbs" which augments the physician's sedative and anesthetizes Antonia into a state resembling death. By virtue of this prescription, Ambrosio effects her rape and eventual murder. This scene — the epitome of tyranny in *The Monk* — centers on the combined forces of lust in the tyrant and anesthesia in the victim.

The crime committed against Antonia is analogous to the crime the French Revolutionaries, according to Burke, had perpetrated against Marie Antoinette: both Ambrosio and the sans-culottes penetrate the sacred lady's bed-chamber with the intent of penetrating the sacred lady (Ambrosio with his sex, the citizens with their sabres). As Ronald Paulson has argued, *The Monk* is typical of that ambivalence so common to writers of the latter half of the 1790s. Ambrosio's sexual liberation from the oppressive regime of the Catholic Church itself becomes oppressive, as he victimizes the symbol of all that is good and true, the virginal Antonia. So while we may applaud his transgression against authority, we recoil at his violent excesses (*Representations* 222).[10] But what Lewis also points to here, besides a straightforward victimization by tyranny, is the role that anesthesia plays in perpetuating this tyranny: sedatives predispose Antonia to greater vulnerability and assist Ambrosio in his deeds. And Antonia is not the only victim of such prescriptions. The hapless novice Agnes, who spends much of the novel in a convent dungeon, is put there by the evil Prioress who had given her an opiate to feign her death and imprison her. Agnes's anesthesia, like Antonia's, is similar to that in Burke, for whom anesthesia acted as a metaphor for the numbing excesses of the Revolution. In the anti-Jacobin Gothic *The Monk*, anesthesia plays a literal role in the moral destruction which Burke had most feared.

Just as Antonia and Agnes are victimized by tranquilizers which diminish their control over their bodies, so is Ambrosio affected by pharmaceutical prescriptions. But the effects of drugs on the Monk point much more clearly to a moral culpability in one's own ill-health. Early in the novel, Matilda declares her love for him. Although he is sexually excited by this proclamation, he checks his bodily desires and declares that Matilda must leave the convent. (Of such self-control Burke would approve.) However, at the moment he picks a rose for her—a moment whose allegorical significance is difficult to miss—he is stung by a deadly insect. Poison fills his veins and he falls unconscious. Father Pablos, the attending physician, declares:

> He cannot recover; . . . All that I can do is to apply such herbs to the wound, as will relieve the anguish: The Patient will be restored to his senses; But the venom will corrupt the whole mass of his blood, and in three days He will exist no longer. (72)

Like the body politic in France, the body of Ambrosio has been infected with a poison, which is transparently linked to the poison of desire, and there seems little hope of recovery.

While the allegory seems clumsy here, the medical treatment that Ambrosio receives is more complexly allusive. In Burke's critique of the Revolution, the promise of reform became an anodyne that actually contributed to the disease; the panacea furthered the plague. The same suspicion of anesthesia pervades *The Monk*. Ambrosio is given pain-killers that "restored him to life, but not to his senses" (72); he regains consciousness, but not good judgment. When he miraculously rallies (for Matilda has sucked the poison from the wound), he is immediately administered a "strengthening medicine" (73), a provocative that, like cantharides in Burke's depiction of the Revolution, is intended to counteract the previously prescribed sedatives by invigorating the patient. As he rests, Matilda attempts to soothe him with her lute, but then to arouse him with her beauty — again making the analogy between sexual passion and chemical stimulation. This combination of drugs is important to Ambrosio's behavior. He "was conscious that in the present disposition of his mind, avoiding her society was his only refuge from the power of this enchanting woman" (82). The "present disposition" here is of a mind first diseased with "poison," then anesthetized by pain-killers, then invigorated with provocatives, then numbed again, then aroused by lust. Like the Revolutionaries, Ambrosio is numbed and aroused, aestheticized and anestheticized, into a "thousand contending passions" (83), and these passions wreak as much havoc on his moral health as they did on the health of France.

The final result of the passions is that Ambrosio breaks his own resolution and allows Matilda to stay in the convent — which is his big mistake. Matilda's presence ultimately allows Ambrosio, in his heightened/weakened state, to entertain more sexual thoughts of her. When he finds out that she vampirized his wound, and that she is "dying" for him from the same poison, he falls into her arms, and begins a life of dissipation that will result in rape and murder. It is not the insect's venom that corrupts his blood, then, but rather the treatment, the anesthesia, that furthers the condition of a blood already tainted. And this anesthetic treatment helps to collapse Matilda's "cure" into Ambrosio's illness, so that panacea and plague again become the same thing. As Burke had warned, the physical disempowerment that results from anodynes and provocatives helps to destroy the moral order.

Ambrosio's poison — both his lust and his disease — and Ambrosio's treatment — both pain-killers and provocatives — weaken his moral will and lead him to ruin; in Burke's words, they wear out "the spring of that spirit which is exerted on great occasions" (154). Interestingly, pain-killers are used elsewhere in the novel, in the Bleeding Nun episode, but with surprisingly different effects. Just as Ambrosio entertains a passion for Antonia, so does Don Raymond attempt to win Agnes. And just as Ambrosio was wounded in the courtship, so is Raymond: while escaping with the woman he believes to be Agnes, he crashes his carriage and suffers two broken ribs, a dislocated shoulder, and a shattered leg. Furthermore, he is emotionally assaulted by the mysterious disappearance of Agnes from the crash site. Like Antonia and Ambrosio, he is ordered to swallow a "composing medicine" and to rest (159), but unlike the other two patients, Raymond receives no comfort from the anodynes:

> That repose I wooed in vain. The agitation of my bosom chased away sleep. Restless in my mind, in spite of the fatigue of my body I continued to toss about from side to side. (159)

Raymond's physical condition degenerates further as he is haunted by the Bleeding Nun. The physician continues to prescribe medicines that, Raymond says, "in some degree tranquillized my spirits," but "My fever seemed rather augmented than diminished; The agitation of my mind impeded my fractured bones from knitting" (161). Unlike Ambrosio, Raymond is impervious to the effects of anesthetics; rather than allowing himself to be numbed — both physically and morally — by pain-killers, he remains fully conscious of the agitated state of his mind and the fractured state of his body. The healing must come from elsewhere.

Both Raymond and Ambrosio are slow to recuperate because of their excessive passions. But it is the source of these passions that marks the distinction between the two. Raymond refuses to heal because he is being haunted by a ghost. That ghost is initially thought to be superstition and hypochondria, which can easily be driven out by proper treatments. But the point of the Bleeding Nun episode is not only a critique of superstition. Rather, we learn that Beatrice, the spectral Nun, is an ancient relative of Don Raymond who had abandoned herself to a scandalous passion for Baron Lindenberg. With all the behavior unbecoming to a lady of her class, she had displayed "the incontinence of a Prostitute" and "had professed herself an atheist" (173). In her dissipation she joined with the Baron's younger brother Otto in murdering the Baron so that he could "make himself Master of the Castle" (174). She is then murdered as well, and her restless spirit roams the earth. As the source of Raymond's illness, Beatrice suggests not merely superstition or even illicit passion (although she is all these things), but also usurpation, the improper seizing of land and property rights. The seizures affecting Raymond are not only medical but manorial as well; it is the usurpation of legitimate authority as embodied in the holding of property that is fragmenting the aristocratic body.

The ghost of Beatrice and its effect on Raymond's illness have, I would suggest, revolutionary overtones. In Burke's *Reflections*, he charges de Pont with excessive concern for ghosts of the *ancien régime* to the neglect of property, which the Revolutionaries are seizing indiscriminately: "You are terrifying yourself with ghosts and apparitions, whilst your house is the haunt of robbers" (248). In fact, Burke's primary concern with the Revolution is that it represents the overthrow of the landed classes. This misuse of property, this French disease, is what haunts Don Raymond, and no amount of opiate or anesthetic can obliterate its importance. Significantly, then, to heal the rupture in property is to heal the human body as well. As soon as Raymond learns the true nature of the Nun's mission, he buries her bones and thereby returns to the new Baron his rightful ownership of the estate he has inherited. He cures the fractured social body of its revolutionary usurpation. And with the reinstituting of property rights and class privilege comes Raymond's medical report that "From this period I recovered my health so rapidly as to astonish my Physicians" (177). Personal health here is, as in Burke's *Reflections*, analogous to the reinstatement of landed succession, the re-empowerment of the aristocracy away from the tyrannical revolutionaries who steal power (or, in the case of Beatrice, those who transgress the demands of their class). The nature of the disease, as Burke had written, has dictated the cure.

In *The Monk*, then, pain and anesthesia are remarkably class-bound. Raymond's body refuses to accept the "anodyne draught of oblivion" that had made the moral order sick instead of better; rather, as Burke had implied, pain is necessary for the aristocrat to get to the heart of social decay. But not so for those outside the aristocracy. Significantly, Ambrosio numbs himself to his own illness so that that illness can continue to rage. As Daniel P. Watkins has pointed out, Ambrosio is the product of a cross-class liaison that the novel explicitly condemns ("Social Hierarchy" 115–124). His mother, Elvira, was a shoemaker's daughter who had disregarded her station by marrying a Spanish nobleman. The unfortunate product of this marriage, Ambrosio, was immediately placed in a monastery where he was forced to repress his bodily desires — a repression that, paradoxically, strengthened them all the more. Thus, with the repression of physicality enhanced by anodynes, with the aesthetic numbed by the anesthetic, Ambrosio becomes the revolutionary par excellence. His inability to feel his own bodily sensations leads to his inability to control them, and like the tyrannical mob at the end of the novel — indeed, like Burke's notorious "swinish multitude" — he loses control. Underneath the anodynes the "galling wakefulness" continues to corrode him, and he finally explodes in revolutionary violence and tyranny. Physical anesthesia ultimately denotes moral anesthesia, and the result is political disaster.

Anesthetics are considered fearfully revolutionary in Lewis's Gothic fiction, then, because they remove the diseased body from its dialogue with the mind; they disturb the natural sympathy that Robert Whytt had argued was the basis of all behavior. But the social implications of Whytt's aesthetic go even further. The "remarkable sympathy . . . between various parts of the body" that Whytt had observed was also the basis for the "still more wonderful sympathy between the nervous systems of different persons" that connected people in physical fellow-feeling (*Works* 583); in Whytt, the sympathetic transmission of pain is what makes social community possible. In *The Monk*, this transmission further marks the class distinctions of pain. As a murderous tyrant, Ambrosio is unable to feel another's pain: he sentences Agnes to the dungeon, murders Elvira, and stabs Antonia — all for his own protection. His own passions anesthetize him to others. The aristocratic Don Lorenzo, on the other hand, exemplifies what Whytt described as the sympathetic transfer of morbid symptoms. As he comes upon his sister Agnes in the dungeon, he does not recognize her, but

> Lorenzo stopped: He was petrified with horror. He gazed upon the miserable Object with disgust and pity. He trembled at the spectacle; He grew sick at heart: His strength failed him, and his limbs were unable to support his weight. He was obliged to lean against the low Wall which was near him, unable to go forward, or to address the Sufferer. (369)

Like Raymond and Ann Radcliffe's bourgeois heroines, Lorenzo here has an intensely *aesthetic* experience, one that feels pain so fully it freezes the observer in horror and helplessness. However, while the Radcliffe women freeze, faint, or swoon in horror — and thereby protect themselves from the community their sentience claims to create — Lorenzo transforms his horror into moral virtue: his "sensibility became yet more violently affected. The first sight of such misery had given a sensible shock to his feelings: But that being past, He now advanced towards the Captive" (370–371). While Burke and Radcliffe know that intense suffering can paralyze and anesthetize us, they also suggest that we can transform it into delight by making it go away: we can relieve our own distress in the benevolent gesture of relieving others. And in this novel, such sentient negotiation is class-bound. The benevolent Lorenzo shares a community of pain in the kind of scene that is never afforded to the lower classes in the novel. Not only does pain connect the aristocrat's body to his own mind, as it did with Raymond, but it also re-unites him with the subjective spaces of others. Pain ultimately heals the fractured body, and the fractured body politic.

Through its exploration of the dangerous terrain of aesthetics and anesthetics, *The Monk* gives us a political directive for our relationship to pain — not only for the way we are to treat violent revolutionaries, but more importantly, for the way we are to view our own sentience and that of others. When we read of Raymond's broken legs or Ambrosio's brutal violences, when we find Agnes chained in her dungeon, we are intended to feel at some level the physicality of their bodies; we are invited to make their aesthetic our own. Because of this tendency to invoke the reader's corporeal responses, the Gothic has traditionally been defined as a series of extremely violent episodes that, while intending to invigorate us, most often end up boring — shall we say, anesthetizing? — us. We get stimulated so often by stock scenes of suffering that we no longer feel their effects; we fall victim to what Maturin parodically calls "the anodyne of my somniferous epistolation" (*Melmoth* 497). But the situation in Lewis is more complex than mere Gothic formula. What we see in Lewis's novel is a fear of the social catastrophe that results when bodies are numbed to their own pain. And in this sense, Lewis translates Burke's antimedical prejudice into a fictional account of antirevolutionary politics. But we also see in the praise of pain an aristocratic virtue that redefines our relationship to our own pain and the pain of others. The aesthetic of pain in this novel is meant to re-acquaint us with a fractured body politic, and to seek in that fracturing what Burke called a "whole, composed of transitory parts." Thus the feeling of pain here acts not as disease but as *inoculation*, an active resistance to the disease of the French Revolution. Burke's ultimate fear, we remember, is that the contagious revolutionary passion would spread to England. The Gothic, to the degree that it is anti-Jacobin, anesthetizes our sympathies against this threatening infection. Like Raymond and Lorenzo, we are granted a modicum of pain; yet the pain we feel is just enough to make us believe that the illness, the *real* source of pain, is other, safely distant, and quarantined.

The Monk's attempt to validate pain may have more at stake than an abstract allegory of the body politic and its revolutionary awareness. The novel's treatment of pain may also be Lewis's attempt to understand his own body. Matthew Lewis was acutely familiar with pain. In a letter to his mother of 14 August 1804, he describes the day's headache as "one of my oldest companions," and indeed it seemed to plague him chronically (*Life* 292). As well, he complained of a sore leg which troubled him when he walked, at one point diagnosing it as an attack of the gout (*Life* 371). Finally, his whole body composition, "Of graceless form and dwarfish stature" (Preface to *The Monk* 4) and severely bothered by myopia of which he often complained, doubtless rendered Matthew Lewis's body a site of limitation, confinement, and compromise. Like the Gothic victim, whose pain is agonizingly immediate and present, Lewis's body continually signified antagonism. But like the aristocracy in the novel, an aristocracy to which Lewis had pretensions,[11] pain can be a confirmation of sensibility and good breeding. Pain affirms not only the life of the body, but also the life of the mind that constantly recognizes its association with the body. Whereas pain destroys the self in so many characters we have seen thus far, in Lewis, pain can help to construct that self as aristocratic.

V

Literary representations of pain in *The Monk* move along that familiar continuum between (aristocratic) sensibility to one's own body and the body of others, and anesthetizing excess (analogously connected to revolutionaries). Without noting the class implications, Lord Byron, Lewis's personal friend, experienced the same tension in his reading of *The Monk*: the novel had some admirable and moving parts, thought Byron, but its worst sections were like "the *philtred* ideas of a jaded voluptuary. . . . They have no nature—all the sour cream of cantharides" (*Letters* Vol. III, 234; emphasis original). That Byron should use the image of cantharides—one of Burke's potent metaphors from the *Reflections*—is interesting, since it sets Byron's reading of *The Monk* within the theatre of medicine, and uses that medical discourse to allude to the problems of revolution. But readers of Byron will also recognize in this short review of *The Monk* a tendency in Byronic figures from Childe Harold to Don Juan: a tendency for stimulation to become jaded and "philtred," for pleasure to sour, for the aesthetic to turn anesthetic. Reading *The Monk* is for Byron an artificial stimulant whose excesses quickly numb, a paradoxical complaint given that, according to Leslie Marchand, Byron's early love of literature can be located in his desire to escape the pain in his right foot (*Biography* Vol. I, 55–56). Despite his cranky review of Lewis, art for Byron was anesthesia, an attempt to silence an omnipresent, pained body. Given this ambivalence to feeling and its lack, Byron, like Lewis, can tell us something about writing—and writing out of—one's own pain. He inscribes his life-long awareness of his sentience in the dual arenas of medicine and war as ways of rendering public what to all of us is most personal: physical pain.

Like Terry Eagleton's definition of aesthetics, Byron's was born as a discourse of the body. His ambivalence toward feeling and anesthesia has a long psychological history. Like Matthew Lewis, Byron himself was constantly tormented by his own body and medical attempts to treat it. The pain in his right foot—a pain that tormented him all his life—proceeded from a deformity that he had reason to believe was not inevitable. At his birth, the attending physician John Hunter pronounced that the deformity could not be cured; it could merely be treated with the right prosthetic shoe (Marchand *Biography* I, 25). However, eleven years later, on 17 July 1799, the young Byron was told by Dr. Baillie that proper treatment in infancy might have corrected the malformation and relieved the child from years of pain (*Biography* I, 54). Whether Baillie was right or not, Byron must have resented the lost opportunity for a cure, and this resentment flowed from his pen almost every time he portrayed the medical profession. But more than just creating—or deepening—an antimedical prejudice, Byron's relations with doctors confirmed for him a life of antagonism against his body. In fact, Byron once claimed to have gone to London, probably during his school days at Harrow, to have the foot amputated, but the surgeon refused to perform the operation (*Biography* III, 1052). Byron's foot, coupled with his perpetual weight problem, hemorrhoids, numerous fevers and catarrhs, all bespoke an awareness of the body as tyrant, a body whose limitations, like Manfred's or Arnold's in *The Deformed Transformed*, constantly reminded him of the Faustian boundaries of living "coop'd in clay" (*Manfred* in *Poetical Works* I,i,7). Byron once confided to Francis Hodgson a rather pathetic wish: "let me live well, if possible, and die without pain" (*Letters* II,89).

Yet if the body always represented for Byron tyrannic pain and limitation (as it did for Lewis), it was also the site of his most pleasurable transgressions. His sexual exploits are recorded in both Leslie Marchand's biography of Byron and his compilation of the letters and journals, making them too well known to require listing. These sexual exploits were, for Byron, part of a larger critique of an *ancien régime* of Calvinist metaphysicians and moralists who advocated temperance and modesty as a way to health. "I shall not live long," he wrote to Hobhouse and Kinnaird on 19 January 1819, "& for that Reason—I must live while I can" (*Letters* VI, 92).

And if the narrator of *Don Juan* is to be trusted, a life of sexual dissipation is a *means* to health, far more effective than anything a doctor could prescribe. The narrator recounts the story of King David whom sex cured of illness:

> 'Tis written in the Hebrew chronicle
> How the physicians, leaving pill and potion,
>   Prescribed by way of blister a young belle,
> When old King David's blood grew dull in motion,
>   And that the medicine answered very well. (I,168,ll.2–6)

Health depends upon exercising the body in every way, avoiding none of the pleasures of the voluptuary. Like Lewis, for whom the body represented the possibility for fulfillment and community (as well as sexual transgression in *The Monk*), so for Byron did physical stimulation validate his sense of being in the world. As Jerome McGann writes, Byron's early life was dedicated to "the high energy of instant sensations and feelings (whether of pleasure or pain makes no difference)" ("Romanticism and Its Ideologies" 586). His body was the central source from which he could live a commitment to individual pleasure, and to his definition of freedom.

It takes little effort, then, to read Byron's bodily ambivalence in political terms. His dedication to a life of freedom and his loathing of any tyrannical description of his body echo his dreams of an emancipated Republic, dreams which, according to Daniel P. Watkins had become his primary fixation by 1821 ("Byron and Poetics" 96; "Violence" 799–816). Such dreams expressed themselves in his fantasy of a liberated Italy, about which he wrote to Augusta in a letter of 18 February 1821, in his praise of America in "Detached Thoughts 112," and in his willingness to volunteer in the fight for Greek emancipation, a political commitment that finally destroyed his health and his life. For Byron, the physical body was not a metaphor for vague political principles, but rather the actual site where political principles could be expressed. As Morse Peckham writes, Byron shared with the Marquis de Sade an overtly *political* sexuality, in that "both of them . . . show the symbolic connection between sexual transgression and moral freedom" (*Beyond* 101). To exercise undue regulation over *either* the sexual body or the body politic is to submit each to an unnatural and immoral governance.

But while Byron's sexual transgression may ostensibly be part of an antiauthoritarian project, his body, by his own admission, is a problematic site for this agenda. As Edward Bostetter has argued, Byron's coterminous

proclamation of physical freedom and enslavement underlies a larger ambivalence Byron felt toward the politics of his own body: Byron, says
Bostetter, both indulged and cultivated his sexual passion (with a good deal
of polymorphous perversity) as a means of living freely, and also hated and
feared those passions as a threat to his will and independence (*Ventriloquists*
269). The powerful body can be both liberating and tyrannical — in much
the same way that the Revolutionary mob can spawn the Reign of Terror.
Just as Byron was suspicious of his own passions, so did he doubt the ability
of any political interest — like Napoleon[12] or the French mob — to gain
power without being corrupted by it. Byron's dually liberating and tyrannical body, then, encapsulates a respect for and fear of the body politic that
Byron was exploring as he devoted himself simultaneously to the war for
Greek emancipation and to the writing of *Don Juan*. In Canto VIII, Byron's
most famous sustained treatment of revolutionary war, he presents the
ambiguities posed by the sentient body in its political manifestations.
Byron brings together in this canto the theatres of medicine and war to
fashion an aesthetic of revolutionary freedom; but with the Terror and
Napoleonic campaigns in mind, Byron depicts this aesthetic as tending
toward the dangerous numbness we saw operating in Burke's ominous
warnings and Lewis's fictionalized reflections.

In Burke's thinking about events in France, medical stimulants meta-
phorically represented the "continual talk of resistance and revolution"
which, in Lewis's Gothic sensibility took on the characteristics of passionate
excess and sexual transgression. In Canto VIII of *Don Juan*, Byron picks up
this medical imagery but resituates it.[13] As the siege of Ismail begins,

> Three hundred cannon threw up their emetic,
>   And thirty thousand muskets flung their pills
> Like hail to make a bloody diuretic. (VIII,12,ll.1–3)

Whereas for Burke, the excessive physical stimulation of war was in the discursive effects of debate and propaganda — what Byron detests as "cant" —
for Byron the horror of war is precisely in its *materiality*, in the flesh-
and-blood presence of battle. No amount of debate and speculation over
plagues, famines, and physicians, he says, can compare to "the true portrait
of one battlefield" (VIII,12,l.8). By situating medical imagery not as a
problem of discourse but as one of material experience, Byron foregrounds
the immediacy of physical pain, and in so doing, combines in Canto VIII
the ontological aesthetic of pain with its literary aesthetic. The battlefield

becomes the site of the most intense aesthetic possible, where the fear of war, "like wind / Trouble[s] heroic stomachs" (VIII,40, 4–5) and presents both soldier and reader with the potential for pain.

The bloody diuretic of war foregrounds the aesthetic immediacy of human pain, in that the description makes graphic the primacy and irreducibility of physical suffering. However, in rendering pain "aesthetic" and immediate, Byron's description threatens to swallow up that immediacy. Byron's depiction of the siege occupies that liminal space that excess creates between physical horror and numbness, between the shocking experience of pain and the inability to feel it. Put another way, the aesthetic of war deconstructs itself, as its sensory elements degenerate into a confusion that obliterates them:

> The very cannon, deafened by the din,
>   Grew dumb, for you might almost hear a linnet
> As soon as thunder 'midst the general noise
> Of human nature's agonizing voice. (VIII,59,ll.5–8)

This revolutionary excess obscures the boundaries of all natural objects so that "the heat / Of carnage, like the Nile's sun-sodden slime, / Engender[s] monstrous shapes of every crime" (VIII,82,ll.6–8). As Ronald Paulson has argued, representations of revolution in Romantic fiction often return to the imagery of Burke's sublime — of the fearfully amorphous and monstrous — and push those images into the exaggeration of the grotesque (*Representations* 171). This amorphousness or sense of the monstrous includes, of course, *people*: we are told that "three thousand Moslems perished here" (VIII,81,l.7) in a magnitude of death that remains incomprehensible to the spectator. Such is the effect on Juan. Throughout the seige, he moves through a heap of dead bodies without being the least affected. He can stumble "backwards o'er / A wounded comrade, sprawling in his gore" (VIII,20,ll.7–8), and not "care a pinch of snuff about his corps," "the greater part of which were corses" (VIII,30,l.8,31,l.8). Thus, war and widespread carnage have that anesthetizing effect that Burke and Lewis describe: they create a vortex into which is sucked all sense of the other, as the most powerful of aesthetic experiences anesthetizes the perceiver.

Yet, at the same time that the magnitude of the carnage threatens to obliterate all perception of the other, it also provides moments of sympathetic identification with that other. Juan can scramble over corpses without caring a pinch, but

> At a distance
> He hated cruelty as all men hate
> Blood, until heated, and even then his own
> At times would curdle o'er some heavy groan. (VIII,55,ll.5–8)

Indeed, Juan is capable of moments of extreme pity — as in the scene with the young Turkish girl (VIII,91–101) or the valiant father fighting with his sons (VIII,116) — because soldiers, in Byron's view, are a "mixture of wild beasts and demigods / . . . now furious as the sweeping wave, / Now moved with pity" (VIII,106,ll.4–6). We see here what Frederick Garber describes as the central problem of individualism in the Romantic hero: a figure who wants to be alone, transgressive, and individualist always finds himself compromised by a vestigial desire to fill social responsibilities. He is plagued by his own moral goodness ("Self, Society" 323). But Byron's depiction of this vicissitude does more than portray the failed individualist; it also contrasts the complete *lack* of sympathetic potential in the sovereignty and the aristocracy. General Markow, for instance, insists on removing and protecting the prince "Amidst some groaning thousands dying near — / All common fellows, who might writhe and wince / And shriek for water into a deaf ear" (VIII,11,ll.3–5). Whereas Burke and Lewis attribute sympathy only to the aristocracy, Byron dispels such a myth by allowing sympathy — however inconsistent — in the soldier classes. In fact, the aristocracy in Byron, like the *mob* in Burke and Lewis, is incapable of feeling its own pain:

> The Prince de Ligne was wounded in the knee.
>   Count Chapeau-Bras too had a ball between
> His cap and head, which proves the head to be
>   Aristocratic as was ever seen,
> Because it then received no injury
>   More than the cap; in fact the ball could mean
> No harm unto a right legitimate head.
> "Ashes to ashes" — why not lead to lead? (VIII,10,ll.1–8)

General Markow is rewarded for his aristocratic anesthesia by having his own leg broken, so that he can suffer like the rest. If pain is pedagogical, as Burke thought it could be, then a broken leg will teach Markow to know better next time.

In Burke and Lewis, losing one's sense of the other *as* other — a loss that precipitated the larger breakdown of the social fabric — was related to the anesthetizing of one's own pain; if one could not feel one's own sentient principle, as Whytt described it, then one could not feel that other, more wonderful social sympathy. To the degree that one's body is the source of the moral order, the mind's relationship to it is homologous to its relationship with *all* others. In *Don Juan*, the kind of social anesthetizing we just saw in General Markow suggests the possibility of losing one's sense of one's own self, by having it swallowed up in the sublime of widespread destruction. Byron directly confronts this tendency by reclaiming in the body the isolating agency of pain that is otherwise lost in the overwhelming carnage. As the scene at Ismail begins to resemble Scarlett O'Hara's hospital grounds in Atlanta, the focus shifts to a particular — and particularly gruesome — scene in which a dying Moslem bites the Achilles tendon of a Russian soldier who is walking over him:

> In vain [the Russian] kicked and swore and writhed and bled
> And howled for help as wolves do for a meal.
> The teeth still kept their gratifying hold,
> As do the subtle snakes described of old. (VIII,83,ll.5–8)

Such power have these dentures that even when the Moslem's head is cut off they do not readily release their grip. Clearly, the soldier's foot here is Byron's own; both author and character have come face to face with their own Achilles heel, the site of their human frailty. But by invoking the individual experience of pain, Byron returns the aesthetic focus to a comprehensible perspective, and rescues the soldier's physical sentience from its disappearance into the black hole of the grotesque. (The grotesquerie committed against the Moslem we are presumably not to notice.) Byron isolates one body in the context of thousands and renders its pain lucid, immediate, poignant. As in Byron's sexuality, the body in this scene employs sentience to reclaim its autonomy from an undifferentiated mass that constantly threatens to obliterate the immediacy of its experience. In fact, as Elaine Scarry argues, pain becomes an aesthetic proclamation of one's existence; by being "so incontestably and unnegotiably present" (*Body in Pain* 4), pain employs its tyranny toward a kind of ontological validation. We see this same proclamation in an earlier scene of *Don Juan* when Juan, as the only survivor of the rowboat disaster, washes up on the shore of a beach "With just enough of life to feel its pain / And deem that it was saved" (II,108,ll.7–8). Whereas pain worked as a reluctant witness to the affirmation of Fleetwood's identity in Godwin's novel, it here becomes a beneficent confirmation — something far from tyrannical oppression.[14] As Byron wrote in a letter to Annabella Milbanke, his future wife, on 6 September 1813, "The great object of life is Sensation — to feel that we exist — even though in pain" (*Letters* III, 109). In pain, we exist not in spite of our sentience but because of it.

In Matthew Lewis's anti-Jacobin Gothicism, pain is employed to construct an aristocratic utopia of sorts. In Byron's more republican sympathies, this utopia is recast: pain is an individual experience that to some degree reconciles us with a much larger community by reducing the hero to the level of the common. As the same Russian officer writhes in pain, the regimental surgeon is called to relieve him. But to no avail: "The Russian officer for life was lamed, / . . . Which left him 'midst the invalid and maimed" (VIII,85,ll.2–4). Similarly, two soldiers who have had their hips and shoulders split open by Juan's sword rush off "to seek / If there might be chirurgeons who could solder / The wounds" (VIII,94,ll.2–4). But Byron refuses to cure or anesthetize the pain: "the fact's a fact," he tells us (VIII,86,l.1), and truth in poetry requires that pain be presented, not numbed. Yet unlike Lewis, Byron's sentience democratizes him at the same time that it individuates him; the soldier's pain makes him one of the countless many, despite the particularity of the close-up. If, with Descartes, we share the body in common, then we all share the potential for pain, a potential that re-enfranchises us as part of the republic (or, reduces us to the common herd, depending on your point of view). Thus, through pain, Byron achieves at least two reconciliations: first, pain provides him a framework within which to situate the individual whose autonomy risks being swallowed up at the same time that it incorporates itself into the larger community (and this reconciliation is *essential* for an individualist turned Republican, and for the Romantic in general); second, it at least partially reconciles Byron to his own painful body. The "fact" of his lameness is a "fact," useless to bemoan and impossible to anesthetize. And more importantly, this pain affirms the life of sensation, which Byron refuses his fictional physicians the privilege of numbing. Through Canto VIII, Byron can to some degree validate both his politics and his ontology by examining the vicissitudes of pain, and thereby transform his tyrannically painful body into an agent of freedom.

Byron's exploration of the ontological aesthetics of pain presents him, naturally, with a problem in literary aesthetics: how does one render in literature the horrors of war and the immediacy of pain? In essence, Byron's problem is the same one we have seen in all the authors in this study: how does one represent physical horror without it becoming anesthetizing and numbing? He puts the case:

> It is an awful topic, but 'tis not
> > My cue for any time to be terrific.
> For checkered as is seen our human lot
> > With good and bad and worse, alike prolific
> Of melancholy merriment; to quote
> > Too much of one sort would be soporific.
> Without, or with, offence to friends or foes,
> I sketch your world exactly as it goes. (VIII,89,ll.1−8)

To avoid the tendency of the "terrific" to become "soporific"—the aesthetic to become anesthetic—Byron reports the facts, but with a reserve that maintains one's interest while reading: "one good action in the midst of crimes / Is 'quite refreshing'" (VIII,90,ll.1−2).[15] But even as he restrains himself from indulging a Gothic sensibility, he charges such restraint with being the "pretty milk-and-water ways" of a readership far too delicate, who prefer rhymes bedewed with ambrosia rather than with the blaze of epic battle (VIII,90,l.4). The English public, he suggests, prefer a hygienic literature, always already anesthetized against the fact of pain. Thus Byron fashions a style that cuts both ways: knowing that mass pain and destruction can do for us what the regimental surgeon *could not* do, that is, anesthetize, Byron edits, focuses, and particularizes the moment of pain. Yet, unwilling to compromise his commitment to the materiality of war, he edits *in order* to keep those horrors fresh and immediate. Like Burke, Byron avoids the anodyne draught of oblivion that comes from excess, but he does so in order to keep our sensibilities alive to the ambiguities of revolution and to the body in pain, rather than to advocate the cant of a clear party line. Burke asks us to feel pain so that we can control it; Byron asks us to feel pain so that we can critique the political structures that inflict it.

In his early life, Byron attempts to escape pain by reading fiction; he supplants one form of the aesthetic (experiential, ontological sentience, the pain in his foot) with another (art). But this move is not a simple deflection or repression. Rather, the fiction he writes in his last days emphasizes his concern for *physical* pain, pain without mitigation. For Watkins, this is a move from ideology to *materiality*, away from Whiggish cant to a focus on the historical conditions that constitute meaning ("Violence" 800). For Jerome McGann, the later cantos of *Don Juan* (particularly those on England) are "the drama of romantic poetry where one becomes what one beholds, where education must be suffered through, where every poet is an Apollyon who must be pierced with his own weapon" ("Romanticism and Its Ideologies" 597). To be pierced with one's own weapons is to become aware that one is trapped by violence, to know that pain is not only inescapable, but compulsory. But with this compulsory pain comes the promise of revolution. Improvements to the quality of life, says Byron, require "weapons such as men / Snatch when despair makes human hearts less pliant. / . . . I would fain say 'fie on't', / If I had not perceived that revolution / Alone can save the earth from hell's pollution" (VIII,51,ll.3–8). We remember here the inevitability of revolution and physical suffering that Alhadra prophesied at the end of Coleridge's *Osorio*. Byron honored his his commitment to revolution by assisting the Italian Carbonari and by volunteering for the Greek struggle. And this same liberation — and the immediacy of pain — await England:

> Think how the joys of reading a *Gazette*
> > Are purchased by all agonies and crimes.
> Or if these do not move you, don't forget
> > Such doom may be your own in after times. (VIII,125,ll.1–4)

England assumes that it is free from revolutionary violence. Indeed, Burke has won. But the inoculation which Burke has given to England is not a cure but an *anaesthetic*, exactly like the kind Burke feared in France, which numbs the body politic to its real tyrannies — the tyrannies of a Castlereagh, a Wellesley, a George III. And it is a temporary anesthetic precisely because the revolution, for Byron, is inevitable; the sentience of the body politic cannot finally be anesthetized. This re-aestheticizing is the role of the poet. Through him, none will forget the "shrieks and groans" that the Russian sovereignty inflicted on the people of Ismail (VIII,135,l.2): "For I will teach, if possible, the stones / To rise against earth's tyrants" (VIII,135,ll.4–5). No longer does the aesthetic risk becoming anesthetic; rather, as a political poetry, it obliterates the numbness of political conservatism and re-enlivens, or re-aestheticizes, the body politic.

Conclusion

Burke knew that an empowered body — in the form of an empowered body politic — could defy the control of its master, and he feared this power. Wordsworth and Coleridge feared it too; Lewis and Shelley were ambivalent about it; Byron hoped for it. For each of these writers, the body holds a political strength that, rightly used, can destroy the old order. Yet this fearful, empowered body is also placed under attack: it is rent, dismembered, afflicted, diseased, maimed. Its power is put in check by pain. And this pain, moreover, can be another agent of a revolution that the Gothics and Romantics wanted to initiate or resist. Byron's revolutionary ideals, for example, required sympathetic identification with the visible, pained body; Wordsworth's conservatism, conversely, depended for its internal regulation and self-surveillance on the absence of the pained body, and relied instead on a body conjured by the imagination and thus regulated by it. Coleridge stood somewhere between Byron and Wordsworth, invoking the visibility of the pained body to further his Tory position. For Coleridge, as for Edmund Burke, the gratuitous spectacle of the pained body could, on the one hand, induce in its excesses a return to the proper order; on the other hand, it could exploit those excesses to destroy the order. There is no politics of the pained body here that is not contested and problematic at the same time that it is effective and forceful.

The political opportunism that circulates around the pained body in Romantic fiction thus expresses itself in the abstract social principles of partisan allegiance and aesthetic theory. But it also goes to the very heart of how one defines the self at the turn of the nineteenth century. Whereas the eighteenth-century discourses of sentimentalism had emptied out the self in an act of sympathetic identification (or, to follow David Marshall's thesis, isolated that perceiving subject in its failure to imagine another), Romantic fiction invokes the pleasures of pain — and the pleasures of being horrified by pain — as a way of constructing identity. I have tried to trace in this book a dialectical movement in tableaux of suffering from imaginative identification (I know how you feel), through appropriation of the isolating effects of that suffering (this hurts me more than it hurts you) to an ontological confirmation that eighteenth-century philosophy urgently needed to re-inscribe (I hurt, therefore I am). As we have seen, this self-fashioning often has implications for class (Lewis's aristocracy, Byron's republicanism) and social theorizing (Fleetwood's epistemological confirmation of judicial theory). But ultimately, pain in Romantic fiction is that apocalyptic moment of revelation and understanding when one moves from naiveté into knowledge. Like Frankenstein's monster and Maturin's Immalee, both of whom begin life in a blissful union with nature that is interrupted by the inexorable consciousness of suffering, the self in Romantic fiction seems to know itself only through acquaintance with physical agony.

This self, as contemporary critical theory since Lacan and Foucault reminds us, is fashioned within conflict and multivalence. In most of the works I have treated here, the representation of Gothic pain exists within contradictions, and across deconstructive vortexes, negotiating both public and private, the expressed and the ineffable, the othered and the selved, the imaginative and the corporeal, the dispersed and the centered. The body in these texts frames and contributes to the self at the same time that it is eclipsed by the self; that is, the body is in dialogue with the mind only then to be recast by the interpretive strategies of the mind. While I would not want to facilely equate Romantic subjectivity with post-structuralist post-subjectivity, I do think we can locate the premises of the post-subjective, antihumanist project in a trajectory that began in the discourses of sensibility: the ineffable self constantly seeking expression through discursive strategy (the *tout dire* strategy of Rousseau's *Confessions*, for example); the decentralized, destabilized self posited in the sympathetic discourses I have discussed here; and most importantly, the notion that there is no physiological process or experience that is not in some way affected by discursive constructions, that bodily mechanisms are always already inscribed with discursive theories and ideological constructions. Thus the self that gets made in these texts is liminal and protean, given its presence and absence through appropriated and inflicted pain. The ontological certainty, the "unnegotiable" and "irreducible" agency of pain decribed by Elaine Scarry, guarantees a process of selving that incorporates the mind-body dialogue as it was established in the 1750s, and in a curious way celebrates the plurality that the antihumanist project of criticism and philosophy has articulated in the last two decades. Pain in Romantic fiction deconstructs the central unified self at the same time that it claims to posit that self.

This deconstruction of the self has had a long history in Gothic criticism to which I can hardly do justice here. In one of the earliest full-length studies of the Gothic, Devendra Varma argued that the late eighteenth century was dominated by a "quest for the numinous" by which writers sought "the recovery of the vision of a spiritual world behind material appearances" (*Gothic Flame* xii). This quest for the spiritual is the same one we saw earlier, in Coleridge's reading of Schiller, Paul Sheats's reading of the young Wordsworth, and in the quest for unification of subject and object that René Wellek identifies as the project of Romanticism proper. The quest for the numinous becomes, in Terry Castle's view, "a crucial feature of the new sensibility of the late eighteenth century": "a growing sense of the ghostliness of other people" in which "the other was indeed reduced to a phantom — a purely mental effect, an image, as it were, on the screen of consciousness itself" ("Spectralization" 237). She concludes that, in this move toward "the spectralization of the other," "everything merges — inside and outside, cause and effect, mind and universe . . . [thus blurring] the line between objective and subjective experiences" (240). Castle shares this reading of the Gothic with Maggie Kilgour (*Communion* 168) and Eve Kosofsky Sedgwick, for whom "both the identification of center with self and the programmatic symmetry of the inside-outside relation are undermined in the same [Gothic] texts" (*Coherence* 13). This obfuscation of the boundaries between inside and outside, and the deconstruction of the central self that such obfuscation implies, are most readily accomplished by the pained body whose experience as other becomes so forcefully one's own.

Thus the pained body in Gothic fiction becomes the conduit through which one's identity vacillates — now felt, now numbed; now empowered, now silenced; now self, now other — and through which one relates to others and invites others to relate to oneself. Unless, of course, you are Beatrice Cenci. The clearest example of a character destroyed and unwritten by pain, Beatrice challenges anything that can be said about the vicissitudes of pain and making in Gothic fiction. For Beatrice, the pain of rape and abuse do not merely mark the tyrannies of parenthood against which all oedipal Romantic children must battle and thus achieve identity; rather, pain in Shelley is that which infects the daughter with the father and destroys the autonomy granted by pain in many of the other texts read in this book. Moreover, Beatrice's physical suffering offers us no laudable binarism of self-construction/deconstruction that can legitimate her subversion of Cenci's patriarchy or Beatrice's conflicted rise to "power." Rather, Beatrice Cenci's pain, like that of Marzio and the other victims of torture, emphasizes the degree to which pain obliterates the self and nullifies the victim's world. Nothing matters in this world but that pain exist and that pain be stopped. It is unnegotiably present, as Scarry says, but it also destroys "voice, self and world." Pain in *The Cenci* is perhaps the antihumanist agency par excellence, not because it bifurcates and problematizes the definition of self, but because it renders the self incapable of being thought about. Pain in this text marks the limits of Romantic and critical consciousness: if pain is apocalyptic for Beatrice, that apocalypse takes more the form of total destruction than of creative rejuvenation.

This destruction of the self, which I have just called the antihumanist agency of pain, is also paradoxically pain's profoundly humanizing effect. I argued in Chapter one that while pain can never be understood outside its culture, and while it is always mediated and defined by a cultural symbolic (indeed, this book has been an attempt to understand that cultural mediation at the turn of the nineteenth century), the experience of pain also institutes in us the ineradicable perception of mind-body antagonism: my *body* is hurting *me*. Pain reinscribes in our experience the mind/body division, and gives the body a mastery that bourgeois society at least since the seventeenth century (if not since Plato) has tried to resist. This mastery gets expressed, I think, in both the Romantic emphasis on the imagination and the post-structuralist emphasis on discursive constructivism: nothing exists but as it is perceived. But pain, by attacking the body, attacks this antihumanist assumption, and poses serious questions about the limits that discourse can have on the body. Is it possible that individual bodies have thresholds of pain over which no discourse can cross? What are the implications of speaking of a culturally constructed "subject" when that subjectivity can be rendered non-existent by its own physicality? Perhaps the most startling thing we can learn from Romantic fiction — that repository of narratives about the limits of physical sentience and the historically determined conditions of that sentience — is that, for the victim of pain, such questions *do not matter*. The phenomenon of pain in the Gothic depicts a fascination for those who are not in it, but rather are imagining, remembering, creating. Yet, these works focus not only on the discursive and invented, but the real and experienced. There are real moments of pain, which not even the most ardent constructivist will deny: indeed, Foucault reminds us that "while there are some very interesting things about the body in Marx's writings, Marxism considered as an historical truth has had a terrible tendency to occlude the question of the body, in favour of consciousness and ideology" (*Power/Knowledge* 58–59). Much the same thing could be said, I think, about post-structuralist theory and ideology that focuses on the body without ever talking about bodies at all. Pain forcefully returns us to that occluded body and reminds us that real pain affords us no ideologies. For all the thinking that we have devoted to pain at least since the mid-eighteenth century, pain is still a phenomenon that remains to a large degree anti-intellectual, antihumanist, and anti-antihumanist.

Notes

Introduction

1. For an excellent study of the gender problems in sensibility, see G. J. Barker-Benfield, *Culture of Sensibility*. On Keats and pain, see Hermione de Almeida, *Romantic Medicine*.

Chapter One

1. Charles Robert Maturin would agree that observed suffering teaches us to value our own position of safety, but he would disagree that such pleasure must be far removed. In *Melmoth the Wanderer*, one of his villains explains:

> It is actually possible to become *amateurs in suffering*. I have heard of men who have travelled into countries where horrible executions were to be daily witnessed, for the sake of that excitement which the sight of suffering never fails to give, from the spectacle of a tragedy, or an *auto da fe*, down to the writhings of the meanest reptile on whom you can inflict torture, and feel that torture is the result of your own power. It is a species of feeling of which we can never divest ourselves, — a triumph over those whose sufferings have placed them below us, and no wonder — suffering is always an indication of weakness, — we glory in our impenetrability. (284–285; emphasis original)

2. Coleridge muses on a similar point in a notebook entry of January 1804:

> Images in sickly profusion by & in which I talk in certain diseased States of my Stomach / Great and innocent minds *devalesce*, as Plants & Trees, into beautiful Diseases / Genius itself, many of the most brillant sorts of English Beauty, & even extraordinary Dispositions to Virtue, Restlessness in good — are they not themselves, as I have often said, but beautiful Diseases — species of the Genera, Hypochondriasis, Scrofula, & Consumption! (*Notebook* Vol.I #1822)

3. Contrary to its name, however, the guillotine was not invented by Guillotin. As Dorinda Outram notes, the guillotine was already a popular tool of execution in fifteenth-century Italy, and appears frequently in art from the period. The guillotine simply became more popular in France because it was more foolproof and less messy than the axe (especially if that axe were in the hands of a reluctant executioner who might flinch at the last minute). See Outram, *Body* 106ff.

4. Indeed, according to the *OED*, "guillotine" also became the late nineteenth-century name for a surgical tool used to remove the tonsils or the uvula.

5. Maturin dramatizes Whytt's point brilliantly. As Moncada relates his escape through the dungeon with the parricide leading the way, he finds himself trapped by the damp walls, his body in a fever. As he fights his way through the dark, he remembers a story about a man in a similar situation getting stuck in a passage and thereby blocking the passage for his fellow travelers, condemning them to certain death. When the fellow travelers threaten to vivisect him and thus remove him from the passage, his body immediately contracts and he frees himself. As Monçada recounts this story, he remembers how "All this detail, that takes many words to tell, rushed on my soul in a moment; — on my soul? — no, on my body. I was all physical feeling, — all intense corporeal agony" (*Melmoth* 267).

6. Excellent explanations of Moral Philosophy's assault on Cartesian rationalism can be found in Charles Taylor's *Sources of the Self: The Making of the Modern Identity* (see 248–349); Mary Poovey's "Ideology and *The Mysteries of Udolpho*" (307–330); and Stephen D. Cox's *"The Stranger Within Thee": Concepts of the Self in Late Eighteenth-Century Literature.*

7. Burke is more suspicious than is Shaftesbury's school about the propensity of human beings to act disinterestedly. For Burke, human self-interest and aggression must be curbed by society and tradition, which is his chief starting point in *Reflections on the Revolution in France*. Whereas the Moral School begins with the premise of benevolent primitivism that assures community and orderly behavior, Burke, like Hobbes, assumes that we act in self-interest and that our primitive tendencies must be curbed by a social construct.

8. The ability to enter fully into someone else's experience is not only assumed by the Gothic, it is also feared by it. In *Between Men: English Literature and Male Homosocial Desire*, Eve Kosofsky Sedgwick locates "homosexual panic" in this ability at the end of the century. For her, homosexual panic in novels like *Caleb Williams, or Things As They Are*; *Private Memoirs and Confessions of a Justified Sinner*; and *Frankenstein* proceeds from the male protagonist's fear that another man is haunting him, that another man is *inside* him. This invasion of the self's private space is the bleak, Gothic rendition of what was, for Burke, the source of moral community.

9. De Almeida argues that "the Romantic physician and Keats's poet were expected to have a dual consciousness of pain — as a patient and as a physician — and healing knowledge, and the comprehending imagination of disease was tied to the actuality and actual experience of pain. As Keats said to his friend Reynolds in May 1818, 'Until we are sick, we understand not'" (57). De Almeida reads this to mean that when we are sick, we automatically know how other sick people feel. I'm not sure our own illness can guarantee this knowledge. Robert Whytt's studies began precisely because people experienced pain differently and, as I have already noted, there are innumerable studies to suggest the class, gender, and religious differences that intrude into the experience of pain, not to mention the linguistic differences in the expression of that pain. When we are sick, we know how we feel; I'm not sure that we can generalize from there.

10. For Eagleton, Mary Poovey, and C. B. Macpherson, this simultaneous sociality and autonomy are linked to the rise of bourgeois capitalism. Together they

define what Macpherson calls "possessive individualism," in that they give one a sense of ownership of one's own body, but ownership that then allows one to sell that body's labor or to contribute in other ways to the social marketplace of trade (*Possessive Individualism* 215).

11. Indeed, as Crompton notes,

> During the period 1805–1835, when the annual number of executions for all crimes dropped from about seventy to about thirty, sodomy was the only crime for which the number of hangings remained more or less constant. (38)

12. In fact, for Immanuel Kant, reliance on the object world obfuscates one's moral alignments as well — that is, the grounding of moral conduct totally within the self, without reference to Nature or political ideology to authenticate behaviour (see Taylor, *Sources of the Self* 363).

13. The same classicism that Outram sees in Jacques Louis David, I would suggest, underlies the depiction of a number of Gothic heroes who, in Paulson's analysis, represent the French Revolutionary and who are condemned by their conservative authors for their passions. Ambrosio in Lewis's *The Monk*, Montoni and Schedoni in Radcliffe's *The Mysteries of Udolpho* and *The Italian* respectively, and even that much later but equally potent threat to British purity, Count Dracula, all share the dubious honor of a classical physical description: aquiline nose, mysterious visage, dark complexion, cool and reserved yet stately demeanor, and so forth. And what makes their descriptions even more interesting in regard to Norbert's notion of *homo clausus* is their consciousness of the people who are watching them, and their response to being watched. Both Ambrosio and Schedoni, for example, refuse to allow their spectator's look to penetrate their being: they constantly force the onlooker to behold the surface, and the surface only.

14. Wellek describes European Romanticism as "a revival of Neoplatonism, a pantheism (whatever its concessions to orthodoxy), a monism which arrived at identification of God and the world, soul and body, subject and object" (150).

15. I am borrowing the title of Helen Neal's 1978 book, *The Politics of Pain*. In this work Neal discusses the various ways in which political considerations determine the pain treatment one receives.

Chapter Two

1. According to John Williams, James Beattie's *The Minstrel* was Wordsworth's most important model during the mid-1790s, when he was experiencing Salisbury Plain and writing about it (*Romantic Poetry* 71). *The Minstrel* is also the poem that provided numerous chapter epigraphs for Radcliffe's novels.

2. James H. Averill notes that the gibbet scene in *The Prelude* focuses on what isn't there — bones, iron, a wooden mast; there is only a tuft of grass which might exist anywhere (*Human Suffering* 245).

3. It is now a critical commonplace that one of *Udolpho*'s most outstanding characteristics is that nothing happens in it. Supernatural events are all exposed as

having natural causes, and perceived dangers are mostly constructions of Emily's frenzied imagination. For discussions of these non-events, see Nelson Smith, "Sense"; D. L. MacDonald, "Bathos"; and Day, *Circles*.

4. For a discussion of Radcliffe's debt to Burke, see Coral Ann Howells, *Love*. On Wordsworth's debt to Burke's *Enquiry*, see W. P. Albrecht, "Tragedy": Patrick Holland, "Wordsworth and the Sublime"; and W. J. B. Owen, "Sublime." On the influence of Burke's *Reflections on Revolution*, see Mary Jacobus, "'That Great Stage'"; and James K. Chandler, *Wordsworth's Second Nature*.

5. In a way, Scarry overstates her case here by making pain the definitive example of an experience that resists objectification in language. Other possibilities suggest themselves: what about "anxiety"? Doesn't anxiety often suggest a state of nervous apprehension with no easily identifiable object? Couldn't a Poe character easily be categorized as "having feeling" but with "no referential content"?

6. Burke's sympathetic connection is echoed by the nun Olivia in Radcliffe's *The Italian*. She says to Ellena:

> I think I could endure any punishment with more fortitude than the sickening anguish of beholding such suffering as I have witnessed. What are bodily pains in comparison with the subtle, the exquisite tortures of the mind! Heaven knows I can support my own afflictions, but not the view of those of others when they are excessive. The instruments of torture I believe I could endure, if my spirit was invigorated with the consciousness of a generous purpose; but pity touches upon a nerve that vibrates instantly to the heart, and subdues resistance. Yes, my child, the agony of pity is keener than any other, except that of remorse, and even in remorse, it is, perhaps, the mingling unavailing pity, that points the sting. (127–128)

7. Also, we remember Vivaldi, the hero of *The Italian*, who is abducted by the Inquisition and is about to be put to the question, that is, he is about to be tortured. As he is led out of the room, the narrative focus switches to Ellena, his beloved, and we are forced to wait for almost 100 pages before we find out whether Vivaldi is wracked in pain from torture. It is such playful narration that Mark M. Hennelly Jr. writes about in "'The Slow Torture of Delay': Reading *The Italian*." Another example of imagining pain — pain which doesn't exist — occurs when Ellena and Vivaldi have been locked in the prison by Jeronimo. As the level-headed Vivaldi tries to procure a means of escape,

> Ellena . . . frequently looked round the chamber in search of some object, which might contradict or confirm her suspicion, that this was the death-room of the unfortunate nun. No such circumstance appeared, but as her eyes glanced, with almost phrenzied eagerness, she perceived something shadowy in a remote corner of the floor; and on approaching, discovered what seemed a dreadful hieroglyphic, a mattrass [sic] of straw, in which she thought she beheld the death-bed of the miserable recluse; nay more, that the impression it still retained, was that which her form had left there. (140)

8. Brissenden uses the *OED* definition of virtue as "refined and elevated feeling" to discuss the moral crisis which such feeling underwent in a fallen material

world. His thesis is that the sentimental response to virtue in distress ultimately collapsed into a pejorative connotation of virtue as "indulgent, superficial emotion" because that virtue was too ambitious. "The sentimental tribute of a tear exacted by the spectacle of virtue in distress was an acknowledgement at once of man's inherent goodness and of the impossibility of his ever being able to demonstrate his goodness effectively" (*Virtue* 29). In Radcliffe's case, the physical response to imagined pain is the "sentimental tribute" but one which must fall short of its goal because of its self-destructive potential as horror which freezes the very sensibility which invited it.

9. The material threat to both body and property in the novel has been the subject of feminist criticism (as I have just indicated), yet it has been lost to those critics who see the novel as satiric. I noted above the critical commonplace that these novels do not go anywhere. Nelson C. Smith, writing on *The Mysteries of Udolpho*, says that "nothing very terrifying really happens. . . . All that happens, indeed, results from Emily's being a high-strung heroine susceptible to the dangers of sensibility" ("Sense" 583). Nothing terrifying happens if we are willing to discount violence, murder, wife-battering, and attempted rape as terrifying.

10. For this reason, Jane Austen's rebuke of Radcliffe in *Northanger Abbey* has always seemed to me slightly unfair. Austen argues that "it was not in [Mrs. Radcliffe's] works perhaps that human nature . . . was to be looked for" (*Complete* 1176), an argument repeated in *Emma* where Harriet Smith is satirized for reading *The Romance of the Forest*. Rather, Catherine Morland is instructed to look for *real* problems, not to invent them through imagination. St. Aubert counsels Emily in something very similar, and Radcliffe is as concerned as Austen about reinstating the value of sense over sensibility. Furthermore, both authors tie that sense into the right to hold land and power. Austen is as horrified as Radcliffe at the thought that one should marry far beneath or above her, and "proper" marriages in Austen always legitimate the owning of estates and lands.

11. This story, changed very little in revisions, becomes "The Female Vagrant" in *Lyrical Ballads*.

12. William Hazlitt was the first to condemn Wordsworth for taking "a subject or a story merely as pegs or loops to hang thought and feeling on," so that the real lives and pains of Wordsworth's characters become nothing but convenient ciphers through which to propound doctrine ("Mr. Wordsworth" in *Lectures* 253). The object is not treated as object, says Hazlitt (*pace* Paul Sheats), but as a source of imaginative speculation. Furthermore, by the publication of *The Excursion* in 1814, that intense feeling borders on becoming what Hazlitt calls "the God of [Words-worth's] own idolatry" (261). This condemnation of Wordsworth's egotism finds its contemporary voice in David Ferry, who initiated the current critical strain that Wordsworth is unable to sympathize with another person without egocentrically assuming center stage in the process. Indeed, Ferry says it is easy to see Wordsworth "not [as] a great lover of man but almost a great despiser of him" (*Limits* 52). Edward Bostetter argues that the French Revolution made Wordsworth aware of the social and political causes of suffering, and so his glossing over them in *The Ruined Cottage* and "The Discharged Soldier" can have no ethical justification (*Romantic Ventriloquists* 53). Bostetter has in mind that controversial line near the end of *The Ruined Cottage* when the Old Man, having just related the sufferings of

Margaret, concludes, "I turned away / And walked along my road in happiness" (in Gill, *Oxford Authors*, 44,ll.524–525).

13. For Eve Kosofsky Sedgwick, this unspeakability is a Gothic convention. She traces in *Melmoth the Wanderer* examples of preterition — that rhetorical device of claiming not to be able to describe something — and concludes that language is "a sort of safety valve between the inside and the outside which being closed off, all knowledge, even when held in common, becomes solitary, furtive, and explosive." To speak, therefore, would be to transgress an artificial barrier that would collapse the outside world of listeners into the inside world of the sufferer. This collapse, in the Gothic, signals chaos (*Coherence* 16–22).

14. In his personal life, Wordsworth was aware of how pain could inhibit the production of language. In 1798 he wrote to Coleridge from Goslar, Germany:

> As I have had no books I have been obliged to write in self-defence. I should have written five times as much as I have done but that I am prevented by an uneasiness at my stomach and side, with a dull pain about my heart. I have used the word pain, but uneasiness and heat are words which more accurately express my feeling. At all events it renders writing unpleasant. Reading is now become a kind of luxury to me. When I do not read I am absolutely consumed by thinking and feeling and bodily exertions of voice or of limbs, the consequence of those feelings. (*Letters* I, 236)

The pain in the stomach and side were no doubt occasional; unlike most other writers of Romantic fiction, Wordsworth did not seem plagued by chronic ill-health. But the link in the final sentence between imagination and sentience is interesting: thinking and feeling (what becomes recollection and emotion in *The Prelude*) are physically exhausting. Bodily exertions of voice and limbs are their consequence. Thus literary endeavors overstimulate the body and tire — or even hurt — it, making writing impossible. Here the imagination of pain seems to destroy itself in the way it did with Radcliffe's heroines.

15. For Enid Welsford, Wordsworth's retreat from the body is inspired by a Radcliffe-like sense of decorum: "The pruning away of much — not by any means all — of the 'Gothic horror' of MS.I may be due to Wordsworth's increased reverence for matter-of-fact as well as the natural development of good taste" (*Salisbury Plain* 28).

16. This is a theme which Wordsworth shares with Coleridge, with whom he co-published part of this poem as one of the *Lyrical Ballads*. For a discussion on Coleridge and the politics of guilt, see the section on *Osorio* and *Remorse* in the next chapter.

17. Seraphia D. Leyda argues that, in the *Sonnets Upon the Punishment of Death*, Wordsworth is combining a doctrine of love with a doctrine of *fear*:

> Blending the "several powers" of Love and Fear implies some imaginative power and clearly challenges any over-reliance on deductive reasoning from a set of utilitarian principles. Man responds to love, but fear is often stronger. Wordsworth, in this sense, is urging the lawgivers to legislate for the "real" world by retaining for the State the "last alternative of Life or Death." ("Wordsworth's *Sonnets*" 50)

18. Andrea Henderson writes that the poem presents the poet as on a threshold; it

> reflects a first and ultimately unworkable response to Wordsworth's personal and political disillusionment. The poem presents a world frozen mid-change, incapable of moving towards an enlightened future or recovering an unfallen past. Wordsworth, finding no clear place for himself, makes himself central in the world of the poem by constructing the poet as the one who restores wholeness by self-consciously and systematically alienating what is at present only partially alienated. ("A Tale Told" 72)

Chapter Three

1. Byron served on the Selection Committee for Drury Lane between 1815 and 1816, when he left England for Geneva. In that time he was inundated with Gothic theatre manuscripts which permanently soured his taste for the theatre. Ironically, the only one of his dramas to achieve any great stage success was *Werner*, which catered to the public taste for melodrama.

2. Earl Wasserman summarizes the history of explanations for the pleasure of tragedy, centering his essay on the question, "Why in the temple of pleasure do we erect the goddess of pain?" See "The Pleasure of Tragedy."

3. Shelley so clearly envisioned this play as being performed that he wrote the principal part of Beatrice for the actress Eliza O'Neill. Not only was her style suited to the representation of Beatrice's passions, but her fame would help ensure the play's commercial success.

4. For a discussion of Byron and Coleridge's dislike of the popular theatre, see John David Moore, "Coleridge and the 'Modern Jacobinical Drama': *Osorio*, *Remorse*, and the Development of Coleridge's Critique of the Stage, 1797–1816."

5. The eighteenth century's suspicion of grand spectacle goes back at least as far as Diderot. As Michael Fried writes,

> Diderot urged playwrights to give up contriving elaborate *coups de théâtre* (surprising turns of plot, reversals, revelations), whose effect he judged to be shallow and fleeting at best, and instead to seek what he called *tableaux* (visually satisfying, essentially silent, seemingly accidental groupings of figures), which if properly managed he believed were capable of moving an audience to the depths of its collective being. (*Absorption* 78)

As Shelley has already indicated, the point of this intense movement is to appeal to the audience's moral being. Mary Jacobus describes how, for Wordsworth, the theatre was threatening because it risked moving the audience too much, and too much excitement would impede the use of the imagination — a danger more likely in those "sickly German tragedies" which exploit so much graphic violence. See "'That Great Stage,'" 353–387. For a more general history of the problem, see Janet Ruth Heller, "The Bias Against Spectacle in Tragedy: The History of an Idea."

6. Paine too is drawing on an antitheatrical prejudice. And like Burke, Paine shares this prejudice with Rousseau. But this time, the prejudice is not just against

theatre, but against the theatre of *sentiment*: "the heart," writes Rousseau, "is more readily touched by feigned ills than real ones, [and] theatrical imitations draw forth more tears than would the presence of objects imitated" (*Letter* 25). For Rousseau, Paine, and Burke, the problem with theatre is that imitations manipulate sentiments for immoral ends. Rousseau strongly objected to the eighteenth-century dramatic tendency (as in Racine) to make the villain sympathetic; such a ploy equates virtue with vice, and destroys the spectator's reason (29).

7. Butwin is quoting Robespierre from *Textes choisis* 150–152.

8. On 12 January 1821, Byron wrote in his journal,

> [John] Murray writes that they want to act the Tragedy of Marino Faliero; — more fools they, it was written for the closet. I have protested against this piece of usurpation (which, it seems, is legal for managers over any printed work, against the author's will) and I hope they will not attempt it. (*Letters* VIII, 22–23)

A month later, on 16 February, he wrote to John Murray and repeated the request.

There is a whole debate about Byron's intentions regarding the staging of the play, a debate to which I do not wish to contribute. For the classic outline of Byron's ambivalence regarding the theatre, see David Erdman, "Byron's Stage Fright: The History of His Ambition and Fear of Writing for the Stage."

9. David Marshall has identified this fear in Diderot as a fear of sympathy as contagion (*Surprising Effects* 91–99). But while Marshall discusses this phenomenon in terms of constructions of self and other, Byron's fear has a very real political element, one of partisan sympathies.

10. Christensen writes: "*Marino Faliero* both represents and enacts Byron's ambivalence about his own social status and about the possibility for effective political action in contemporary England" ("Fault" 321).

11. For Daniel P. Watkins, this ambivalence represents Byron's wish to "[plunge] beneath surface considerations such as episode and spectacle in an attempt to develop a coherent imaginative portrayal" of the "unifying principles" of political life ("Poetics of Revolution" 104). But such ambivalence also makes a political statement of its own. What we see is an image of a peasant rebellion as somewhat prurient, slow, bombastic, and ineffectual.

12. For discussions of this question, see John David Moore; Watkins, "'In That New World'"; and Elizabeth Sewell, "Coleridge and Revolution."

13. For a more complete discussion of the class determinants in the depictions of Alhadra and Albert, see Watkins, "'In That New World'."

14. After 1800, Coleridge focused almost solely on a definition of politics and revolution as occurring internally, in the imagination, a definition which he explores more fully in the *Biographia Literaria*. For a discussion of this move and its implications for politics, see the group of essays "Coleridge: The Politics of the Imagination," ed. Carl Woodring.

15. One aspect of this self-delusion was his condemnation of Maturin's *Bertram* as a Jacobinical drama, a condemnation which comprises Chapter 23 of the *Biographia Literaria*. As Hazlitt was the first to point out, Coleridge's unfair review

of Maturin was not only sour grapes (Maturin's play was produced while Cole-ridge's *Zapolya*, the play which followed *Remorse*, was rejected), but an obvious attempt to cover up his own Jacobin past by accusing Maturin of subversion. For a more complete discussion of this, see Alethea Hayter, "Coleridge, Maturin's *Bertram*, and Drury Lane" in Donald Sultana, ed., *New Approaches to Coleridge*. For Coleridge's own account of his anti-Jacobinism, and its debt to Burke, see chapter 10 of *Biographia Literaria*.

16. For Moore, this nostalgia for Gothic spectacle is Coleridge's attempt to appropriate Gothicism for an attack against Napoleon. He argues that Coleridge's problem was not with spectacle, but with the Jacobin use of spectacle (464). But Coleridge's problem is complicated by the anxiety over what constitutes "Jacobin" as opposed to anti-Jacobin use, since the plays seem not quite clear on the distinction.

17. Julie Carlson argues that

> Coleridge's awareness of the conflicting claims of old and new distin-guishes him from both poles of the revolutionary debate in England. Neither Burke's traditionalism nor Paine's radicalism adequately meets the contempo-rary challenge. For the day's challenge is unique, the French Revolution represents a wholly "new event"; and the task of politics is to learn how to adapt old principles to new circumstances. To do this means to view history philosophically; to do this requires a synthesis of reason and sensitivity. In this context Coleridge promotes imagination and recommends the Bible as the stateman's manual. By recording eternal truths and the "temporal destinies of men and nations," it exemplifies the proper interactions between principles and circumstances. ("An Active Imagination" 25)

While I agree with Carlson's description of what Coleridge attempts to do, I find the attempt less successful than does she, and precisely because the "eternal truths" of sensitivity — in the sense of bodily feeling — are so strikingly at odds with the eternal truths of the transcendent and imaginative.

18. For Stuart Curran, Shelley inherits from Calderon the suspicion that everywhere you look is illusion — your own or someone else's — and that the drama can be a distorting perversion rather than a clarifying prism. See Curran, "Shelleyan Drama," in Richard Allen Cave, ed., *The Romantic Theatre* 69.

19. As Robert F. Whitman writes, "In Count Cenci . . . Shelley saw a symbol of that tyranny, whether domestic, social, political, or religious, which he felt it was his lifelong duty to attack" ("'Pernicious Mistake'" 250).

20. For a discussion of the echoes of *Macbeth* in *The Cenci*, see Alan Richard-son's *A Mental Drama* 117.

21. This familiar position anticipates the quotation from Maturin which I have included in Chapter one.

22. See for example Stuart Curran, *Shelley's "Cenci"*; Earl Wasserman, *Critical Reading*; Ronald Tetreault, *Poetry of Life*. Curran and Wasserman also set up the classic debate, picking up from Shelley's own statements on the "Preface," as to whether Beatrice is morally guilty in the murder of her father.

23. This well-worn phrase from Berkeley re-emerges in Shelley's "A Defence of Poetry" as "All things exist as they are perceived" (505).

24. For Alan Richardson, this collapse of the self into the other repeats Hegel's Master-Slave dialectic from the *Phenomenology of Spirit*. For Richardson, the

> drama of Hegel's account begins with his insistence that self-consciousness cannot arise in isolation and is inconceivable apart from a social context; moreover, it emerges only through a struggle with another (or rather an other) consciousness. (13)

However, as the master battles the slave, he loses his autonomy over that slave, needing his weakness to make the master strong. Similarly, as the slave battles the master, he wins mastery only in the sense that he appropriates the master's polluted strength. Thus does the Romantic hero lose his integrity, and "the quest for autonomy [is] ultimately self-defeating" (14). Romantic drama is for Richardson a critique of self-consciousness, in that the self is always other-defined, other-infected.

25. For Michael Worton, this preterition marks "the essential paradox of the play: there is a consistent and deliberate refusal by the playwright to *name* the catalysing action within the tragedy." Thus, when a character cannot find a language for thought, he or she will invariably "be forced to find expression in a non-verbal way — in action" ("Speech and Silence" in Miriam Allott, ed., *Essays on Shelley* 107–108; emphasis original).

26. Paine here is defending the National Assembly in France by arguing that it did not persecute its conspirators; rather, it was preoccupied with the contemplation of a constitution based on the authority and rights of the people. Paine's optimism seems rather misplaced in the light of the Terror in 1793, a year after the publication of his tract.

Chapter Four

1. Hanson discusses this problem in terms of an epistemology of "discovery" which sought to draw truth from the body, but which was troubled by the very truth it sought to draw. Since Renaissance torture was looking for confessions of treason that proceeded from a spiritual site which, by definition, could not be trusted, "every project of discovery, 'successful' or not, revealed the impenetrable sanctum it had created. Thus, the victim's positive assertions of his truth were never treated as a discovery that he possessed no subversive secrets" ("Torture and Truth" 77).

2. They also appear in the criticism and commentary on that reform. Spierenburg's book sets out to correct Foucault's, which itself had wanted to demythologize the benevolent humanism which had proceeded from notions of Enlightenment "progress."

3. Lewis, Shelley, and Godwin offer only a small sample of the instances of torture in the Gothic novel. Godwin's is one of some thirty Gothic novels produced between 1790 and 1830 in which scenes of torture figure prominently. For a complete list, see Ann B. Tracy, *The Gothic Novel 1790–1830: Plot Summaries and Index to Motifs*. Tracy subdivides these novels into those dealing explicitly with torture and those merely showing the instruments of torture or chambers.

4. The utterly barbarous countries of which Beccaria speaks are, for the Gothic novel, synonymous with Roman Catholic countries: Italy, Spain, and, at times, France. By depicting torture as the state agent of Catholicism, the Gothic novel, as Joel Porte argues, articulated a Protestant suspicion of Catholicism's sinister influence on the continent and helped to legitimize the strength of Protestantism in England ("In the Hand of an Angry God," in G. Richard Thompson, ed., *The Gothic Imagination* 43). By imagining another's pain, the English Gothic novel could proclaim against the tyrannical source of that pain — Catholicism. The crowning irony of this suspicion of Catholic barbarity is that the British use of torture in the Renaissance was *by* Protestants trying to rout out Catholic heretics and to check the spread of Catholicism. Therefore the Gothic's use of torture to depict Catholic barbarity is a ludicrous projection of guilt.

5. Sade was one of the first to argue that the Gothic novel was an expression of European revolutionary unrest rather than conservative moralism. In *Ideas on the Novel*, he writes that the Gothic,

> whatever may be said about it is undoubtedly not without merit. It was the inevitable fruit of the revolutionary shocks felt by the whole of Europe. For one who knew all the miseries with which the wicked can afflict humanity the novel became as difficult to create as it was monotonous to read. There was not a single individual who had not experienced more misfortune in four or five years than the most famous novelist in literature could paint in a century. (*Selected* 287)

6. Fleetwood's construction of Mary as theatrical piece makes this scene analogous to what Michael Fried calls an "absorptive tableau." An "absorptive tableau" is a certain mood in eighteenth-century French painting in which the spectator is simultaneously absorbed by the realism of the action on the canvas and made aware of his inability to enter that action. Thus, says John Bender, the absorptive tableau defines "a spectator who is at once isolated and irrevocably fascinated with the sensations and thoughts of the beings he confronts — a spectator simultaneously at one with an imagined consciousness yet incapable of direct entrance into its realm" (*Imagining* 232). This dialectic seems to me to characterize Fleetwood perfectly, except that the fascination and frustration of denied entrance are rendered all the more potent by his being the artist, the actual creator of the scene.

7. The privileging of mental sufferings over physical ones also occurs early in *Caleb Williams*, during one of Caleb's musings on Falkland's power. As he fears the implications of Falkland's wrath, Caleb declares:

> I envied the condemned wretch upon the scaffold. I envied the victim of the inquisition in the midst of his torture. They know what they have to suffer. I had only to imagine everything terrible, and then say, The fate reserved for me is worse than this! (167)

I suspect the torture victim himself would have a different opinion on what hurts more: mental or physical abuse.

8. Angela Carter says something like this in her discussion of torture in Sade's *Justine*. She writes:

The heart's egoism sees itself suffering when it sees another suffering and so it learns sympathy, because it can put itself in another's place; then the heart comes a little way out of its egoism and tentatively encounters the world. But, before the prospect of its own suffering, the heart melts completely and retreats into egoism, again, to protect itself. (*Sadeian Woman* 52)

For Carter, or Carter's Sade, sympathy here is a moral failing. In my reading of the Gothic, the failure is more physiologically based.

9. The "boots" were metal footwear that could be tightened by driving wedges into the straps located between the boots and the victim's legs. When tightened, they crushed the shin bones. This "contrivance . . . to squeeze the truth out of a man" is just one of a large lexicon of techniques that literalize the metaphor of "extracting" the truth from the body. For a more complete description of these techniques, see Parry, *History of Torture*.

Chapter Five

1. This cooperation really began much earlier, with the establishment of the Royal College of Physicians in England in 1522. But advancements were slow until the eighteenth-century, when legislation and societies began to proliferate. See Wyndham E. B. Lloyd, *A Hundred Years of Medicine* 53; and Lester S. King, *The Medical World of the Eighteenth Century* 2.

2. Actually, the construction of the body image in France did *not* proceed regardless of class. As Outram points out, the revolutionary imaging of the body was a particularly middle-class phenomenon which remained at a loss to understand the peasant body from which it was alienated. Hence the peasant body was usually figured as fat, poorly defined, and disgusting, thereby leaving class stratification still intact (60).

3. As Outram writes, Bordeu sought in his attack on Descartes "a much more holistic view of the organism as a self-propelling, self-regulating entity, whose 'vital force' came from within its interior, instead of as a result of receptors to stimuli applied from outside" (54). The result of this search was the all-important elevation of the concept of "sensitivity":

> Without attributing all this [i.e., reactions to stimuli] to any metaphysical entity, Bordeu saw the organism as possessing something one may call a force, capable of executing functions that no blind mechanical motor could. This was the force to which Bordeu gave the name "sensitivity," a property which he considered to be diffused by the nerves, not only to some parts of the organism, but throughout the whole of it. (55)

4. One particular illustration of this is the surgeon William Cheselden (1688–1752), who not only made sure that his knives were perfectly sharp before he performed surgery, but was actually nauseated the night before the operation over the pain that he was about to inflict. For this anecdote, see Daniel de Moulin, "A Historical-Phenomenological Study of Bodily Pain in Western Man," 545–546.

5. Priestley did not discover anesthesia, merely a safer form. The first non-narcotic anesthesia to be introduced to England was a nerve compression machine, which was invented by James Moore in 1784. Though not generally respected, this method was further developed by Benjamin Bell, whose *System of Surgery* became a standard eighteenth-century medical text. See Bernard Seeman, *Man Against Pain* 103.

6. Narcotics were the chief form of *physical* analgesic to be associated with quackery and to be dismissed. The popular contemporary form of *psychological* analgesia came in the work of Franz Anton Mesmer (of our current "mesmerism") whose complex system of anesthetizing hypnosis and magnetic treatment of illness was known to be effective in 1778 but was not widely used until 1829 (Moulin, "Historical" 543–544).

7. For J. G. A. Pocock, the seat of this concord is a respect for church estates ("Political Economy" 334); for James T. Boulton, it is centered in the concept of Natural Order (*Language of Politics* 110); and for Gary Kelly, it is a respect for gentry ("Revolution" 16–32). While these fixations appear somewhat disparate in the separate critics, they contribute to defining Burke's overall love of the idea of the traditional. For Burke, as for Pope, whatever is, is right.

8. The information Burke got in these early days was specious to say the least. According to William Palmer, Burke got most of his information from the British newspapers, and thus was subject to their biases and interpretations ("Edmund Burke and the French Revolution" 181–190). The limitations which the media imposed upon Burke's political position seem not that much different from our own, as we witness world events solely through journalistic interpretation.

9. Faith Wallace at McGill's Osler Library has pointed out to me that such medical over-prescription was common in the eighteenth century, and was called "heroic treatment." Heroic treatment denotes "an aggressive, daring procedure which in itself may endanger the patient but which also has a possibility of being successful, whereas lesser action would result in failure" (*Stedman's Medical Dictionary*). For "heroic treatment" in this definition, read "political revolution" and one has the justification for radical, violent uprising.

10. This ambivalence is replayed in the mob's stoning of the Prioress near the end of the novel. As an evil tyrant she deserves what she gets, but the image of a mob out of control is terrifying, for they become completely indiscriminate in their slaughter.

11. As Howard Anderson notes in his Introduction to *The Monk*, Lewis always enjoyed moving in high society, and amusing the assembled company with his fascinating anecdotes. However, as Byron makes clear, Lewis's anecdotes were more amusing to himself than to anyone else, and he had the reputation of being a notorious bore. See Byron's *Letters* IX,18.

12. For a more complete discussion of Byron's ambivalent relation to Napoleon, see Jurgen Klein, "Byron's Idea of Democracy: An Investigation into the Relationship Between Literature and Politics," in Erwin A. Sturzl and James Hogg, eds., *Byron: Poetry and Politics*, 58–59.

13. I am not suggesting a *conscious* re-writing of Burke here. There is no evidence to suggest that Byron actually read the *Reflections*, although it is inconceiv-

able that he didn't. Steffan, Steffan, and Pratt suggest that Byron no doubt had enormous respect for Burke, and "was probably attracted to him by Burke's efforts on behalf of India and the American colonies, his passionate lack of restraint, his lifelong support of the traditional order and of free parliamentary processes, and especially by his formal eloquence" (613). While I question Byron's wholesale "support of the traditional order," I do think Byron admired Burke's love of gradualism in political reform: like Burke, Byron respected Americans because they "acquired their freedom by firmness without excess" (*Letters* IX,17). While Byron's thoughts on the efficacy of revolutionary excess changed as he grew older, he did advocate a peaceful change whenever it was possible.

14. This is not the only instance in *Don Juan* where bodily infirmity can act as a blessing. When Juan and a group of others are set adrift in the famous rowboat scene which comprises much of Canto II, the passengers are forced into acts of cannibalism as a means of staying alive. After they have eaten Juan's spaniel and his tutor Pedrillo, they turn to the first mate, who is the fattest—and therefore healthiest, in a pre-aerobics culture—of the survivors. The mate is saved from Pedrillo's fate, however, by pointing out that

> He had been rather indisposed of late,
>   And that which chiefly proved his saving clause
> Was a small present made to him at Cadiz,
>   By general subscription of the ladies. (II,81,ll.5–8)

Normally, one does not wish to be stricken with venereal disease, but in this case illness is actually a *protection*, an assurance of life at the same time that it threatens it. In other words, contagion can be its own prophylactic.

15. It would seem that Byron bequeaths his own challenge here to Mary Shelley when he charges her at the Villa Diodati to write a ghost story. As Shelley contemplated the genesis of *Frankenstein*, she knew she wanted a story that would appeal directly to the body, one "which would speak to the mysterious fears of our nature, and awaken thrilling horror—one to make the reader dread to look round, to curdle the blood, and quicken the beatings of the heart" (Introduction to *Frankenstein*). Yet, as she writes in the Preface, "my chief concern . . . has been limited to the avoiding the enervating effects of the novels of the present day" (25). Out of this delicate balancing act Shelley produces her "hideous progeny"—her text and her monster.

Works Cited

Abrams, M. H. *Natural Supernaturalism: Tradition and Revolution in Romantic Literature*. New York: W. W. Norton, 1971.

Addison, Joseph, Richard Steele, and Others. *The Spectator*. Ed. Gregory Smith. New York: Everyman's Library, 1967.

Albrecht, W. P. "Tragedy and Wordsworth's Sublime." *Wordsworth Circle* 8, 1 (1977): 83–94.

Allott, Miriam, ed. *Essays on Shelley*. Totowa, NJ: Barnes and Noble, 1982.

Austen, Jane. *The Complete Novels of Jane Austen*. New York: Random House, n.d.

Averill, James H. *Wordsworth and the Poetry of Human Suffering*. Ithaca, NY: Cornell University Press, 1980.

Barish, Jonas. *The Antitheatrical Prejudice*. Los Angeles: University of California Press, 1981.

Barker-Benfield, G. J. *The Culture of Sensibility: Sex and Society in Eighteenth-Century Britain*. Chicago: University of Chicago Press, 1992.

Barker, Francis et al., eds. *1789: Reading, Writing, Revolution — Proceedings of the Essex Conference on the Sociology of Literature, July 1981*. Essex: University of Essex Press, 1982.

Beccaria, Cesare. *On Crimes and Punishments (Dei Delitti e delle Pene)*. Trans. Henry Paolucci. New York: Bobbs-Merrill, 1963.

Beer, John. *Wordsworth and the Human Heart*. New York: Columbia University Press, 1978.

Bender, John. *Imagining the Penitentiary: Fiction and the Architecture of Mind in Eighteenth-Century England*. Chicago: University of Chicago Press, 1987.

Benedict, Barbara M. "Pictures of Conformity: Sentiment and Structure in Ann Radcliffe's Style." *Philological Quarterly* 68, 3 (1989): 363–77.

Benjamin, Walter. *Illuminations*. Trans. Hannah Arendt. New York: Schocken Books, 1969.

Bewell, Alan. *Wordsworth and the Enlightenment: Nature, Man, and Society in the Experimental Poetry*. New Haven, CT: Yale University Press, 1989.

Blackstone, Sir William. *Commentaries on the Laws of England*. Vol. IV. New York: Garland, 1978.

Blake, William. *Blake's Poetry and Designs*. Ed. Mary Lynn Johnson and John E. Grant. New York: W. W. Norton, 1979.

Bostetter, Edward E. *The Romantic Ventriloquists: Wordsworth, Coleridge, Keats, Shelley, Byron*. Seattle: University of Washington Press, 1963.

Boulton, James T. *The Language of Politics in the Age of Wilkes and Burke*. Toronto: University of Toronto Press, 1963.

Brissenden, R. F. *Virtue in Distress: Studies in the Novel of Sentiment from Richardson to Sade*. New York: Macmillan, 1974.

Brooks, Peter. *The Melodramatic Imagination: Balzac, Henry James, Melodrama, and the Mode of Excess*. New Haven, CT: Yale University Press, 1976.

Brown, Marshall. *Preromanticism*. Stanford, CA: Stanford University Press, 1991.

Bruns, Gerald. "Wordsworth at the Limits of Romantic Hermeneutics." *Centennial Review* 33, 4 (1989): 393–412.

Bryson, Norman. *Tradition and Desire from David to Delacroix*. New York: Cambridge University Press, 1987.

Burke, Edmund. *Letter to a Member of the National Assembly*. In *The Writings and Speeches of Edmund Burke*. Vol. 4. Boston: Little, Brown, 1901.

——. *A Philosophical Enquiry into the Origin of our Ideas of the Sublime and Beautiful*. Ed. James T. Boulton. London: University of Notre Dame Press, 1986.

——. *Reflections on the Revolution in France*. Ed. Conor Cruise O'Brien. Markham, Ont.: Penguin Books, 1986.

Butwin, Joseph. "The French Revolution as *Theatrum Mundi*." *Research Studies* 43, 3 (1975): 141–152.

Byron, George Gordon, Lord. *Byron's Letters and Journals*. Ed. Leslie Marchand. New York: Alfred A. Knopf, 1973.

——. *Byron: Poetical Works*. Ed. Frederick Page and John Jump. New York: Oxford University Press, 1987.

——. *Don Juan*. Ed. T. G. Steffan, E. Steffan, and W. W. Pratt. Markham, Ont.: Penguin Books, 1987.

Carlson, Julie. "An Active Imagination: Coleridge and the Politics of Dramatic Reform." *Modern Philology* 86, 1 (1988): 22–33.

Carter, Angela. *The Sadeian Woman and the Ideology of Pornography*. New York: Pantheon Books, 1978.

Castle, Terry. "The Spectralization of the Other in *The Mysteries of Udolpho*." In *The New Eighteenth Century: Theory, Politics, English Literature*. Ed. Felicity Nussbaum and Laura Brown. New York: Methuen, 1987.

Cave, Richard Allen, ed. *The Romantic Theatre: An International Symposium*. Totowa, NJ: Barnes and Noble, 1986.

Chandler, James K. *Wordsworth's Second Nature: A Study of Poetry and Politics*. Chicago: University of Chicago Press, 1984.

Christensen, Jerome. "*Marino Faliero* and the Fault of Byron's Satire." *Studies in Romanticism* 24, 3 (1985): 313–333.

Ciccone, Madonna and Patrick Leonard. "Hanky Panky" from *Madonna: I'm Breathless*. Warner/Chappell Music, Los Angeles, 1990.

Coleridge, Samuel Taylor. *Biographia Literaria, or Biographical Sketches of My Literary Life and Opinions*. Ed. George Watson. London: Everyman's Library, 1987.

——. *The Collected Works of Samuel Taylor Coleridge*. Vol. 4, Pt. II. Ed. Barbara Rooke. Princeton, NJ: Princeton University Press, 1969.

——. *The Complete Poetical Works of Samuel Taylor Coleridge*. Vol. II. Ed. Ernest Hartley Coleridge. Oxford: Clarendon Press, 1957.

——. *Letters of Samuel Taylor Coleridge*. London: William Heineman, 1895.

——. *The Notebooks of Samuel Taylor Coleridge, Vol. I, 1794–1804*. Ed. Kathleen Coburn. London: Routledge and Kegan Paul, 1957.

Cox, Stephen D. *"The Stranger Within Thee": Concepts of the Self in Late Eighteenth-Century Literature*. Pittsburgh: University of Pittsburgh Press, 1980.

Crompton, Louis. *Byron and Greek Love: Homophobia in 19th-Century England*. London: Faber and Faber, 1985.

Curran, Stuart. *Shelley's "Cenci": Scorpions Ringed with Fire*. Princeton, NJ: Princeton University Press, 1970.

Day, William Patrick. *In the Circles of Fear and Desire: A Study of Gothic Fantasy*. Chicago: University of Chicago Press, 1985.

de Almeida, Hermione. *Romantic Medicine and John Keats*. New York: Oxford University Press, 1991.

de Moulin, Daniel. "A Historical-Phenomenological Study of Bodily Pain in Western Man." *Bulletin of the History of Medicine* 48, 4 (1974): 540–570.

Derrida, Jacques. *Dissemination*. Trans. Barbara Johnson. Chicago: University of Chicago Press, 1981.

de Sade, Donatien Alphonse. *Justine, Philosophy in the Bedroom, and Other Writings*. Trans. Richard Seaver and Austryn Wainhouse. New York: Grove Press, 1965.

———. *Selected Writings of De Sade*. Trans. Margaret Crosland. London: Peter Owen Limited, 1964.

Doughty, Oswald. *Perturbed Spirit: The Life and Personality of Samuel Taylor Coleridge*. Toronto: Associated University Presses, 1981.

Durant, David. "Ann Radcliffe and the Conservative Gothic." *Studies in English Literature, 1500–1900* 22, 3 (1982): 519–530.

Eagleton, Terry. *The Ideology of the Aesthetic*. Oxford: Basil Blackwell, 1990.

Erdman, David. "Byron's Stage Fright: The History of His Ambition and Fear of Writing for the Stage." *ELH* 6, 1 (1939): 219–243.

Fawcett, Mary Laughlin. "Udolpho's Primal Mystery." *Studies in English Literature, 1500–1900* 23, 3 (1983): 481–494.

Ferry, David. *The Limits of Mortality: An Essay on Wordsworth's Major Poems*. Middletown, CT: Wesleyan University Press, 1959.

Foucault, Michel. *The Birth of the Clinic: An Archeology of Medical Perception*. Trans. A. M. Sheridan Smith. New York: Vintage Books, 1975.

———. *Discipline and Punish: The Birth of the Prison*. Trans. Alan Sheridan. New York: Vintage Books, 1979.

———. *Power/Knowledge: Selected Interviews and Other Writings*. Ed. Colin Gordon. Trans. Colin Gordon et al. New York: Pantheon Books, 1980.

Fülop-Miller, René. *Triumph over Pain*. New York: Bobbs-Merrill, 1938.

French, R. K. *Robert Whytt, the Soul, and Medicine*. London: St. Ann's Press, 1969.

Freud, Sigmund. *The Standard Edition of the Complete Psychological Works of Sigmund Freud*. Vols. 14 and 17. Trans. James Strachey. London: Hogarth Press, 1955, 1957.

Fried, Michael. *Absorption and Theatricality: Painting and Beholder in the Age of Diderot*. Berkeley: University of California Press, 1980.

Fuss, Diana. *Essentially Speaking: Feminism, Nature, and Difference*. New York: Routledge, 1989.

Garber, Frederick. *The Autonomy of the Self from Richardson to Huysmans*. Princeton, NJ: Princeton University Press, 1982.

———. "Self, Society, Value, and the Romantic Hero." *Comparative Literature* 19, 4 (1967): 321–333.

Gervais, David. "Suffering in Wordsworth." *Cambridge Quarterly* 16, 1 (1987): 1–14.

Godwin, William. *The Adventures of Caleb Williams, or Things as They Are*. San Francisco: Rinehart Press, 1960.

——. *Enquiry Concerning Political Justice and Its Influence on Modern Morals and Happiness*. Ed. Isaac Kramnick. Markham, Ont.: Penguin Books, 1976.

——. *Fleetwood; or The New Man of Feeling*. London: Richard Bentley, 1853.

——. *Travels of St. Leon*. London: Henry Colburn and Richard Bentley, 1851.

Habermas, Jurgen. *Communication and the Evolution of Society*. Trans. Thomas McCarthy. Boston: Beacon, 1979.

Hale, David George. *The Body Politic: A Political Metaphor in Renaissance English Literature*. The Hague: Mouton, 1971.

Hanson, Elizabeth. "Torture and Truth in Renaissance England." *Representations* 34, 1 (1991): 53–84.

Hazlitt, William. *Lectures on the English Poets, and Spirit of the Age: or Contemporary Portraits*. New York: Dutton, 1963.

Heller, Janet Ruth. "The Bias Against Spectacle in Tragedy: The History of an Idea." *Eighteenth Century* 23, 3 (1982): 239–255.

Henderson, Andrea. "A Tale Told to be Forgotten: Enlightenment, Revolution, and the Poet in 'Salisbury Plain.'" *Studies in Romanticism* 30, 1 (1991): 71–84.

Hennelly, Mark M., Jr. "'The Slow Torture of Delay': Reading *The Italian*." *Studies in the Humanities* 14, 1 (1987): 1–14.

Holland, Patrick. "Wordsworth and the Sublime: Some Further Considerations." *Wordsworth Circle* 5, 1 (1974): 17–22.

Howells, Coral Ann. *Love, Mystery, and Misery: Feeling in Gothic Fiction*. London: Athlone Press, 1978.

Hume, Robert D. "Gothic vs. Romantic: A Revaluation of the Gothic Novel." *PMLA* 84, 2 (1969): 282–290.

Jacobus, Mary. "'That Great Stage Where Senators Perform': *Macbeth* and the Politics of Romantic Theatre." *Studies in Romanticism* 22, 3 (1983): 353–387.

Jones, [Henry] John [Franklin]. *The Egotistical Sublime: A History of Wordsworth's Imagination*. London: Chatto and Windus, 1964.

Keats, John. *The Letters of John Keats*. Ed. Maurice Buxton Forman. New York: Oxford University Press, 1935.

Kelly, Gary. "Revolution, Crime, and Madness: Edmund Burke and the Defense of the Gentry." *Eighteenth-Century Life* 9, 1 (1984): 16–32.

Kilgour, Maggie. *From Communion to Cannibalism: An Anatomy of Metaphors of Incorporation*. Princeton, NJ: Princeton University Press, 1990.

King, Lester S. *The Medical World of the Eighteenth Century*. Huntington, NY: Krieger, 1971.

Lacan, Jacques. *Écrits: A Selection*. Trans. Alan Sheridan. New York: W. W. Norton, 1977.

Lamb, Charles. *Poems, Plays, and Miscellaneous Essays of Charles Lamb*. London: Macmillan, 1884.

Lawrence, Christopher. "The Nervous System and Society in the Scottish Enlightenment." In *Natural Order: Historical Studies of Scientific Culture*, ed. Barry Barnes and Steven Shapin. Beverly Hills, CA: Sage Publications, 1979.

Lewis, Matthew Gregory. *The Castle Spectre (1798)*. Intro. Jonathan Wordsworth. New York: Woodstock Books, 1990.

———. *The Monk; A Romance*. Ed. Howard Anderson. New York: Oxford University Press, 1987.

———. *Romantic Tales*. London: Longman, Hurst, Rees, and Orme, 1808.

Leyda, Seraphia D. "Wordsworth's *Sonnets Upon the Punishment of Death.*" *Wordsworth Circle* 14, 1 (1983): 48–53.

Lloyd, Wyndham E. B. *A Hundred Years of Medicine*. New York: Humanities Press, 1968.

Locke, John. *An Essay Concerning Human Understanding*. Ed. Peter Nidditch. Oxford: Clarendon Press, 1988.

———. *Two Treatises of Government*. Darmstadt: Scientia Verlag Aarlen, 1963.

London, April. "Ann Radcliffe in Context: Marking the Boundaries of *The Mysteries of Udolpho.*" *Eighteenth-Century Life* 10, 1 (1986): 35–47.

MacDonald, D. L. "Bathos and Repetition: The Uncanny in Radcliffe." *Jounal of Narrative Technique* 19, 2 (1989): 197–204.

Macpherson, C. B. *The Political Theory of Possessive Individualism, Hobbes to Locke*. Oxford: Clarendon Press, 1962.

Mann, Ronald, ed. *The History of the Management of Pain from Early Principles to Present Practice*. Park Ridge, NJ: Parthenon Books, 1988.

Marchand, Leslie. *Byron: A Biography*. New York: Alfred A. Knopf, 1957.

Marshall, David. *The Figure of Theatre: Shaftesbury, Defoe, Adam Smith, and George Eliot*. New York: Columbia University Press, 1986.

———. *The Surpising Effects of Sympathy: Marivaux, Diderot, Rousseau, and Mary Shelley*. Chicago: University of Chicago Press, 1988.

Maturin, Charles Robert. *Melmoth the Wanderer: A Tale*. Ed. Alethea Hayter. Markham, Ont.: Penguin Books, 1984.

McCracken, David. "Godwin's Literary Theory: The Alliance between Fiction and Political Philosophy." *Philological Quarterly* 49, 1 (1970): 113–133.

———. "Godwin's Reading in Burke." *English Language Notes* 7, 4 (1970): 264–270.

McGann, Jerome. "Romanticism and Its Ideologies." *Studies in Romanticism* 21, 4 (1982): 573–599.

Moore, John David. "Coleridge and the 'modern Jacobinical Drama': *Osorio, Remorse*, and the Development of Coleridge's Critique of the Stage, 1797–1816." *Bulletin of Research in the Humanities* 85, 4 (1982): 443–464.

Morris, David B. *The Culture of Pain*. Berkeley: University of California Press, 1991.

Mullan, John. *Sentiment and Sociability: The Language of Feeling in the Eighteenth Century*. Oxford: Clarendon Press, 1988.

Myers, Mitzi. "Godwin's Changing Conception of *Caleb Williams.*" *Studies in English Literature, 1500–1900* 12, 4 (1972): 591–628.

———. "Godwin's *Memoirs* of Wollstonecraft: The Shaping of Self and Subject." *Studies in Romanticism* 20, 3 (1981): 299–316.

Neal, Helen. *The Politics of Pain*. New York: McGraw-Hill, 1978.

Nietzsche, Friedrich. *The Birth of Tragedy and The Genealogy of Morals*. Trans. Francis Golffing. Garden City, NY: Doubleday, 1956.

Nuttal, A. D. *A Common Sky: Philosophy and the Literary Imagination*. Berkeley: University of California Press, 1974.

Outram, Dorinda. *The Body and the French Revolution: Sex, Class and Political Culture*. New Haven, CT: Yale University Press, 1989.

Owen, W. J. B. "The Sublime and Beautiful in *The Prelude.*" *Wordsworth Circle* 4, 2 (1973): 67–86.

Paine, Thomas. *The Rights of Man.* Markham, Ont.: Penguin Books, 1985.

Palmer, William. "Edmund Burke and the French Revolution: Notes on the Genesis of the *Reflections.*" *Colby Library Quarterly* 20, 4 (1984): 181–190.

Parry, Leonard Arthur. *The History of Torture in England.* Montclair, NJ: Patterson Smith, 1975.

Paulson, Ronald. *Representations of Revolution (1789–1820).* New Haven, CT: Yale University Press, 1983.

Peckham, Morse. *Beyond the Tragic Vision: The Quest for Identity in the Nineteenth Century.* New York: G. Braziller, 1962.

Peters, Edward. *Torture.* New York: Basil Blackwell, 1985.

Pocock, J. G. A. "The Political Economy of Burke's Analysis of the French Revolution. *Historical Journal* 25, 2 (1982): 331–349.

Poovey, Mary. "Ideology and *The Mysteries of Udolpho.*" *Criticism* 21, 4 (1979): 307–330.

Praz, Mario. *The Romantic Agony.* Trans. Angus Davidson. New York: Oxford University Press, 1970.

Punter, David. "1789: The Sex of Revolution." *Criticism: A Quarterly for Literature and the Arts* 24, 3 (1972): 201–217.

Radcliffe, Ann. *The Italian; or The Confessional of the Black Penitents.* Ed. Frederick Garber. New York: Oxford University Press, 1986.

———. *The Mysteries of Udolpho.* Ed. Bonamy Dobrée. New York: Oxford University Press, 1986.

———. *The Romance of the Forest.* Ed. Chloe Chard. New York: Oxford University Press, 1986.

Rather, L. J. *Mind and Body in Eighteenth Century Medicine: A Study Based on Jerome Gaub's De regimine mentis.* London: William Clowes, 1965.

Richardson, Alan. *A Mental Theatre: Poetic Drama and Consciousness in the Romantic Age.* University Park: Pennsylvania State University Press, 1988.

Robespierre, Maximilien. *Textes choisis.* Vol. II. Ed. Jean Poperen. Paris: Éditions Sociales, 1965.

Robinson, Victor. *Victory over Pain: A History of Anesthesia.* New York: Henry Schuman, 1946.

Rousseau, G. S., ed. *The Languages of Psyche: Mind and Body in Enlightenment Thought.* Berkeley: University of California Press, 1990.

Rousseau, Jean-Jacques. *Basic Political Writings of Jean-Jacques Rousseau.* Ed. Donald A. Cress. Indianapolis, IN: Hackett Press, 1988.

———. *Letter to M. d'Alembert on the Theatre.* Trans. Alan Bloom. Ithaca, NY: Cornell University Press, 1968.

Scarry, Elaine. *The Body in Pain: The Making and Unmaking of the World.* New York: Oxford University Press, 1985.

———, ed. *Literature and the Body: Essays on Populations and Persons.* Baltimore: Johns Hopkins University Press, 1988.

Sedgwick, Eve Kosofsky. *Between Men: English Literature and Male Homosocial Desire.* New York: Columbia University Press, 1985.

——. *The Coherence of Gothic Conventions*. New York: Methuen, 1986.

——. "Jane Austen and the Masturbating Girl." *Critical Inquiry* 17, 4 (1991): 818–837.

Seeman, Bernard. *Man Against Pain: 3000 Years of Effort to Understand and Relieve Human Suffering*. New York: Chilton, 1962.

Sewell, Elizabeth. "Coleridge on Revolution." *Studies in Romanticism* 11, 4 (1972): 342–359.

Sheats, Paul D. *The Making of Wordsworth's Poetry, 1785–1798*. Cambridge, MA: Harvard University Press, 1973.

Shelley, Mary. *Frankenstein, or The Modern Prometheus*. Ed. Johanna M. Smith. Boston: St. Martin's Press, 1992.

Shelley, Percy Bysshe. *The Complete Works of Percy Bysshe Shelley, Vol. X: Letters 1818–1822*. Ed. Roger Ingpen. New York: Gordian Press, 1965.

——. *Shelley's Poetry and Prose*. Ed. Donald H. Reiman and Sharon B. Powers. New York: W.W. Norton, 1977.

——. *Zastrozzi and St. Irvyne*. Ed. Stephen C. Behrendt. New York: Oxford University Press, 1986.

Simms, Karl N. "Caleb Williams' Godwin: Things as They Are Written." *Studies in Romanticism* 26, 3 (1987): 343–363.

Singer, Peter. "Unspeakable Acts: *The Body in Pain: The Making and Unmaking of the World* by Elaine Scarry and *Torture* by Edward Peters." *New York Review of Books* (February 27, 1986): 27–30.

Smith, Adam. *The Theory of Moral Sentiments*. Ed. D. D. Raphael and A. L. Macfie. Oxford: Clarendon Press, 1976.

Smith, Nelson C. "Sense, Sensibility, and Ann Radcliffe." *Studies in English Literature, 1500–1900* 12, 3 (1973): 557–570.

Smith, Olivia. *The Politics of Language 1791–1819*. New York: Oxford University Press, 1986.

Smith, W. Lynn et al. *Pain: Meaning and Management*. New York: SP Medical and Scientific Books, 1980.

Spector, Jack J. *Delacroix: The Death of Sardanapalus*. London: Penguin Books, 1974.

Spierenburg, Pieter. *The Spectacle of Suffering: Executions and the Evolution of Repression from a Preindustrial Metropolis to the European Experience*. New York: Cambridge University Press, 1984.

Stedman, Thomas Lathrop. *Stedman's Medical Dictionary*. Baltimore: Williams and Wilkins, 1982.

Sternbach, Richard, ed. *The Psychology of Pain*. New York: Raven Press, 1986.

Sterne, Laurence. *A Sentimental Journey Through France and Italy*. Ed. Graham Petrie. Markham, Ont.: Penguin Books, 1984.

Storch, Rudolph. "Metaphors of Private Guilt and Social Rebellion in Godwin's *Caleb Williams*." *ELH* 34, 2 (1967): 188–207.

Sturzl, Erwin A. and James Hogg, eds. *Byron: Poetry and Politics; Seventh International Byron Symposium, Salzburg, 1980*. Salzburg: Institut für Anglistik und Amerikanistik, 1981.

Sultana, Donald, ed. *New Approaches to Coleridge: Biographical and Critical Essays*. Totowa, NJ: Barnes and Noble, 1981.

Swann, Karen. "Suffering and Sensation in *The Ruined Cottage*." *PMLA* 106, 1 (1991): 85–95.

Taylor, Charles. *Sources of the Self: The Making of the Modern Identity*. Cambridge, MA: Harvard University Press, 1989.

Tetreault, Ronald. *The Poetry of Life: Shelley and Literary Form*. Toronto: University of Toronto Press, 1987.

Thompson, G. Richard, ed. *The Gothic Imagination: Essays in Dark Romanticism*. Pullman: Washington State University Press, 1974.

Todd, Janet. *Sensibility: An Introduction*. New York: Methuen, 1986.

Tracy, Ann B. *The Gothic Novel 1790–1830: Plot Summaries and Index to Motifs*. Lexington: University of Kentucky Press, 1981.

Tysdahl, B. J. *William Godwin as Novelist*. London: Athlone, 1981.

Varma, Devendra. *The Gothic Flame: Being a History of the Gothic Novel in England: Its Origins, Efflorescence, Disintegration, and Residuary Influences*. New York: Russell and Russell, 1966.

Wasserman, Earl. "The Pleasure of Tragedy." *ELH* 14, 4 (1947): 283–307.

———. *Shelley: A Critical Reading*. Baltimore: Johns Hopkins University Press, 1971.

Watkins, Daniel P. "Byron and the Poetics of Revolution." *Keats-Shelley Journal* 34 (1985): 95–130.

———. " 'In that New World': The Deep Historical Structure of Coleridge's *Osorio*." *Philological Quarterly* 69, 4 (1990): 495–515.

———. "Social Hierarchy in Matthew Lewis's *The Monk*." *Studies in the Novel* 18, 2 (1986): 115–124.

———. "Violence, Class Consciousness, and Ideology in Byron's History Plays." *ELH* 48, 4 (1981): 799–816.

Watson, George. "Burke's Conservative Revolution." *Critical Quarterly* 26, 1–2 (1984): 87–99.

Wehrs, Donald R. "Rhetoric, History, Rebellion: *Caleb Williams* and the Subversion of Eighteenth-Century Fiction." *Studies in English Literature 1500–1900* 28, 3 (1988): 497–511.

Wellek, René. "The Concept of 'Romanticism' in Literary History." *Comparative Literature* 1, 2 (1949): 147–172.

Welsford, Enid. *Salisbury Plain: A Study in the Development of Wordsworth's Mind and Art*. Oxford: Basil Blackwell, 1966.

Whitman, Robert F. "Beatrice's 'Pernicious Mistake' in *The Cenci*." *PMLA* 74, 3 (1959): 249–253.

Whytt, Robert. *The Works of Robert Whytt*. Edinburgh: Balfour, Auld, and Smellie, 1768.

Wilde, Oscar. *The Complete Plays, Poems, Novels and Stories of Oscar Wilde*. London: Magpie Books, 1993.

Williams, John. *Wordsworth: Romantic Poetry and Revolutionary Politics*. New York: Manchester University Press, 1989.

Woodring, Carl, ed. "Coleridge: The Politics of the Imagination." *Studies in Romanticism* 21, 3 (1982): 445–474.

———. *Politics in English Romantic Poetry*. Cambridge, MA: Harvard University Press, 1970.

————. *Politics in the Poetry of Coleridge*. Madison: University of Wisconsin Press, 1961.

Wordsworth, William. *The Fourteen-Book Prelude*. Ed. W. J. B. Owen. Ithaca, NY: Cornell University Press, 1985.

————. *The Oxford Authors: William Wordsworth*. Ed. Stephen Gill. New York: Oxford University Press, 1989.

————. *The Poetical Works of William Wordsworth*. Vol. I. Ed. Ernest de Selincourt. Oxford: Clarendon Press, 1944.

————. *The Prose Works of William Wordsworth*. Vol. I. Ed. W. J. B. Owen and Jane Worthington Smyser. Oxford: Clarendon Press, 1974.

————. *The Salisbury Plain Poems of William Wordsworth*. Ed. Stephen Gill. Ithaca, NY: Cornell University Press, 1975.

Wordsworth, William and Dorothy Wordsworth. *The Letters of William and Dorothy Wordsworth, Vol. I, The Early Years, 1787–1805*. Ed. Ernest de Selincourt. Oxford: Clarendon Press, 1967.

Index

This book has been set in Linotron Galliard. Galliard was designed for Mergenthaler in 1978 by Matthew Carter. Galliard retains many of the features of a sixteenth-century typeface cut by Robert Granjon but has some modifications that give it a more contemporary look.

Printed on acid-free paper.